GRANNY SNATCHING

How a Ninety-Two Year Old Widow Fought the Courts and Her Family to Win Her Freedom

RON WINTER

Nightengale Press
A Nightengale Media LLC Company

GRANNY SNATCHING

For information about Nightengale Press please
visit our website at www.nightengalepress.com.
Email: publisher@nightengalepress.com
or send a letter to:
Nightengale Press
370 S. Lowe Avenue, Suite A-122
Cookeville, Tennessee

Library of Congress Cataloging-in-Publication Data

Winter, Ron,

GRANNY SNATCHING/ Ron Winter
ISBN 13: 978-1933449-83-8
Non-Fiction

Copyright Registered: 2010
First Published by Nightengale Press in the USA

January 2010

10 9 8 7 6 5 4 3 2 1

Printed in the USA and the UK

foreword

Elder Abuse and a related phenomenon termed "Granny Snatching" are increasingly common afflictions, and are growing across the United States at a near exponential rate.

Granny Snatching refers to efforts by family members, and in some cases mere acquaintances, to gain control of an elderly person's financial affairs, often across state lines, by convincing the courts to place the person into an elder care facility while the "guardian" has complete control over their life and finances.

It doesn't matter whether it is assisted living, a nursing home or an Alzheimer's facility, so long as the victims no longer have a say in the management of their finances. That it has become a nationwide problem—and embarrassment—is reflected by ongoing efforts to enact a uniform national law governing the rights of the elderly.

But national afflictions generally don't show up in the driveways and homes of individuals. National afflictions are something you read about in the papers; they happen to other people. Right?

Sometimes. But this is a story about "us" and how a national affliction became "our" problem.

There was no advance warning, no alarm bells sounded, and frankly we weren't prepared for it. In a matter of weeks our home went from safe, sound and somewhat predictable to a war zone with lives, finances and reputations at stake.

Even when the main battle was over, the sniping and skirmishing continued.

Here's an example.

Shortly after noon on June 30, 2009 a sedan bearing official State of Connecticut license plates pulled into the driveway of our home in rural eastern Connecticut.

The driver opened the door only an inch or so when she was greeted by a barking hundred-pound male black Labrador/Golden retriever mix. He was aided and abetted by a fifty-pound Heinz 57 mix of chow, Finnish Spitz, Golden Retriever and who-knows-what else. The dynamic duo is used to delivery men and occasional visitors trying to buy them off with dog treats of one kind or another. It doesn't work.

The noisy reception is what you usually get when you arrive at the Winter residence—our home—and as usual it alerted me, Ron Winter—that I had a visitor. I was just sitting down to lunch with Mom, Ella Winter, who moved in with our family the previous December after being hospitalized in Albany, New York, suffering from dehydration and potassium deficiency. Her admittance form at Albany Medical Center said she was in an "altered mental status," which is a common side affect of dehydration.

I walked to the door of the car, and was informed by the woman inside that she was a social worker from the State of Connecticut Department of Social Services, investigating a complaint of elder abuse against M. Ella Winter.

I asked her, "What is my sister saying now."

"The complaint is anonymous," the social worker replied.

"Well, there is only one person in the world who would make a complaint like that," I said, "and that person is Nancy Patrick, my sister. Is that in your records?"

"It's an anonymous complaint," the social worker insisted, but asked why I believed the complaint came from my sister.

"Because ever since Mom moved here, my sister has been trying to have her committed to an Alzheimer's facility. She filed suit against Mom and wants to be named guardian and take over all of Mom's assets. She claims that Mom has Alzheimer's and dementia. She even insisted that Mom stand trial in Albany.

"But come on in. Meet Mom and find out for yourself."

The social worker wended her way past the dogs, and entered the house. She was escorted to the kitchen where Ella was preparing her lunch. She was about to dig into a container of yogurt and was making herself some tea and toast.

"Mom, this lady is a social worker from the state," I told her. "Nancy sent her here. She says you're being abused."

Ella looked askance at me, then at the social worker as if she couldn't believe her ears. In fact, she couldn't.

"Why would she say a thing like that?" Ella demanded.

I shrugged and the social worker began asking questions. She encouraged Ella to sit down at the kitchen table and continue with her lunch as she went through her list of questions to determine whether Mom understood what was happening.

Ella correctly answered who she was, where she was, the date of her birthday, and if asked she could have rattled off her Social Security number with no problem.

I sat quietly as most of the inquiry progressed, but gave the social worker a rundown on the lawsuit that my sister Nancy, with help from Mom's oldest son Wilson Winter III—also known as Skeeter—filed against our mother in January.

The suit was filed within a month of the time that Mom moved from her apartment in Menands, New York to Connecticut. That was a few days after Mom was released from Albany Medical Center.

Thus far it cost Mom tens of thousands of dollars—a vast chunk of her savings—to fight the charges against her, even though there never was a shred of medical or any other viable evidence that she had Alzheimer's.

The ongoing harassment also was taking a huge toll on her emotionally. The legal battles extended outside the courtroom after Nancy and Skeeter tried to saddle her with a nearly $9,000 legal bill from a court appointed evaluator whom she had not hired, used, nor wanted. That fight—over the legal fees—ended in a settlement in Mom's favor only three weeks before the social worker showed up at our door.

After that bit of unpleasantness was over Mom spent the rest of the month of June relaxing, planting flowers and enjoying their growth and color in the yards—trying to keep her mind off of her family and legal issues. She was successful until the state investigator showed up.

Although the social worker never acknowledged that it was Nancy Patrick who had made the "'anonymous" elder abuse complaint, the conversation that day continued in the vein that it was Nancy's doing, and that everyone at the table knew it.

"I know why she's doing this," Mom declared. "She's mad because I won't call her. But I haven't called her because I don't know if I'll get screamed at like the last time. And, to tell you the truth, I still don't know how I feel about what my son and daughter are trying to do to me."

It was the first time Ella spoke from the heart about the attacks on her from her own children, and it went to the heart of the issue.

The social worker left soon after that comment, and told me on the way out the door that she would check with Mom's doctor, but that she didn't see anything that should cause concern.

Nonetheless, Mom was not reassured. She continued to talk about Nancy's most recent attack, and her fear that Nancy would never stop finding ways to harass her. Her reaction to the social worker's visit was eerily similar to a reaction she had to an early legal ruling that went against her in February. Mom's lawyer attempted to have Nancy Patrick's lawsuit dismissed on jurisdictional grounds, arguing that Ella was a resident of Connecticut, not New York, had not been served in New York, and that the New York courts did not have control over her. The judge ruled against Mom, allowing the lawsuit to go forward.

Mom was not conversant with the courts and was devastated at what was little more than a procedural victory for her daughter.

On the February night when she learned of the judge's ill-advised decision against her, we found Mom awake in the early morning hours saying she was fearful that her daughter would send thugs from New York to force her into the Alzheimer's ward.

Mom's reaction to the social worker showing up was similar. She couldn't stop talking about it, worrying about it, examining it over and over from every angle.

My wife Jennifer and I tried to reassure her that Nancy was about to find out that filing false charges in Connecticut was not a smart tactic. But by dinner time Mom was complaining of being extremely tired and she decided to go to bed early rather than eating dinner.

An hour later her condition had grown worse. Jennifer checked on her and called me. "Mom has something wrong with her," she said. "She's talking but nothing she says is making any sense."

I checked Mom's vital signs, found them to be relatively normal, and determined that she was not showing any signs of a stroke. Her words were understandable, but they were out of context. She could not answer a question, and she could not articulate her own concerns.

I considered, and then rejected, the idea of calling an ambulance or taking Mom to the emergency room. I kept an eye on her vital signs but let her get as much sleep as possible. Finally, at 5 a.m., with Jennifer sleeping on the couch just outside the bedroom door, Mom arose and began making sense.

As soon as her doctor's office opened I called and was told to bring Mom in for an examination. The doctor gave her a thorough exam, including an electrocardiogram to check her heart, and scheduled a CT scan of her brain to ensure there had not been a stroke.

What happened to Ella Winter that day in June 2009 occurred often while she lived in New York, according to statements, surprisingly enough, from her daughter, Nancy Patrick. She testified in court that there were numerous times in the recent past when Ella would get confused and disoriented, even noting that each time

Nancy herself was directly involved in a conflict with her mother.

Nancy also testified that she provided daily care for her mother for nearly ten years. Mom relates a different relationship, and says that Nancy called her on average every other day, but generally saw her only once each week, usually on Sunday morning. Occasionally Nancy and her husband James also took her out to dinner mid-week, Mom said.

In addition, for nearly a year prior to her move to Connecticut Mom paid a service that arranged for a woman to visit her two mornings each week. Those regular visits included help in doing her laundry, trips to the grocery store, and assistance with light housework.

Mom also took the senior citizen's bus on a roughly forty-mile round trip to her hair appointment in Clifton Park, New York each week. Otherwise her only regular personal contacts were with other tenants in her apartment building.

Nonetheless, Ella's episodes of confusion and disorientation directly coincided with her contacts with Nancy. Nancy testified that such episodes often came as she argued with Mom about some minor item, such as the time of an appointment.

Nancy also attributed Ella's episodes to Alzheimer's. But even a cursory review of the symptoms of Alzheimer's show that they don't fit Mom's condition.

Mom's doctors in New York didn't agree with Nancy or Skeeter when they claimed during office visits that Ella was suffering from dementia or memory loss. At least twice Ella's doctors wrote "none noted," on diagnosis reports after Skeeter and Nancy claimed that she was suffering from memory issues.

In the end, Mom's family in New York and the Supreme Court system in Albany would have been far better off if they just let her live her life in peace, because Ella Winter is a diminutive nonagenarian, but that doesn't mean she is a pushover. Ella fought back, aided by her Connecticut family, and a small but strong circle of friends and legal advisers.

It cost her, make no mistake about that. It cost her personally and it cost her financially. But the cost to fight for her freedom is significantly less than what it would cost to institutionalize her against her will.

It would be easy by now to say "so what?" and write off the indignities suffered by Ella Winter at the hands of her family—and the New York State Supreme Court system—as an oddity, her problem, just one of those things.

Statistically, she is just a minor cog in a very large wheel.

But Ella Winter is not a statistic. She is a living, breathing, functioning human being who has made a significant contribution in her life, has seen her share of triumphs and tragedies, and has much she still can teach us.

Ella Winter is an intelligent and knowledgeable lady who grew strong in her youth while living and working on her father's farm in upstate New York. The twin fires of the Great Depression and World War II taught her determination and perseverance.

In the long run she needed it all.

In the coming pages you will meet Ella Winter and learn a bit of her history. It is important to know who she is and what she endured previously in her life, to fully appreciate the travesty that she encountered in the winter of 2008 and throughout much of 2009. She should have enjoyed her lunch on that summer day, and then retired to the outside porch to get some sun, absorb the aroma and bask in the bright colors of the flowers, the butterflies and the hummingbirds that inhabit our backyard, rather than being grilled by a state investigator following up on a false complaint. Ella has spent the vast majority of her life outside of the limelight, trusting her family to do right by her, as she did by them, and believing that the good she did for her children in their younger years would somehow be repaid when she reached advanced age. So first we'll learn about Ella—Mom—and then we'll review the legal assault against her spearheaded by her only daughter.

I wish this were a unique situation, one that would have people shaking their heads, but secure in the knowledge that it was an oddity. Unfortunately, it isn't.

What happened to Ella can happen to anyone, and as Ella's story will show, no one can consider himself safe and secure when money, family and old age collide.

Dedication

To Ella Winter, Mom, with appreciation for a life lived long and well, for her faith, perseverance, and indomitable strength in the face of unexpected and unrelenting assaults on her person, her character and her well being.

Acknowledgements

The first people who should be thanked for their support are my wife Jennifer and daughter Heather. They agreed without hesitation or question to open our home, and their hearts to Mom. Both knew that major changes were in the offing; both knew their lives and routines would be forever altered; and neither knew what was really in store for them. But they stood tall and strong and have never wavered.

I would be remiss if I didn't also point out that without the involvement and day by day assistance of Ella Winter herself, this book would not have been possible in this form. It was Ella who first broached the concept of writing the story of her life, and it was only through daily interviews for more than six months that a reasonably complete story was possible. In these interviews Ella was forthcoming about the good and the bad, was remarkably adept at recalling details of her life from long ago, and provided daily input and encouragement as the project progressed.

Also at the top of the list is John Tuttle who provided support ranging from long distance trips to acting as a sounding board when frustration and aggravation were just about to boil over. John's friendship and support were instrumental in the fight to keep Ella free.

Atty. Tom Sousa provided invaluable legal assistance for Mom from day one. His expertise was instrumental in helping Mom declare her independence and after a lawsuit was filed against her he was a willing and highly capable source of legal expertise.

Atty. Jack Casey represented Mom in Albany Supreme Court. He was tough, relentless and fiercely defended Mom from the legal assaults against her. Casey knew legal technicalities and also was adept in the courtroom.

Bob Soloyna showed once again the meaning of true friendship. He provided advice and assistance whenever called upon, and helped apply his personal knowledge of elder care to outline what was possible on a range of scenarios.

Rich Rodriguez surfaced at the best possible time, even though we had not seen each other or spoken in forty years. His knowledge of the legal scene in the Albany, New York area saved us considerable time and effort in locating an attorney who would provide the best possible representation.

Our neighbors Louis and Sally Dominiski have been supportive from the beginning, and have responded to requests for assistance with virtually no advance warning.

My cousin Floyd Haber and his wife Kay, and my cousin Bob Haber provided constant reassurance, information and support. They were in contact with Mom and Uncle Bob before his death, and saw firsthand many of the situations described in this book. Their continuing support of Mom, through phone calls and visits is invaluable.

Janet Rossman, Kay and Floyd's daughter made sure Mom was snug and warm in her new home literally from the time Mom arrived in Connecticut.

Uncle Vic and Joyce Brimmer. They were the anchors in Mom's life while so much else was upheaval. Mom's regular chats with her brother and our visit to their home on the anniversary of Dad's death helped immensely in keeping Mom's spirits up.

Pete and Anita Comrack my in-laws who befriended Ella and supported her in her time of need are owed a special thanks. Through them Mom has made new friends, and has made a seamless transition to a new home.

The Dziedzic and Manna families, who folded Mom into their embraces as seamlessly as if they knew her forever.

State Rep. Pam Sawyer and State Sen. Edith Prague for their support and assistance.

Physicians Kristin Gildersleeve, Katarzyna Pomianowski, Jennifer Taylor and the highly capable staff at Hebron Family Physicians including Kathy, Mary, Maryann, and Stacey for their superb medical care and the personal attention they gave to Mom and her issues.

The Hebron, Connecticut Senior Citizen Center, Town Clerk's office and other agencies for their help in making Mom's transition to our community easier.

The Hebron Resident Troopers and the Hebron Town Constables for ensuring Mom's security. Also Connecticut's Department of Social Services and the department's Aging Division; Chief State's Attorney Kevin Kane; Attorney General Richard Blumenthal; and former 2nd District Congressman Rob Simmons for providing guidance and support.

The surrounding communities and businesses for helping in the adjustment process and making Mom feel that she is truly welcome in her new home. A special thanks to Stephanie for her attention and friendship during Mom's weekly hair appointments.

And a huge thank you goes to Valerie Connelly, publisher (and editor) at Nightengale Press. This really is a case of "if not for her" because she toiled long and hard, with great suggestions on both the writing and the content. Writing, editing and producing Granny Snatching is a true collaboration of efforts thanks to Valerie's abilities and work ethic.

GRANNY SNATCHING

PART ONE

Knowing Ella Winter

CHAPTER ONE

The Early Years

A terrible snowstorm was raging the day Ella Winter was born and the doctor didn't arrive until late in the afternoon. By then, her mother and a midwife had collaborated to deliver the bouncing baby girl, with Ella's mother doing most of the work and the midwife taking a nip from time to time. Rumor had it — and Ella is only too happy to pass the story along — that the midwife hid a bottle of her favorite adult beverage under the bed, but close enough at hand to calm her nerves when necessary.

Ella debuted on January 4, 1917 in her family's home in Waverly, New York, the second daughter of Maude Ann and Archibald Eugene Brimmer. Waverly is located northwest of New York City, between Binghamton and Elmira, right on the Pennsylvania border. It was and still is in farm country, although it has changed some since the time Ella was born. The formal name listed on her birth certificate is Maude Ella Brimmer, but Ella dropped her first name when she was in high school, and she still goes by Ella today.

In Waverly the Brimmer family inhabited a large former roadhouse/inn, built in classic colonial style. An old photo from that time shows white clapboard siding, and Ella remembers that it had some additional features including a ballroom with polished hardwood on the top floor. There were windows at the end of the ballroom, but it usually was lit with oil lamps as electricity had not been installed. Ella lived there until she was four, quite happily as she remembers it. She loved the country, the sights and smells of the farm, and life in that big old house. Her sister Olive and brother Vic putting her into a baby stroller and then sending her rolling from one end of the ballroom to the other is a favorite memory. Pastures and large Elm and maple trees surrounded the house, and there were green swaths of grass to run on, a smaller yard in the front and larger yards on the sides and in back. The yards were never too large though, as they would have taken up room needed for growing crops. In back, a large pine tree sported a rope swing with a wooden seat that the children played on for hours. Ella remembers that a sweet cherry tree stood in the swing's path and the objective of every turn on the swing was to go high enough to touch its branches. "I don't know how Mom let us get away with that," Ella says. In the summer when the cherries ripened the tree provided plenty of fruit for pies and desserts.

The farm included a barn for the dairy cattle, and a pig pen - a boarded enclosure off one side of the barn that housed two pigs. The ground in the pen was usually wet and muddy which kept the pigs cool in the hot summer months. It also had a stench all its own and the children avoided it as much as possible. The family always kept two pigs through spring and summer, and Archie butchered them in the fall to provide ham, bacon, and pork for the family. "I hated that time of year," Ella says. "I always ran up to my bedroom and stuck my head under the pillow. But I could still hear the pigs squealing when Dad killed them. I can still hear them today."

Ella's early memories also are of generous parents who cared about the welfare of others. Her father was a successful farmer, and

Ella recalls her mother giving meals to strangers who passed that way. It was well before the Great Depression, but America was a mobile land and riding the rails was a common form of transportation. The railroad tracks weren't exactly nearby, but they were within walking distance and passenger trains slowed down when approaching a stream crossing. "When the train slowed, transients jumped off and soon passed by our house, looking either for work or a meal," Ella says.

"I remember Mom inviting a man in on Thanksgiving Day," Ella recalls. "He must have been pretty surprised to ask for a little something to eat and find himself invited in to sit down to a full meal, with a linen tablecloth and all."

Other family type incidents of the kind that seem intense when they occur, but generate gales of laughter when viewed from a distance, also marked their time in Waverly. One such incident occurred on a Sunday morning when Maude and the children exited the front door all cleaned, shined and ready for the walk to church. Ella's brother Vic ran down the path, ignoring Maude's call to "slow down before you ..." Vic tripped and fell headlong into a mud puddle before Maude could finish her sentence. Maude had spent the previous hour working to get her children ready for church and for an instant her face took on a look of total dismay. "It was early summer and Mom had us all dressed in white," Ella says. In Vic's case it was a white shirt and white slacks. But Maude, seeing her work undone in an instant, overcame her initial shock and reacted with understandable frustration by picking Vic up under her arm and marching straight for the barnyard. Her jaw was set, her brow was furrowed and she made it very clear that Vic was about to go swimming in the pig pen. "I told you to be careful. I told you not to run. I told you that just once I wanted you all clean and presentable when we got to church. Was that too much to ask? Well young man, if you want to be dirty, then you'll do it right. If you're going to look like a pig you may as well just jump in the pen with the rest of the pigs."

But Ella's older sister, Olive, who always had a protective streak, ran off the porch screaming "Stop Mom, stop!" The children didn't doubt for an instant that Maude really would drop Vic in the mud. But Olive didn't get more than a half-dozen steps before she too fell face first in a mud puddle, putting an end to both Maude's feigned march to the pig pen, and any plans they had for attending church that day. Maude turned and strode purposely back into the house, muttering "I give up," while the children stood motionless. After a few minutes Vic and Olive timidly made their way back into the house, where Maude silently helped them clean up and change.

As stern as she was that day, Maude also had a fun-loving streak and was fond of entertaining her children. It was near Christmas one year that Maude dressed up as Santa Claus and suddenly appeared before her children. As she intoned a somewhat higher than expected "Ho, Ho, Ho" punctuated by an occasional "Merry Christmas," Maude made for an entirely believable character, at least to the older children who screamed with delight. Ella, however, at three years old and the least familiar with the seasonal elf, had never seen Santa Claus. As Maude continued with the "Ho, Ho, Ho" routine, Ella erupted with screams of fear while running as fast as her little legs would go into the house and up to her bedroom where she hid her head under the pillow. "Bob, Olive and Vic told me much later that it really was Mom playing Santa Claus," Ella says, but for years she feared the jolly old elf.

As much as they enjoyed the home in Waverly, the Brimmers, both Archie and Maude, were a long distance from their immediate family members, and thus moved to a ninety-nine acre farm in Center Brunswick, New York, when Ella was four. That farm became the focal point of her life and to a great degree the lives of her children too. According to family lore, Archie travelled alone to Center Brunswick to look over the farm, with an eye to buying it. When Archie returned he reported that the farm was beautiful, had a large home in good repair, outbuildings that were mostly in good shape, a source of water and just shy of 100 acres of fields that could be used both for grazing and crops. His report was well-received by Maude and they agreed to the move.

While they were in Waverly the Brimmers loved to entertain, but did not approve of going overboard. Their impending move to Center Brunswick provided two opportunities at one time to display their values. One evening in particular, Ella says, a goodbye party was in full swing in the upstairs ballroom, with neighbors from miles around enjoying the music, dancing and each other's company. However, some of the neighbors also were enjoying nips from jugs of hard liquor they brought with them even though temperance movement leaders had successfully pressed for the passage of Prohibition. The jugs were left outside on a stone wall near the front door, and the male guests would go out periodically to "get some air." When Archie smelled alcohol on the breath of one of his guests, and learned by further inquiries of other guests that the "air" was tainted with ninety-proof or above he responded quickly and decisively — rushing down the stairs from the ballroom and out onto the porch. There he found jugs of alcohol lined up on the stone wall and he responded by smashing every single jug on the stones. Archie's message was clear: merriment was fine, drunken merriment was not! He also was not going to give the local law enforcement a reason to spoil their move to Center Brunswick.

Archie lived most of his life in the Troy, New York area where the Brimmers were well established, especially east toward the Vermont border, in towns including Grafton. Archie had several brothers and sisters, but like many young men of his generation who were seeking better opportunities, he left home, taking the train from Troy, to Albany and then to New York City where he found employment driving truck and delivering block-ice to homes, businesses and taverns. But his sister, Ella, known as Aunt Ella to Archie's children, was well aware that many young men of that era who left Grafton for New York came back alcoholics, and she was determined that Archie would not fall victim to the same fate. So Aunt Ella went to New York City, found Archie and marched him right back to Grafton. Life in the country may not have been as exciting as New York City, but it was safer and Archie found steady work on the farms throughout the area. Eventually the move back to the Troy area positioned him to meet Maude.

Archie's wife—the first and only marriage for him, the second for her—was Maude Ann Clarke when she first came to America from Ireland at the age of sixteen. Maude went home at seventeen, but only to say goodbye to her family in Ireland. It must have taken considerable courage to leave home and journey across the Atlantic alone on the way to America. But Maude apparently was spunky, despite being what was then referred to as a "mere slip of a girl," never growing over five feet tall or weighing much over 100 pounds.

On the voyage over, their steam-powered passenger ship encountered a strong Atlantic storm with seawater cascading over the top decks, sending the bow plunging deep into the troughs between waves one minute and climbing to the top of the next one a minute later. Maude, a Protestant, settled down on a bench below decks, where many of her fellow passengers were seasick, staggering past her, desperately searching for bathrooms. Maude looked to her left and found that her seat mate was a Roman Catholic nun who was fingering her rosary beads and praying. Seeing Maude watching her, the sister said she had an extra set of beads and Maude could use them if she wished.

"No ma'am," Maude retorted, her face set and determined. "When I pray I go straight to the top." The nun reacted as though she was stung, and stared at Maude for a long ten seconds before wordlessly returning to her prayers.

Arriving back in America Maude joined her brother Rob, and her sister Elizabeth, known as Aunt Lizzie, who was already living in America with her husband Charlie Johnson on a mid-sized dairy farm on the outskirts of Troy. Later, Maude's sister Minnie also came to America to be with her siblings, and she too settled in the Troy, New York area. The Clarke family already knew the Brimmers because Aunt Lizzie and Uncle Charlie employed Archie on their farm.

Soon after Maude Clarke arrived in America to stay she met a Navy doctor named Robert Mandeville. Eventually they married and had a son, also named Robert. Maude and her family lived in Sayre, Pennsylvania after her husband left the Navy. But her husband fell ill, possibly with cancer, and died when little Robert was only a toddler. Maude stayed in Pennsylvania for a time after his death, primarily because her in-laws lived nearby. She trained as a nurse soon after arriving in America, and after her husband's death she found work in that profession. Her in-laws cared for her son if she worked extended shifts with terminal patients.

Maude was an especially good caregiver, and never lacked employment. She honed her cooking skills during this period and later told stories of taking care of young patients with rich parents, and spending time in the kitchen with the cook when the children were sleeping. Depending on the requirements of her various clients, Maude also performed additional duties, and in at least one household was required to perform menial tasks such as sweeping and scrubbing the sidewalk!

But her days as a live-in nurse came to an end when she realized that her own son needed her skills too. Although Bob's grandparents loved him and cared well for him while his mother was away, Maude arrived home one day to find him sitting on the kitchen floor spoon feeding himself from a can of condensed milk. Although it was tasty and kept him occupied, it was not the best thing for his health and Maude decided to find employment that would allow her to be with her son on a daily basis.

Maude rarely took time off but on one such occasion she travelled north to Troy to visit her siblings. By chance, her future husband Archie was working on Aunt Lizzie's farm when she went to visit. Maude used to joke that when she met Archie, he was standing on a manure pile, which in a sense he was, because he was spreading the substance on the fields when Maude came by to visit her sister. Despite the questionable beginnings it didn't take long for the two to marry and start a family. Archie, Maude and young Robert initially lived on Aunt Lizzie's farm, and they had three children — Olive who was a twin, and Victor.

Olive's twin brother died tragically as a baby when he was exposed to whooping cough from an unthinking neighbor. The woman brought her infected child to the farm to view the twins, but Maude forbade them from entering the room where they were sleeping. But when she turned her back the child slipped into the room. Only a moment later Maude found the sick child leaning over the crib, breathing right in the baby's face. The baby, named Eugene for his father's middle name, caught the disease and died.

After the death of their child, Maude and Archie moved to Waverly, where Ella was born, right across the border from Sayre,

Pennsylvania. They stayed there for nearly five years before returning to the Troy area. The Brimmers were hard working, thrifty and generous people, and did well both in Waverly and when they purchased the farm in Center Brunswick in 1921. In Center Brunswick Archie grew vegetables — especially potatoes, tended an apple orchard, managed a herd of dairy cattle, and raised pigs.

One of the very few painful memories of the time involved what became Ella's lifelong love of chocolate. It was common for relatives who lived in the cities to visit the Brimmers on the farm during the heat of the summer. One year when Ella was four, her relatives came and brought a huge box of chocolates as a gift. They were sitting on blankets in the back yard under a large maple tree enjoying the shade and the cooling breeze, when rumbling thunder announced the arrival of a fast-moving storm. The sunny skies quickly turned dark and threatening, forcing the adults to gather up the blankets and lemonade glasses and run for the house. But no one realized until they were inside and settled that little Ella was left behind — along with the box of chocolates.

"Mom and the other women were talkers," Ella says, "and once they got going no one could get a word in edgewise. They were on to something and they didn't realize I was still outside until the rain started and someone looked out the window." Having settled comfortably in the parlor, they immediately jumped up, running outside again to retrieve the candy and the child, only to find that Ella helped herself to nearly the entire box. Besides being soaked, Ella's face and the front of her white blouse were covered with chocolate, as were her hands. She remembers that eating so much candy was fun at first, but she soon became so sick that her parents feared she had appendicitis, and they rushed her to the doctor, who correctly diagnosed the cause of her stomach ache. Despite the pain, the pleasure of consuming the candy far outweighed the inconvenience and nearly ninety years later Ella will tell anyone who inquires "Chocolate is wonderful. I highly recommend it!"

The farm in Center Brunswick was well established by the time the Great Depression hit, and self-sustaining to the point that the family was able to escape the worst of the privation that struck much of America in those years. Maude's work week evolved into an established routine that included wash day on Monday, ironing on Tuesday, and baking on Thursday. She cooked for her family as well as at least two regular hired hands, and occasionally much larger crowds of workers. That routine continued well into the last decade of her life, and in addition to her capabilities as a nurse, Maude was known far and wide as an excellent cook and baker.

That is not to say life was easy. Ella well remembers her father telling her to take occasional days off from school to help her mother. Ella says washing day alone, especially from spring to fall when two hired hands worked alongside Archie and the boys, could be a crushing burden. Maude did the laundry for her family and the hired men, and Ella remembers the heavy overalls that could become caked with dirt. The size of the extended family also created difficulties for Maude, especially with the weekend visits during the summer. "One Sunday there were so many people at the farm escaping the heat that Mom ended up cooking for 28 people," Ella recalls. "She just went down to the basement and brought up jars of fruits, vegetables and even meat. She could 'put up' nearly everything we raised - even fresh eggs. She had a method for preserving eggs that they would last for six months. And the odd thing was, no one ever gave her advance warning that they would be coming. They all just showed up." Maude took it all in stride, but Ella says it also was exhausting.

"I can remember Mom being so tired that she would go to bed, and sometimes she would just lie there crying," Ella said. The change in her lifestyle from being a nurse, and before that a doctor's wife, to working on the farm was striking, and yet Maude saw it through, especially with help from her daughters. Maude's work ethic and resilience had a deep impact on Ella, and in later years, when called upon to defend herself against family members, she effortlessly switched to a "work" mode, assisting in her defense, and even taking the offense to ensure her security.

As a child and teenager Ella stepped up when the situation required and helped with the heavy work. She saw the difficulties her mother faced, and she saw that occasionally the load seemed more than Maude could bear. But with some rest and assistance from her daughter, Maude would bounce back and pick up where she left off.

Many years later, when she was in the battle of her life, Ella too would have her 'down' moments. But she has a long memory and the lessons she learned in childhood stayed with her. She too bounced back after a little rest, and she never forgot that she also had help at hand.

While Ella's parents tended to the overall direction of their farming lifestyle the youngsters also had their chores. The boys helped with the dairy herd, which was hard work, requiring twice a day milking, seven days a week and deliveries to the dairy. There simply were no holidays. When Vic became old enough to drive, he took over delivering the milk containers to a processor in Cropseyville, about ten miles away. Ella remembered that when he allowed her to accompany him, Vic smoked a cigar he hid away in the delivery truck. "Vic told me I could ride with him as long as I didn't squeal about the cigar. I never did."

Although much of the heavy work was done by the men, the family also expected Olive and Ella to make a contribution both inside the house and in the fields too. During her teen years Ella became adept at handling a team of horses pulling loaded hay wagons from the fields to the barn, as well as operating the hay fork inside the barn.

Ella developed upper body strength that was unusual for women and she stunned the physical education teachers who tested her in gym class at Troy High School. One test involved throwing a ball, which was not the best event for most women, but Ella threw it the length of the basketball court, clearing the bleachers at the end and bouncing it off the wall near the ceiling. It was an impressive show of strength that drew considerable commentary from her teachers.

From spring to fall on the farm, mid-day mealtime could bring a crowd into the dining room, especially if there were special chores requiring extra hands, such as filling the silos, cutting hay, or harvesting. Maude cooked huge meals, with the girls serving the family and the temporary workers. Ella remembers developing a crush on one of the hired hands, and while serving dessert at lunch time "I came up behind him with a slice of blueberry pie. But he turned to help me just as I reached over his shoulder and he hit the plate with his hand. The pie went right down his shirt and I retreated to the kitchen. My face must have been as red as a beet. I couldn't even look at him after that. He was nice and didn't blame me for the accident, but that wasn't exactly the way I wanted to get his attention."

Maude and Archie developed an unspoken sense of teamwork that they applied to every action throughout the day. Both arose before five in the morning, with Archie stoking the stoves. A huge Kalamazoo range with an oven for baking, and a wide cooking surface on top was the dominant feature of the kitchen, while a pot-bellied stove stood in the center of the living room. Archie used kindling wood to get them started in the cold weather to restore heat to the house, and then added coal that burned hotter and longer. The living room stove was used only in cold weather, but the kitchen stove was operated summer and winter for cooking. Regardless of the season,

Maude began perking a huge pot of coffee first thing each morning. The coffee sat on the Kalamazoo range all day, to be accessed at will. Archie roused the boys for the daily milking chores and Maude had breakfast ready by the time they finished. After breakfast, depending on the season, the boys left for school, or went out to work with Archie.

Although Ella's teen years coincided with the Great Depression, life in the country was fruitful. Ella often said, "We didn't have a lot of money, but we weren't poor." While the farm was virtually self-sustaining she also remembers that her father was a generous man who routinely gave surplus potatoes and milk to the less fortunate. Ella's many happy memories from those days include a small but loyal circle of friends who remained close throughout adulthood. Among her best friends were Clara Wilson, who became Clara Davis when she married, and Eleanor Wager, who became Eleanor Gustafson. Ella stayed close to both women for her entire life. The three girls shared many adventures in their youth that continued right on through their adult years. When she wasn't working or spending time with her friends, Ella also loved roaming the fields that stretched along both sides of what is now Town Office Road in Center Brunswick from the section immediately surrounding the farm house, up the hill going toward Eagle Mills. Ella enjoyed the solitude she found on those walks.

"Sometimes I would take a book and go up the hill to a little knoll and sit there alone to read," she says. "Sometimes I wouldn't read I would just lie on my back and watch the clouds, making up forms and shapes."

On that side of the farm she remembers the sweet smell of hay, or the honeysuckle that grew in tangles along the edge of the woods that bordered the fields.

On the other side of the farm house, going up a slight rise toward Rt. 7, the state highway that runs through Center Brunswick, Ella loved to pick wild strawberries that flourished on the hillside. In spring the farm's apple orchards would burst with blooms that filled the air with perfume, and in the summer there was nothing better than being sent up the hill to gather strawberries for that night's dessert. Later in the summer wild raspberries grew in abundance, and they too added their special tastes and aromas to the outdoors and the dinner table. Rhubarb flourished in several patches and Maude would boil it down mixing it with heaps of sugar for a dessert that was at once both sweet and tart.

When the aromas of wild and cultivated fruits and vegetables were absent in the winter, Maude came to the rescue for her husband and children with her weekly baking marathons. The family ate at a large round center-pedestal oak table in the dining room, but on Thursdays, Maude opened up the leaf that doubled its size, and spread a soft white linen tablecloth across the top. As baking day progressed fresh loaves of bread covered the table, then cookies, including oatmeal raisin, molasses or ginger snaps, then cakes, and finally pies. Maude could bake a lemon meringue pie from scratch that literally melted in your mouth. Many years later when Ella emulated her mother's success in pie baking, she considered it the highest of compliments when another family member said she had matched her mother's skill level with the lemon meringue.

Ella was a bouncy and joyous child who developed into an outgoing young woman. She loved the life she lived in Center Brunswick, and looks back on these years with an understandable sense of longing and nostalgia. She knows that she lived in a very special era that had its share of hardships, but also provided her with the time and opportunity to grow as both a dreamer and a doer.

The Brimmer girls were hard workers and contributed to the overall family success, but that is not to say that they didn't have a bit of what Maude called "malarkey" in them too. Ella particularly remembers that when they were teens, she and Olive shared an upstairs bedroom. Olive, who was seven years older than Ella, developed a fancy for reading True Romance magazines that Maude banned in the Brimmer house.

Olive solved that dilemma by standing in front of her bureau each night with the True Romance magazine sitting inside the open top drawer, and her Holy Bible just above, sitting on top of the bureau, next to an oil lamp. Olive would read the latest gossip and scandal stories by the light of the lamp, until Maude, seeing the light from downstairs would come up to put an end to the session.

Olive, hearing her mother on the stairs, would close the drawer, and Maude always found her reading from the Bible.

"That's enough for tonight, dear," Maude would say. "The Good Book will always be there for you. But now it's time to get some sleep."

Ella, meanwhile, remembers that "I would bury my head in the covers so Mom wouldn't see how hard I was laughing. She always talked so nicely and sweetly to Olive. Mom was a task master and she could be very stern if you crossed her. She didn't believe in corporal punishment — Dad took care of that — but she still could give you a dressing down that made you feel just as bad as if you'd been spanked. It was hard to pull the wool over her eyes but I don't think she ever caught on to what Olive was doing. She really believed that every night before she went to sleep, Olive would stand at the bureau, reading her Bible by the light of the oil lamp. It made for a good picture, but the next day Olive would always have the latest Hollywood gossip or a story to share from her magazine. I didn't hear her talk much about the Bible though."

Ella acknowledges that in modern America it would be nearly impossible to duplicate her upbringing. America has become a far more dangerous place, she says, and the once common practice of letting the children run out the front door for a morning of unsupervised play now could be regarded as reckless or irresponsible. Referring to the modern practice of communities spending multiple millions of dollars to build facilities that provide tightly supervised and controlled 'recreation,' Ella muses, "Kids need time to be alone."

There was a lifelong benefit to having time to just be alone, reading a book or dreaming, she says, thinking her own thoughts and coming to her own conclusions.

She remembers a childhood that was full of people, including her immediate family and her friends. There also was an extended family structure, especially on the Brimmer side, and Ella remembers a constant coming and going of family members who lived in the area. The Brimmer family settled in what then was the wilderness of towns like Petersburg and Grafton prior to the Revolutionary War.

The Brimmer family history includes stories of children being kidnapped by Indians, and more than a century later, feuds with other families in the remote section of New York that borders the still rural Green Mountains in adjacent Vermont. In addition to his sister Ella, Archie's brothers married into other families whose ancestors were among the early settlers of the area. Ella's cousins had names including Burdick, Bulson and Miner.

And then there was Uncle Rufus.

Uncle Rufus Burdick was married to Aunt Ella. They lived on Hoosick Road — Rt. 7 — but he was an ordained minister with a church in Postenkill, several miles southeast of Center Brunswick. Ella remembers that Uncle Rufus could preach a spell-binding sermon — "people said he could make a grown man cry," Ella recalls

— and that he and Aunt Ella would go to area jails to preach and sing hymns for the prisoners. She also said Rufus was a carpenter and Ella suspects that he had something of a Jesus complex. But Archie, for reasons that are best left buried in history, did not like Rufus, and considered him a hypocrite. Ella remembers Rufus leaving his wife behind while he went on a preaching tour of America, taking a "parishioner" with him. "But I remember that when a young chicken we adopted as a pet was killed by a neighbor's dog, Rufus came and said a sermon for it when we buried it."

However, there also was a somewhat grievous incident when Archie's brother Abe — Uncle Abe as Ella recalls him — died suddenly when he was only thirty. "He was my favorite uncle," Ella says. "He would bounce me on his knee and tell me stories when I was a little girl. I don't remember why he died so young, but I was devastated." At Uncle Abe's wake, however, seeing that Ella was despondent, Uncle Rufus picked her up, held her over the open coffin, and urged Ella to give her uncle's corpse a kiss goodbye. "I didn't want to do it," she says, "but Uncle Rufus was so insistent, and everybody was watching, so I finally bent down and kissed him. But it wasn't anything like I expected. His skin was cold and didn't seem like the uncle I remembered at all. I was so upset I screamed and ran out of the room." Nonetheless, Ella and Vic still remember Uncle Rufus fondly and they have far more good stories than bad. Even today, merely the mention of his name will bring a smile to their faces.

But Archie and Rufus did not get along and there were times when other members of the family went to visit Rufus and Aunt Ella, but Archie would not enter their house. Ultimately, as both men aged, whatever caused the animosity between them dimmed, Ella remembers, and in their later years both Archie and Rufus buried the hatchet.

Kissing a corpse notwithstanding, the bulk of Ella's childhood memoires are pleasant. But there was another unhappy event in her formative years that had a lifetime impact on her — a decision made when she was in the seventh grade, to move Ella ahead in her schooling. Ella was extraordinarily smart and was on target to be the eighth-grade valedictorian of the area school district. She maintained straight A's and her average was in the high nineties. But her seventh-grade teacher, for reasons that seem inexplicable from the vantage point of history, was adamant that Ella could advance further by taking two grades simultaneously. The teacher convinced her parents to let Ella double up. For most of the courses the extra work probably would not have been all that difficult, but the eighth grade was the point where students at that time began studying Algebra. However, as a seventh grader, Ella had not finished the requisite preliminary math to prepare her for Algebra and she struggled with mathematics for the first time in her education.

Ultimately she graduated a year early, but with a B average instead of the A level she previously maintained. Ella regretted the decision to take two grades at once for the remainder of her life, and often wondered what the world would have been like for her if she had stayed with her class and maintained her A average.

After elementary school, she attended Troy High School and again did very well. High school was essentially a fun time for Ella. She had her close friends who grew up with her in Center Brunswick, she made new friends at school, she liked most of her teachers and was well liked in return. Like her mother Ella never grew very tall, topping out at four feet eleven inches during this period. She weighed less than a hundred pounds throughout her high school years.

Public school transportation was not a universal concept at the time and Ella vividly recalls her early morning walks from the farm house to the state road, about a quarter mile away, where a neighbor who drove that route to work would stop and give her and Vic a ride into the city. "But he always dropped us off on 8th Street," Ella says, "even in the coldest weather or when it was snowing. It wouldn't have taken him five minutes out of his way, but he would not alter his route, so we had to walk the last half-mile no matter what the weather was like."

Ella, who was fashion conscious and not inclined to wear ungainly snow boots that were common footwear at the time, Arctics as they were called, preferred to walk several blocks risking frostbitten toes than to be seen in those boots. It would take a snowstorm to convince her to forego fashion in favor of warmth. Archie finally relented, Ella says, and allowed Vic, who was in his senior year, to drive them both to and from school. The trip home took a bit longer because Vic also drove his girlfriend home after school each day. Once again, Ella never told on him, and Archie never found out.

During this time Ella attended the Epworth League — which much later became the Methodist Youth Fellowship — at the Center Brunswick Methodist Church. She was allowed to go on retreats both for weekends and occasionally for week-long events during the summer. Ella enjoyed this aspect of her religious upbringing very much, and her church activities combined with her 4-H membership gave her the base for her later career as a public speaker. The chaperones and instructors she met were good people who cared about the youth with whom they were entrusted, but they were not overbearing. She learned about her religion, about work on the farm, and about life, and had a good time doing it.

Ella sailed through her classes for the four years of high school, and expected to graduate high in her class. But she was not able to take her final exams due to a severe bout with Scarlet Fever that hit her just at exam time, and left her bedridden for more than a week. Ella remembers that her mother stayed by her bedside throughout her illness, taking care of her daughter without complaint, and still tending to the rest of the family too.

"I planned to go back to school in the fall and take the finals the following January, but my cousin — also named Maude — was hospitalized with a long term illness and her father asked me to come look after her." Ella ended up moving to Maude's home in Cohoes, across the river from North Troy, to care for her cousin's two toddlers. (For clarity purposes, there were three people named Maude in Ella's early life. Her mother was Maude Ann, she was Maude Ella and then there was her cousin Maude.)

Ella's cousin Maude was the daughter of her Aunt Lizzie and Uncle Charlie, who had been instrumental in Ella's parents meeting. Aunt Lizzie was talked about often in Ella's life, and Ella saw her aunt as a person who personified the immigrants' dream. She came to America with little in the way of personal wealth, but worked hard and she and Uncle Charlie succeeded in every way. They lived in a large house, drove a touring car, and had hired help — yet they were down to earth, likable people.

Aunt Lizzie made sure that her daughter Maude had a proper upbringing and Ella remembers her older cousin as a beautiful and very classy young woman. But one afternoon when Ella was quite young, Uncle Charlie and Aunt Lizzie drove to Maude's high school to pick her up at the end of the day. Aunt Lizzie stayed in the car while Uncle Charlie went inside for their daughter. When Charlie and Maude emerged a short time later they found that Aunt Lizzie had died of a heart attack while she waited in the car. In addition to the expected impact that such a horror would have on an only child in a close knit family, there was a more practical impact too

— Maude had to take over her mother's extensive business duties. Maude was only about sixteen but she stepped up to the job.

A few years later she married Sam Hall, and bore him two children — Betty and Wendell. But over time the stress caused a significant and negative impact on Maude's health. As Maude neared her thirtieth birthday she began to need the help of her younger cousin Ella, and during this time period she also was hospitalized for an operation. Ella said the nurse later told Maude's husband Sam that the doctor botched the operation, and from that point on Cousin Maude was never quite the same. She needed far more assistance at home and extensive medical care too. Maude was placed in a rehabilitation hospital for a time, and Ella moved to her cousin's home to care for Wendell and Betty.

Ella loved her older cousin and it is likely that her fashion sense developed from their association. More than seventy years later, in a courtroom in Albany, New York, with her life on the line, one of the first things observers noted about Ella was that she was impeccably dressed and groomed. The judge noted it too and there is no reason to doubt that Ella's closeness to her cousin had a positive and lifelong impact upon her. Ella never minded the work involved with caring for Maude and her children. But she also knew it couldn't last forever.

CHAPTER TWO

The War Years

Ella cared for her cousin Maude from the fall through to the following Easter. She might have continued helping out for much longer, but when it became obvious that she would never be going back to school, Ella strongly felt a need to contribute to her immediate family's finances. Her older sister, Olive, arranged a job interview for Ella at Frear's Department Store in downtown Troy, and Ella made a good impression. The manager hired her immediately and she reluctantly told Sam that she would be taking the job in Troy. Sam was unhappy with her decision, but accepted it as inevitable and scrambled to find a replacement. "I had mixed feelings about leaving," Ella says. "I really loved my cousin and felt responsible for her care. I liked Wendell and Betty too, so in a sense I felt that I was abandoning them. But it was the Great Depression and my immediate family needed me too. Ultimately they took precedence over my cousin."

The job in Frear's was the beginning of Ella's working career, and the end of her formal education. Ella remarked many times in the future that "Girls still didn't necessarily need a high school diploma to get by in those days. But times were changing and twenty years later it would have made a big difference. I always wondered what I might have become if I had continued with my schooling. I was only a few months away from my high school diploma, and in the long run, the work I did instead wasn't really more important."

That sense of regret also goes back to her parents' decision to let her combine Grade Seven and Grade Eight. "I was on track to be the valedictorian, and that in turn could have led to college. I just needed to take math one step at a time instead of jumping ahead the way I did. I wonder why that was so important. My teacher even came to the house to convince my parents to move me ahead. They saw it as an honor, but it had the opposite affect. I lost ground trying to catch up on my math."

Ella's formal schooling ended with her senior year in high school, but her informal education continued throughout her life. She had a natural curiosity and never hesitated to ask probing questions in new situations. Two decades later, when she became a manager for Stanley Home Products, she took college graduate level management courses, and applied what she had learned with considerable skill.

"I could talk to just about anyone," she says, "and if I could talk to them, I could sell them something. I worked at so many jobs in those early years, at department stores, or the shirt factories in Troy, and the automotive factories too. I always met people I liked and I always had a good time on the job, but I never felt as though I was doing what I was intended to do. There was always something missing."

Ella enjoyed her post high school years, dating often and even receiving marriage proposals along the way. She was lively, fun loving and was often invited to fraternity parties at Rensselaer Polytechnic Institute in Troy. Before you get any ideas, these were not "Animal House" type parties, but instead were formal affairs that required heels, gowns and were well attended by chaperones as well as students.

Ella enjoyed the single lifestyle, but side-stepped potential long-term relationships. One example was a boy she met at an RPI social event. They dated exclusively for several months and then he invited her home.

"I spent a weekend on Long Island meeting Eddie's parents. I liked them and they liked me, and Eddie really wanted to get married. His folks were very disappointed when I said no. He was a great guy, but the spark just wasn't there." The spark finally arrived when her friend, Jimmy Marshall, introduced Ella to Wilson Winter in the early 1940's.

Wilson emigrated from Scotland when he was in elementary school, and was raised in New York City. He too left high school before graduation, in his case so he could enroll in a machinist apprentice program at the National Can Company.

After completing his apprenticeship, "The foreman told me to pack my tools and hit the road," Wilson said. "When I asked him why, he said 'so you can learn your trade.' He said the apprenticeship was just the beginning and I still had a lot to learn."

Wilson packed his tools and his belongings, said goodbye to his family and headed north, finding work at the U.S. Army Arsenal at Watervliet, New York, a short distance up the Hudson River from Albany and directly across the river from Troy. Wilson and Jimmy worked together at the Arsenal, Jimmy's sister Millie dated and then married Ella's brother Vic, and Jimmy was responsible for the first meeting between Wilson and Ella.

They hit it off immediately, and began dating. "When I met him he had ulcers from eating all his meals in a diner," Ella says. "He ate way too much fried food so I started bringing him home for dinner." Their courtship opened a world to Wilson that he had not appreciated when he lived in New York City—the country.

"We used to drive out in the country on weekends," Wilson said of his family in New York City, "and I saw the farms and animals from a distance. But I never gave much thought to how much work was involved in a successful farm nor in the risks involved."

Soon after Wilson and Ella began dating, he and Archie attended an estate sale at a farm near Archie and Maude's that was being sold off by a bank. "Everything they had gained in their entire life was being sold out from under them," Wilson said.

But he didn't see the end of the sale because he came down sick, including a high fever, right in the middle of the auction. Archie brought him back to the farm where Maude took pity on him and gave him a dose of "liniment" which probably could not be sold legally today.

"He fell asleep on my bed and woke up three hours later completely drenched with perspiration," Ella says, "But the fever was gone. We never figured out whether Wilson was coming down with something before he went to the sale or if he encountered something there that hit him so hard. But he never forgot that dose of liniment and never found out what was in it."

Wilson also had to become accustomed to fields, field hands, farm equipment, seasonal work, milking schedules and feeding the stoves in the winter. He had a pretty steep learning curve initially, but he stuck with it and he and Ella continued to date. They finally married on August 23, 1942, and rented an apartment in Troy for several months. But well before their first anniversary World War II intervened. It happened because Wilson was expecting a raise in his hourly wage at the Arsenal, but when he got it, the amount was far less than what he believed he deserved.

"His boss called him in and made a big deal out of giving him two cents. Wilson told him exactly what he could do with those two cents and stormed out," Ella recalls. "He was sure he would be working at a better job with a better wage by the next day. General Electric was hiring and he planned on applying there. But the next day before he could, a telegram came from the draft board telling him to report for induction to the Army," Ella says. "I'm sure his boss at the Arsenal called the draft board before he was out the door."

Wilson wasn't too keen about becoming a foot solider, and instead followed centuries of family seagoing tradition by joining the US Navy. He spent the summer of 1943 in basic training at Camp Sampson in upstate New York, then departed for the Great Lakes training center for further schooling.

Ella travelled to Chicago to be as near to her husband as possible, and landed a job at the Marshall Fields department store. "I liked it there, and learned a hard lesson too," Ella says. "I already had more experience than some of the people who had been hired before me, so I got a higher salary going in. But the first time our paychecks came out, one of the girls looked over my shoulder to see how much I was making. When she found out it was more than she made, she went to the other girls and started a ruckus. The boss called me upstairs and told me that I had to be careful who was looking when I opened my check. But I didn't get fired and he didn't dock my pay."

Ella did well at Marshall Fields and was promoted, but when Wilson was given orders to report to the west coast for deployment, Ella returned to Center Brunswick. Their parting was sad and Ella feared for Wilson's safety—appropriately as it turned out. But it was World War II and more than ten percent of the total American population of 140 million was serving on active duty. By the end of the war some fifteen million Americans served in the Armed Forces and Wilson was not one to stay at home when so many others were serving.

Much later in her life Ella revealed that she always suspected Wilson had staged the walkout at the Arsenal so he would have an excuse to join the service without angering her. "I had a suspicion that he really wanted to join and didn't want to stay back when his friends were already in the service," she said.

Wilson reported aboard the USS Princeton, (CVL-23) a small aircraft carrier, known as a "baby flattop." He set sail for the western Pacific in 1944 while Ella took jobs first at a defense plant, working on airplane parts, and later at the local ration board in Troy, New York. But in October 1944 Ella heard the news on the radio that the Princeton had been sunk in the Battle for Leyte Gulf. It was more than a week before she received word that her husband had survived. Ella was nearly in shock, and couldn't eat or sleep well until she finally received word from the War Department that Wilson was alive. Wilson lived because the bomb that hit the Princeton exploded below decks, on the same deck where he was working. He said many times in later years that he wasn't killed because the explosion went upwards and outward, wreaking havoc on the decks above. Wilson and a comrade, choking on thick smoke, donned gas masks and groped their way across decks that were strewn with debris, their arms wrapped around each other so neither would be lost. They clambered up broken stairways, occasionally bumping into other survivors who also were climbing upwards, and at times passed the bodies of sailors who were killed in the blast.

After what seemed like an hour, but probably was no more than fifteen minutes, they emerged from a hatchway onto the hangar deck, where burning aircraft were laden with fuel and torpedoes. "The smoke was so thick we couldn't see," Wilson said. "But then we saw a faint light and we started for it, figuring it must be an opening to the outside. All we wanted then was to breathe fresh air." The light was coming from one of the aircraft elevators which fortunately was in the down position, providing unfettered access to the outside of the ship. As they reached it a tremendous explosion sent them flying out into the waters of Leyte Gulf.

Wilson suffered shrapnel wounds to his back, burns to his neck, and his shoes were ripped off of his feet. But after three hours in the water he eventually was rescued. Wilson was eligible for, but refused to apply for, the Purple Heart medal for his wounds. Shrapnel was found in his back when he was x-rayed during a medical exam more than forty years later, but even then he would not discuss applying for the medal. He once told his son that he had seen so many other sailors whose injuries were so much worse than his that he could never in good conscience accept that medal, regardless of his sacrifices.

There was one other thing about his three-hours in the blue, shark-infested waters of Leyte Gulf. "I was terrified," Wilson said late in his life. "The water was warm so I wasn't worried about hypothermia. And I was wearing a lifejacket so I wasn't worried about drowning. But I was worried about the Japanese strafing us, and I was terrified of the sharks. I just wanted to go home."

Finally a rescue boat appeared, but Wilson's rescue nearly got his comrade a court martial. They had been treading water within arms reach of each other for three hours when a lifeboat from a destroyer reached them. Wilson's friend was pulled from the gulf, but just then the Boatswain's Mate—Bos'n in Naval parlance—who was in charge of the boat, received a call from the ship that another Japanese attack was inbound. The boat began to turn back to the ship, leaving Wilson still in the water, but his friend threatened to flatten the Bos'n if Wilson wasn't rescued too. With a shrug the Bos'n ordered the boat to turn back, Wilson was pulled aboard and no one spoke about the incident again.

Back home, life had come to a standstill for Ella and the Brimmers as they waited for word from the western Pacific. She made her daily trip to the Troy ration board, doling our ration cards for meat, cheese, gasoline and other essential items that were regulated according to the national defense needs. "But I went to work and came home in a daze," Ella says. "I'm sure I went to church that Sunday, but I really don't remember it." She does remember when the telegram arrived announcing that he had survived, and the immense sense of relief that flooded over her and her other family members as well.

"Those were the longest eight days of my life," Ella recounted. She later discovered to her dismay that a lifelong friend from Center Brunswick, Peter Bulson, had been killed on the cruiser USS Birmingham, that had pulled alongside to help fight the fires on the Princeton. A second massive explosion on the Princeton engulfed both ships and hundreds of sailors on the Birmingham were killed.

Decades later Ella would recall how as kindergarteners she and Peter sat on a bench outside the two-room schoolhouse in Center Brunswick on a sunny afternoon in the fall, waiting for their older sisters to walk them home. They weren't allowed to walk alone on Rt. 7—the school and Rt. 7 are both still there—but Peter had a small amount of money and an idea.

"He asked if I liked chocolate, and when I said yes, he said 'Let's go to Hayner's and get some candy,'" Ella recalled. So they walked a quarter-mile up the forbidden road to the local candy store, and bought the chocolate. "It was warm and sunny and the chocolate melted all over us. It ended up smeared all over our faces. But on the way back we saw our teacher, Mabel Keyes, and she took pity on us. She cleaned us up and had us back on the bench before our sisters arrived to walk us home. No one ever told on us." That exploit is one of the many fond memories of Ella's childhood.

Peter figured prominently in another incident in her early life, this time when she was in her mid-teens. Peter's mother had died and Ella and her friends often gathered at his house in the evenings, in what many decades later would be termed a support group. "We played board games, talked and listened to the radio," Ella says. "It helped him deal with the death of his mother. We hadn't experienced unexpected death like that and we all felt it was important to be there for him." Peter's mother was well liked in Center Brunswick and it seemed natural for his friends to help provide him with emotional support. On an evening in late summer Ella left her house to join with her friends at Peter's.

"Be home by dark," Archie admonished her as she was leaving.

"I'll be home by nine o'clock," Ella responded.

"Be home by dark," Archie repeated ominously.

Ella went to Peter's house and was absorbed in a card game with her friends when she looked at the clock and saw that it was 8:40 p.m. "I had this sense that I let too much time go by, but when I saw the clock I felt relieved. Then I looked outside and it was pitch dark. My heart went right up into my mouth."

"I literally flew out the door of Peter's house," Ella says, and her friends quickly followed her. "I ran for the intersection," of what now are Rt. 7 and Town Office Road. It was only about a quarter-mile away, and the one street light in town provided a landmark as well as illumination.

The streetlight also provided a glimpse of Archie, waiting impatiently, occasionally sending out a piercing whistle, accomplished by putting two fingers in his mouth and blowing through them. He used that whistle when working in the fields and it was well known that it carried an urgent message—*look this way,* or *get over here!* "I ran up to Dad, but as soon as I was within arm's reach he grabbed me, spun me around and walloped me right on the rump. It was bad enough that I was fifteen and considered myself way too old to be spanked, but we knew everyone who lived by that intersection. There were a half-dozen houses there, maybe seven, and we knew everyone. They were our friends and neighbors and they were all out on their porches. I couldn't see them, but I knew they were there."

"I was so humiliated. I don't remember whether I felt any pain, but to be handled like that, to be spanked like a little child right in front of the whole community! All my friends had caught up just as Dad hit me. But I couldn't even look at them. I took off running down the road, and didn't even stop when I passed right by Mom. She was worried about me, because she had seen how angry Dad was so she was coming up to the intersection to talk to him. But it was too late. I remember tears running down my cheeks and I think my face stayed red for a week. I was so embarrassed, so humiliated. I didn't want to leave the house, I didn't want to look at my friends. I felt so grown up when I went to Peter's house, to help out that way. But Dad made sure I did get 'too big for my britches' as they used to say. He brought me back down to earth, and maybe I needed it, but I never forgot what a horrible feeling it was to be disciplined like a child right out in public where everyone could see."

The next afternoon, after school, Archie entered the kitchen where Ella was working on her homework. "I hope you learned a lesson last night," he intoned dryly. Ella doesn't remember whether she answered him, but she certainly remembers what was on her mind, and it wasn't a kindly thought. The next day Archie approached her again, and gave her a quarter. "Go up to Hayner's and get yourself some candy," he told her. "It was obviously a peace offering," Ella says. "He had gotten over his anger at being disobeyed and maybe was feeling a little guilty about spanking me. In the long run I got over it, and we were close again, but I have never forgotten that night and how it made me feel. I can still see that street light, I can still feel the blood going to my head and I can still remember the tears on my cheeks."

If that incident reminds Ella that she was still a child in her parents' eyes, it is the memory of Peter's death that serves as a poignant benchmark of Ella's transition to adulthood.

Several years later, as WWII raged, Peter, now also in the Navy, stopped by her house to say goodbye before he shipped out. Wilson had already survived several battles in the Pacific, but "this was Peter's first time out." She had no way of knowing that in a few short weeks her husband and her friend would be within yards of each other in the midst of the last great sea battle between modern navies. Nor could she have imagined that only one would survive. She would often muse on the twist of fate that spared her husband as his ship exploded, but took the life of a friend on a nearby ship that was trying to help save the Princeton. Even though it was decades ago, a sense of lingering sadness still surfaces when Ella remembers her long ago childhood friend and his untimely demise. Her voice grows low, she looks downward, and after a moment or two she'll look up and remind listeners, "It all was so long ago. So much has happened since then. But I can see every bit of it as if it was just yesterday."

Ella was already married and in her mid-twenties, but she sees the sinking of the Princeton and the death of Peter Bulson as the time when she truly became an adult. She realized that she could not have changed anything that happened, and she had to toughen herself emotionally to overcome the sadness she felt about the loss of a friend.

"You have to adjust," Ella says decades later. And she sees the adjustment she made in the 1940's as very similar to the adjustment she made sixty years later when she was locked in a legal battle with some of her own children.

"You realize that life is continually changing," she says. "Some changes are more dramatic than others, and some require a new approach. You have to learn to go on. I still remember Peter, and I still remember life before my children took me to court. But in both cases life is different now and you have to live in the present."

While Ella and the rest of the family waited for news on Wilson he was experiencing his own drama, and was oblivious to the death that occurred on the Birmingham. He treaded water, floated, swam a bit, and kept his spirits up for three hours until he was rescued. He was brought to the destroyer, given hot coffee and food, and was issued replacement clothing. He then began a series ship-to-ship transfers ending with his return to the states. Wilson was given shore leave while he waited to be assigned to a new ship, which turned out to be another aircraft carrier, the USS Siboney. It was under construction at the naval installation in Bremerton, Washington, and when his leave was over Wilson reported in.

Ella took a troop train across the US and joined him a short time later. Her stories of that trip are amazing in that she often relied on and received, as Tennessee Williams once put it, "the kindness of strangers."

She remembers that even though she travelled alone, "Soldiers and sailors were very protective. They made sure I had a seat in the dining car, that I had food, that I wasn't bothered. They were great guys. It is amazing to realize that once I travelled all over this country alone, and didn't think anything of it. I don't think a young woman can do that now, at least not with the same sense of safety."

Photos from that period show a very pretty and perky young woman with dark wavy hair and a friendly smile. Her sparkling blue eyes and friendly demeanor made Ella easy to talk with and easy to like, but she also was determined and strong. The thought of travelling across the breadth of the United States in a troop train full of strangers so she could be with her husband never fazed her. However, when she arrived on the West Coast she found that life in Bremerton was very much on the wilder side, as the town was crammed full of sailors and Marines, bars and brothels. Friday and Saturday nights meant that huge numbers of servicemen would be in town on liberty, and fights between the services were common, as was drunkenness. Wilson also talked of "Zoot Suiters," thugs who dressed in the fashion of the time with wide-shouldered suit jackets, pants that were extraordinarily narrow or "pegged" at the ankles, and wide-brimmed hats. They preyed on the servicemen, mugging and robbing them of their wages.

"Sailors never walked alone, and we never walked on the sidewalks, because the Zoot Suiters would drag you into the alleys and rob you. We always went in groups and walked down the middle of the street to be safe," Wilson said.

But they also found decent people, who weren't involved in the seamier activities of the town, who rented a home to them, although it was across the street from the Navy brig. "I'd start my day with a cup of coffee while the prisoners did their morning run and exercises on the other side of the wire," Ella says.

When the Siboney was completed it sailed out for a weeks-long shakedown cruise, during which Ella was alone and not exactly happy. She was lonely, she didn't know anyone except her landlords, and she dared not go out by herself. Once again Ella made friends, but she was happy to leave Bremerton to meet up with Wilson in California. The ship then sailed for San Diego and Ella took a long bus trip to join her husband there. She met and long remembered not only fellow passengers, but people along the way at rest stops who helped make the trip both bearable and memorable. She arrived in Los Angeles, California after nearly three days and two nights in a forerunner of modern passenger buses. Comfort was limited, there were no on-board restrooms and the bus made frequent stops to pick up new riders, or for meals at rest stops. When Ella arrived in Los Angeles she took a taxi to a small town about an hour away, where her second cousin Anna, and Anna's husband Albert, lived. But then fate intervened on Ella's behalf and what had seemed like a simple act of friendship several years earlier resulted in a stay in a Hollywood mansion and an inside look at filmdom in America.

A few years before Ella met Wilson her brother Vic's wife Mildred—Millie—was working as a clerk in the Troy, New York offices of the Hollywood Curler Company. One of the firm's founders Tommy Thompson visited her office and Vic and Millie accompanied him to dinner that evening. Although the executive was married, his wife was back in California, so to even off the party, Ella, who was in her late teens, came to the rescue, agreeing to accompany them as a dinner companion. Ella handled the assignment with grace and dignity and Tommy had a wonderful evening, enjoying good food, good conversation and good companionship - which he did not forget. The next day they gave Tommy a tour of the hills east of Albany, New York driving as far as Bennington, Vermont. Ella said it was an all around pleasant day, with blue skies, fair temperatures, and the top down on Vic's convertible. Tommy, who had never been to the east, immensely enjoyed his stay.

Several years later, while she was staying with Anna and Albert and waiting for word on when the Siboney would arrive in San Diego, Ella mentioned her encounter with Tommy Thompson and that he lived in Hollywood.

"I told cousin Anna that Tommy had said to call them if I ever came out west, but I didn't think he'd remember me. But Anna insisted that I make the call. She said someone who lived in Hollywood would be able to show me far more of the area than she could at her age."

Ella responded that she was a young woman when she was Tommy's dinner companion, and she didn't take the invitation seriously. But Anna, who was in her mid-seventies and still drove a truck along what then were narrow roads often along steep canyons, urged Ella to make the call. Ella was enjoying her stay with family, especially Anna's husband Albert, who was eighty-nine and blind, but had a wealth of life experiences and stories to share. Ella felt at home staying with Anna and Albert and was reluctant to call someone who might not remember her. But ultimately Anna prevailed, and Ella made the call. She was not only remembered, but very well received!

"Tommy and his wife came to Anna and Albert's within an hour in a touring car, picked me up, took my suitcases, and drove me from the hills outside Hollywood to the hub of California's film industry." For the next two weeks she lived in a home that to her was a mansion, in Hollywood.

Ella remembers a wonderful diversion that included Wilson as soon as the Siboney arrived in San Diego. Mrs. Thompson was a school teacher and her students included Bing Crosby's children who lived right next door. They also had a neighbor on the other side who cultivated orchids. When the call came one morning that the Siboney was docking that afternoon, the neighborhood sprang into action.

The Thompsons gave Ella a ticket for her first airplane ride, the orchid-growing neighbor fashioned a corsage from fresh orchids and Tommy drove her to the airport for the trip to San Diego. Ella remembers that airplane ride as if it were yesterday.

"I was really surprised at how low we were," Ella says. "I didn't think I'd be able to see the ground from way up there, but I could see fine. In fact I could see so far that I spent the entire trip glued to the window next to my seat. I really loved that flight. It was my first time in an airplane and it was wonderful."

When the ship docked Ella was waiting, and she was able to give Wilson a pleasant shock when she informed him where he would be staying. They returned to Hollywood for several days, and were given a whirlwind tour of film land. She particularly remembers their visit to Grauman's Chinese Theater which has since been renamed, but sixty years later still stands right where it was in 1945.

Ella and Wilson also visited with Anna and Albert, and got to hear more of Albert's stories—including his taking a steamer to the Alaskan gold fields during the gold rush of the 1890's—before they left for San Diego. But soon the leave was over and the Siboney was scheduled to sail. Ella and Wilson, still relative newlyweds, and still very much in love, left the Los Angeles area and took a bus to San Diego where they rented a room for their last few days together. Those few days flew by and then it was once again time for Wilson to leave. Ella expected a few last minutes together on the dock after Wilson reported aboard and before the ship set sail, but the ship's captain decided against granting further shore leave and Ella was forced to watch Wilson sail away to war without a final goodbye. She was left standing on the dock with hundreds of other wives and family members, hoping for a glimpse of Wilson. But the flight deck where sailors were allowed to stand at attention while the ship departed was several stories above ground level and it was impossible for her to see him.

"I was left standing on the dock, waving my handkerchief, tears streaming down my face," Ella says. "It must have looked like a scene out of a movie but I wasn't thinking about that. I was thinking that I didn't want him to go, I didn't want him to go into battle again. I'd hoped to have a few last minutes with him, just a few, just one last goodbye, but the Captain wouldn't allow it. I was so sad, and so afraid of what was waiting for him. I knew there was a real possibility that I would never see him again, and my heart was breaking." The ship sailed, Ella returned home to Center Brunswick by train and then, a month later learned that she also was pregnant!

She worried that Wilson might not survive to see his first child, but fate intervened in their favor. The battles of Iwo Jima and Okinawa were fought while Ella and Wilson were in Washington, and Germany surrendered before the Siboney was cleared for war duty. The entirety of the US Armed Forces was gearing up for the invasion of the Japanese homeland which was expected to be bloody beyond anything anyone had ever experienced in human history. But on August 6, 1945 as the Siboney headed out into the Pacific, President Harry S. Truman ordered the ***Enola Gay*** B-29 Superfortress bomber to launch from the airstrip on the island of Tinian and drop the first atomic bomb, code-named "Little Boy," on Hiroshima, Japan. That was followed on August 9, 1945 by the detonation of the second atomic bomb, Fat Man, over Nagasaki, Japan. Prior to the use of the atomic bombs the Japanese homeland was the target of a months-long fire bombing campaign that all but destroyed sixty-seven Japanese cities and killed an estimated 500,000 Japanese, leaving up to five million homeless. The atomic bombs killed as many as 70,000 people in Hiroshima and 40,000 in Nagasaki outright, with those numbers doubling by the end of 1945. The extent of the destruction and the loss of human life convinced the Japanese to surrender on August 15, 1945, sparing Wilson and millions of other Americans.

Despite Japan's surrender, the Siboney continued on and the Navy assigned Wilson to a few months of occupation duty in Japan.

In later years he would tell of his tour of a Japanese factory that was building one-man submarines, hundreds of which were ready and waiting for use. They were to be loaded with explosives and piloted by suicide drivers beneath the American warships in the invasion fleet, blowing them up from underneath much like the kamikaze aircraft did from the air at Okinawa. Tens of thousands of Americans would have died before setting foot on the Japanese homeland, Wilson maintained.

But if that was Wilson's most enduring memory of Japan, the one that stuck with Ella was the time he and a buddy didn't make it back from liberty and hired a Japanese fishing boat to take them far out in Tokyo Bay to catch the Siboney which already was underway. "Missing a movement" as their escapade was called was a court-martial offense, but Wilson got off with a month on mess duty, peeling potatoes on the night shift for a Marine cook.

Wilson said for the rest of his life that he had more fun on mess duty than the ship's captain ever intended. "Every night I dumped huge sacks of potatoes into the automatic peeler, delivered the peeled potatoes to the cook, and threw away the peels," he said. "That Marine would give me anything I wanted to eat, so for the next month I had steak and fried potatoes every night. I'd sit and talk with the cook while I ate." As Wilson remembered the "punishment," it didn't seem like punishment at all.

The one thing he never revealed is what he was doing when he missed the movement. He had been in Japan for a few months and should have known his way around. He certainly knew Navy regulations and what would happen if he was late getting back to the ship.

"He said they got lost," Ella said. "At least, that's his story. And he is stuck with it."

CHAPTER THREE

Post World War II

It wouldn't be naïve of a person who was born in the late 1940's through the early 1960's to assume that everything in America immediately after World War II was one big party, judging from the photos and news coverage of the time. Sailors were kissing pretty girls in Times Square, people were celebrating the end of the war all across the country, Europe was grateful, and neither Wilson, nor millions of other war veterans ever wavered from their assertion that we were spared a million casualties by dropping two atomic bombs on Japan, rather than invading the main islands.

But by the time Wilson returned from occupation duty he experienced what veterans of other wars have encountered when the threat is gone and the fighting is over.

"You couldn't buy a drink in any bar in San Diego if you were in uniform before I shipped out in '44 and again '45," Wilson said. "But by the time I got back after the bomb was dropped, it changed to 'Sailors and Dogs Keep Off the Grass.'"

When he returned to California in late November, 1945, Wilson wasted no time in travelling across America by train, back to upstate New York. Millions of veterans were heading home and looking for jobs. Wilson and Ella lived briefly with her family in

Center Brunswick, and then purchased a two-family home on Hoosick Street in Troy. Wilson had many plans when he first got back, Ella related, even considering starting a chicken farm.

"I have no idea how he figured he would be a good chicken farmer," Ella would laugh later, noting that the smell alone would have discouraged him the first day.

But Wilson was a skilled machinist and began seeking employment in a field where he had some expertise. The competition was brutal, as many veterans who were stationed in the states had a jump on job hunting since they often were discharged long before Wilson and others who were overseas got home. Wilson searched for work unsuccessfully into January, but soon realized that he should do what he knew best and successfully applied for his old job at the Watervliet Arsenal! As a result of going back to work for the federal government, Wilson's time in the Navy counted toward his seniority, which would work in his favor in the future.

The government passed the GI Bill in 1944, the largest and most expansive of its kind in American history, and millions of vets enrolled in college, living in government built housing, paying for books and tuition with government checks, and even receiving a monthly stipend that didn't make anyone rich, but did help with the readjustment.

But college was not for Wilson. Besides, he had a family now. Ella's pregnancy, which she discovered shortly after he shipped out in August 1945, resulted in their first child, a son, on April 29, 1946. Wilson's full name was Wilson Winter Jr., since his father and namesake in New York City was Wilson Winter Sr. Thus, Ella and Wilson's first son was aptly named Wilson Winter III. Somewhere along the way the baby picked up the nickname Skeeter and that moniker stuck with him for the rest of his life.

Shortly after Skeeter's birth Ella and Wilson purchased the house on Hoosick Street. They rented part of the house to another family and even took in borders from Rensselaer Polytechnic Institute nearby. They kept the house for about a year before deciding that it was too crowded and too hectic. They sold it at a profit and moved back in with Archie and Maude in Center Brunswick.

Maude and Archie rented out part of the big farmhouse during and after the war to supplement their income, but family took precedence over money and they accommodated Ella and her growing family. Activity on the farm dwindled since the mid-1940's when an anthrax outbreak in dairy herds across the country resulted in the destruction of a portion of Archie's milk producing stock. As a result of the costs and loss of income Archie sold off most of his acreage, leaving a roughly ten-acre plot surrounding the main house. He sold some land to the Town of Brunswick, and a few plots that had once been hay and cornfields eventually became house lots.

The farm still looked essentially the same, with flat land surrounding the house and rolling hills rising up on the east. The acreage remaining—after the land sale—was bordered on the east and north by a small stream and a long stand of huge willow trees marked the boundary. In the next three decades only three houses were built on the fields—a red-brick cape, a white clapboard cape, and a ranch-type house, all at the top of the hill to the east. Other farmers still used the land for hay or corn, so there was little to show that it now belonged to someone else. Archie also rented out his remaining acreage to other farmers, and each spring and fall the crews would come for planting or harvesting. Some years the fields would sprout even rows of field corn, with the tassels reaching well above six feet and higher before harvest time. Archie never planted the same crop two years running and in other years oats or timothy were the favored crop with the green sprouts of spring topped by golden seeds in August.

Although life settled into a far more normal routine than they experienced during the war, Ella said that Wilson changed in the years he had been away, and not for the better. He had, after all, experienced combat and nearly been killed.

"He wasn't the happy-go-lucky guy I married," she said. Studies decades later showed that a huge percentage of returning World War II veterans suffered from the impact of combat. But compared to the later openness—and criticism—of Vietnam veterans who agitated for Veterans Administration recognition and treatment for combat stress, many veterans from the World War II generation were left to deal with their ghosts alone. Wilson's demons followed him throughout the rest of his life, and Ella bore the brunt of his war experiences. They were manifested primarily through a white-hot anger that could flare at an instant's notice with little to no warning and often no noticeable provocation.

"One minute he would be fine," Ella says, "and then he would be so angry that you couldn't talk to him. The only thing you could do when he got like that was avoid him. He had never been like that before he went to war, and I am convinced that what happened to him in the Navy changed him permanently."

Despite the difficulties, Wilson and Ella worked on his readjusting to civilian life together, and settled into family life. Nine months after Skeeter was born Ella became pregnant again, and on October 10, 1947 their son Ron was born. Archie and Maude could well have been excused if they had seemed confused about the makeup of their household in this period, as not only Ella and Wilson, but her brother Bob and his wife Irene, their two children, Gladys and Paul; and her brother Vic and his wife Millie also lived there at various times. The farmhouse was a two-family building with a central entrance door to the main house. It had a center staircase and four chimneys, two in Archie and Maude's side, and two more in the side occupied by Wilson, Ella and their family. Additions had been built on both sides of the house to accommodate separate kitchens that truly made it a two-family home. It had clapboard siding when Archie and Maude first moved in, but in the 1940's they covered it with brown asphalt shingles that remained in place for nearly two decades. The house sat on a slight knoll that fell away to fields on the north and west sides, the road on the south, and an unused building that later became Bob's home on the east. The farmhouse also had two bathrooms, with water supplied from a shallow well on the north side next to Ella and Wilson's kitchen. Archie and Maude occupied the ground floor on the south side, with a kitchen, dining room, living room, bedroom, bath and porch, while the upstairs rooms were for Ella's brothers and their wives.

Maude surrounded the house and the yards with a wide variety of flowers that bloomed from early spring to late fall, and warm weather always brought the aromas of blossoms in the spring that were supplemented by the smell of new mown hay in the summer.

Across the road on the south side stood the barn that once housed Archie's dairy herd on the lower level, as well as a huge hay loft on the upper level. The barn was unused, unpainted and the boys were forbidden from playing there. It belonged to someone else from the late 40's onward, and Wilson feared that the unused equipment on the first floor and trap doors in the hayloft provided far too many opportunities for injury.

The farmhouse on the other hand provided plenty of opportunities for both play and mischief. It was commonplace for the children downstairs to climb the center staircase to visit their relatives upstairs, until an incident in 1949 when Skeeter kicked Ron under the chin knocking him down the stairs and breaking his nose. Six decades later, Ella still grimaces when describing the incident.

"First I heard a thud, then a scream. I found Ron at the bottom of the stairs and rushed him to the hospital. The doctor had to set his nose without anesthesia. He just put one hand on one side and the other hand on the other side and snapped it back in place—SNAP—just like that. Ron let out a blood-curdling yell, but it was over so quickly that he didn't cry for long. I still remember it though," she adds with a shudder.

The near overcrowding was resolved when Bob began converting the building on the east side—on the same side of the road and just downhill from the farmhouse—into a house. In previous years it was used as a garage and chicken coop. Vic raised turkeys there, and Maude lost her diamond engagement ring when she was casting feed to the chickens one day.

"We all went down there and looked for hours, but we never found Mom's ring," Ella said.

After Archie discontinued dairy farming, with the children grown and working elsewhere, the building was used only occasionally as a garage. No one minded that Bob wanted to turn it into a house, in fact they encouraged him. Bob worked steadily on the conversion, and when he finished, the old farm building was transformed into a tidy cape with kitchen, living room, one bedroom and a dining room on the first floor, and more bedrooms on the second floor. A porch on the back of the house was accessed from the kitchen and Bob closed it in with storm windows and screens so the family could enjoy the cool breezes in the summer. Bob moved his wife Irene, his daughter Gladys and his son Paul into their new home, close enough to see his parents and siblings every day, but just far enough away to have a life of his own. Uncle Bob, as he was known to Olive and Ella's children, would occupy that home for nearly sixty years. Vic and Millie, also looking for a little space and privacy, found a farm in Grafton and moved there.

Ella and Wilson occupied the larger side of the farmhouse, which provided them with a kitchen, dining area, separate dining room for formal meals, living room, bathroom and two bedrooms. The L-shaped kitchen had a pantry on the far end of the short side that provided plenty of storage space for canned and dry goods. In the early 1950's Wilson installed black tiling over the wood kitchen floor, and painted the wainscoting that ran along the entire interior wall. Since the kitchen also had a door to the outside, he built a small entryway on the outside "stoop," so the winter winds wouldn't blow straight into the kitchen when someone entered. A propane stove was used for cooking in the kitchen, and a coal stove that was centrally located in the dining room heated that side of the house in the winter. Eventually they also would have use of another bedroom upstairs, which more than accommodated their growing family.

In time life in the farmhouse in Center Brunswick settled into an agreeable routine. Wilson worked while Ella stayed home with the boys.

Maude still maintained her lifelong routines, and arose early every morning. The first sounds heard in the house every day were the clanks of the stove tops being opened to make room for more fuel, and they were quickly followed by the aroma of percolating coffee. Nearly simultaneous with the aroma of coffee came the sounds of the early morning farm report on the kitchen radio on weekdays and the music of hymns on Sunday mornings. For reasons she would not discuss later in her life, Maude stopped going to church, but that didn't mean she was not religious. She just decided to keep her religion to herself and practiced it in her kitchen rather than in the church. She knew the lyrics to dozens of hymns and would sing along with the radio. When she didn't know the words, she hummed as she went about her work. In addition to her inside work, Maude often tended the vast flower beds that included tulips and daffodils in the spring, poppies, roses, irises, hollyhocks and other perennial flowers that bloomed right through the fall. Aromatic shrubs lined a pathway from the front yard around to the kitchen door on Archie and Maude's side.

The central gathering area for the boys outside of the house was the creek, or "crick" as they called it, that bordered Archie's last 10 acres. The small stream could be dammed to make pools, it was wide and deep enough in some spots for small boys to sit in it on hot summer days, and there was sufficient imagination to turn it into the playground of choice on an instant's notice. The boys would scrape gravel from the creek bed to form the outlines of the dams, and then finish them off with mud and clay that were dug out of the banks. The standing rule was that once a day's playtime was ended, the dam would be opened up and the stream would return to normal. On the far side of the crick the land turned swampy and occasionally the dank smell of rotting vegetation would waft over the boys as they played in the water. They examined frogs, tried to catch water striders or minnows, and set leaves to sailing down the current. Muskrats built burrows in the banks and occasionally the boys would catch a glimpse of one before it disappeared under the water, or into the bank. Willow trees, standing well over fifty feet tall lined the stream and it was nearly always in the shade. The crick ran straight on an east-west plane for about two hundred yards upstream from the road. Then it took a ninety degree turn to the north, continuing to the end of Archie and Maude's property, and from there bordering their neighbor, Milo Hyde's farm. Further upstream it crossed under Rt. 7 and went on northward from there. Most of the time the boys played on the side bordering the corn field, but occasionally they crossed Town Office Road and played under the willows on the downstream side, where a large natural pool provided wider opportunities to build dams. Sometimes they would cross the crick near the spot where it turned to the north and explore a small feeder stream that led into it. The boys never went more than a few hundred yards into the dense woods on that side, but once they traversed a few yards into the woods they were out of sight, and the isolation gave them a sense of time and distance away from the farmhouse. Between the house and the crick, the rows of field corn made an excellent playground for endless hours of hide and seek for the Winter boys. They would run through the rows, hidden from view since they were small and the corn would grow to well over six feet high. If the fields were planted in timothy that later would be cut and baled for winter feed, the boys made "tunnels" that ran throughout the fields like a maze.

In 1950 Ella gave birth to her first and only girl, Nancy Arlene. Ella, believing that Nancy was her final child, was happy to finally have a daughter, and doted on the only other female in the family, then and right through adulthood. Three months after Nancy's first birthday, Ella put Ron in kindergarten and he started his formal education when he was four years old. This arrangement provided Ella with a few years where childcare seemed easier for her.

Then in 1954 Ella became pregnant again and gave birth to her last child Laurence Alan on April 9, 1955. The family welcomed Larry into the fold and enjoyed several good years living on the farm. From kindergarten through grade four Ron and Skeeter attended the same two-room schoolhouse on Route 7 where Ella went to school in her youth. Then for the higher grades up to grade 6, they went to a newer school built at the end of Keyes Street, a small lane that was named after the teacher who had once cleaned chocolate off of Ella's face, and now was still teaching Ella's children.

One benefit of Wilson's continued employment with the federal government was at least a week's vacation each summer, and the family often went away during that week. A cottage on Brant Lake, north of the Capitol District near Lake George, became a favorite retreat. It was a white two-story Cape style building, with a private beach a few yards outside the front entrance door, and a private dock at the end of a path through a small wooded patch to the right of the beach. A boat was tied at the dock for the family to use, and rowing on the lake was a frequent activity. The Winter family vacationed at the Brant Lake cottage for several years. When Wilson was back to work, there also were several lakes within easy driving distance of the farm and the family often spent summer days at their beaches swimming and sunning. The winters were especially fun times as the hill where strawberries bloomed in the summer also made an excellent launching point for sledding and tobogganing when the snows came. On occasion, Milo Hyde, the neighbor who lived on the other side of the hill to the north, brought his toboggan over and two families of children would pile on for the rides of their lives. The toboggan also packed down the snow making a solid track that gave extra speed to the boys' sleighs later on. Wilson often reminisced about the winter day he was leaving for work at 7 a.m., and out of the corner of his eye saw something on the field.

"It was just a red blur," he said. "And then I realized Skeeter had been out sledding since before I even had my coffee."

The toboggan track from the night before had hardened and now resembled a bobsled run. The hill went down at a steep grade for about 100 yards, and then flattened out for another two hundred yards until it reached the crick. "But Skeeter kept going all the way across the field and across the crick too. I couldn't believe how fast that sled was going."

Theirs was a good life in all respects, but America was changing and in the mid-1950's, to help cope with rising costs, Ella took a job as a saleswoman for Stanley Home Products. Headquartered in Westfield, Massachusetts, the company was founded by F. Stanley Beveridge, who had worked for the Fuller Brush company but had left with a handful of former Fuller associates, and formed his own company. By 1950, a few years before Ella joined the firm, Stanley Home Products outsold the rival Fuller Brush. Working for Stanley, as the company was called in the Winter home, Ella sold household cleaners and cleaning tools, personal hygiene and related products. Ella's outgoing personality and clear-minded intelligence helped her find a niche and quickly become one of the top sales earners in the area. Her work involved holding "parties" where the minimum requirement was a hostess, three other people and "a pot of coffee." It was this sales concept that was so successful and proved to be a better model than the door-to-door method used at Fuller Brush. Other companies including Tupperware quickly mimicked the Stanley sales model after seeing its success.

Ella took at least two display suitcases with her to each Stanley party, containing a wide selection of the firm's goods. She learned to deliver a spiel that enabled her to converse with her customers and at the same time demonstrate the products and their use, one at a time. Ella thrived in this environment. It gave her independence, the opportunity to meet new people and simultaneously return regularly to repeat customers, and also provided a decent income to the Winter household. In a one-week period early in her career, she sold more goods than many others did in several months, winning an award and getting the attention of the company management. She also won valuable merchandise, and all-expenses paid sales trips. Ella even travelled to Connecticut for several days, staying at the former Frank Davis Resort in a little town called Moodus, where many years later her son Ron would live.

Ella soon moved into the management circles to a position labeled Unit Manager, in which she was responsible for recruiting, training and supervising several other dealers. She was able to handle all of her work from her home and once a week a delivery truck would pull up to the farmhouse laden with the goods she had sold the previous week. At this point most of the family helped out, with the boys taking boxes of goods to a now empty upstairs bedroom where they were unpacked and the stocks set out in an orderly array designed by Wilson. He then set up an assembly line, taking the order forms from Ella's parties and calling out the products on each order sheet to the boys who passed the products to him. They placed the merchandise into bags provided by the company and on Saturdays, Wilson and the boys delivered the packages to the hostess's homes for distribution to the customers.

On occasion either Skeeter or Ron would travel with Ella to parties in the city or far out in the country, especially if it was a night party. Eventually Ella was offered another step up the corporate ladder to the Branch Manager position, in which she would have been in charge of several Unit Managers. But the new job required far more time away from home and her family and Ella decided to stay where she was. Although her job selling Stanley products provided a welcome boost to the household income, it was not always a joy for her. Ella remembers with a shudder travelling long distances out in the country on bitterly cold and snowy nights and having parties turn out to be a "bust."

On one occasion when she did not take either of the boys with her Ella felt uneasy as the adult son of a hostess stared at—or more accurately, ogled—her all night long from the doorway leading from the kitchen to the living room of the house where she was demonstrating. After the party, only a matter of minutes after she left the house for what she anticipated would be a long ride home along mostly empty country roads, a car with its high beams on sped down the road after her, coming so close to her bumper that Ella could no longer see the headlights. The car stayed glued to hers and the driver did not take several opportunities to pass her in passing zones. Ella was terrified of what the other driver might be planning, but maintained control and held both her speed and position on the road. Finally she entered a more populated area and seeing a house where she knew the occupants, pulled into their driveway. The car sped away and only after a decent interval did Ella finally pull out of the driveway and resume her trip home. After that incident she did not travel out into the country alone again.

Ella also had several occasions where for reasons that were never fully explained, she set out on the road to a night party only to find that she was nearly out of gas. All-night gas stations did not hug every intersection as they do now and more than once Ella said she was sure she arrived home on a prayer and a tank full of fumes. But the country parties weren't the only ones where she had misadventures. Ella followed the parties wherever they took her and on occasion that was in less than desirable city neighborhoods. There were occasions where she carried her suitcases past groups of tough-looking city kids who eyeballed her as she went into nearby apartments. But she kept her commitments to the company and the family, doing her best to ignore the stares of the rough boys lounging on the sidewalks. Her work ethic was strong and Ella rarely passed on an opportunity to demonstrate. Once again, Ella's upbringing helped her deal with adulthood, and that in turn was preparing her for future difficulties that she never would have foreseen as a young wife and mother.

Throughout this period the family regularly attended the Center Brunswick Methodist church, although neither Wilson nor Ella could be described as especially religious. Ella was very active in the Women's Club, and Wilson took part in many Men's Club activities, but his favorite was bowling. At some point in this time Wilson began bowling on Monday nights, and continued that pastime for the rest of his life. Looked upon from the vantage point of history this was a halcyon time for the Winter family. Three of the children were in school, Wilson was permanently employed at the Arsenal, Ella was highly respected for her abilities as a saleswoman and also was comfortable in the community where she had been raised.

But it all came to a sudden end in the summer of 1957. On what can best be described as an obscure day, Ella's mother Maude walked into the Winter side of the farmhouse and spoke with Ella for a few minutes, asking whether she and Wilson would be interested in buying the property. Life became difficult for Maude and Archie after the anthrax outbreak. They never returned to full-time farming and at one point Archie took a job with the town road crew. But he was aging and in ill health. Ella and Wilson didn't realize that her parents were very worried about mounting bills and were looking for a way to ensure that they could keep their home.

Ella said she didn't think the family was in a position to buy the farm outright, not knowing that her sister Olive already made an offer to do just that. Olive, her husband Floyd, and their two sons, Floyd Jr., and Bob, lived in a nice home off South Lake Avenue in nearby Sycaway, a Troy suburb. But Olive apparently was missing life on the farm too, and upon hearing that her parents were having a difficult time, offered to buy the farm, move into the side occupied by Ella and her family, while allowing Maude and Archie to live on the other side for the rest of their lives.

Maude decided to give Ella a chance to buy the farm before accepting Olive's offer, but didn't tell Ella exactly what was hanging in the balance. When Ella declined to consider the proposal, Maude accepted the offer from Olive. The news that the family would have to move was devastating in many ways, some anticipated and some not recognized until decades later. But on October 7, 1957, three days before Ron's tenth birthday, the Winter side of the farmhouse was emptied out, and Ella's family moved to a house they found ten miles away in the town of Wynantskill. The Winter family never wanted to leave Center Brunswick and it didn't help matters when Ella and Wilson realized that the money they raised to buy the house in Wynantskill would have been more than enough to buy the farm in Center Brunswick.

Ella enrolled three of the children in the Wynantskill Elementary School, which perhaps was the best symbol of the difficulty the move imposed on the family—even though they all tried to make the best of it. Compared to the country school houses in Center Brunswick, the Wynantskill Elementary School was huge. It accommodated grades kindergarten through eight, had a principal's office on-site, and an indoor gymnasium that also doubled as a cafeteria during the noon hour. The children could purchase full lunches, sandwiches or just milk to supplement their bagged lunches. Outside, the school sported a huge paved playground in the back, and fields for baseball, softball and other games in lot alongside the playground. The Winter children knew enough about playground games and rules, but having few friends in such a huge population was the most difficult adjustment for them. Each day they walked a half-mile from their new home along a heavily travelled Main Street, entering a large L-shaped, tan brick building housing hundreds of strangers. Some were friendly, some were not, and finding out the difference often was a painful lesson. Among the children, only Larry, who was still a few years from starting kindergarten, was spared the stress of making new friends in a new place.

Things were also different in their new home. The Winter family moved into a forty-year-old house, a large two-story affair with a full attic as well as a full, but very old basement, and a huge wrap-around front porch. It was located at 12 Van Woert Court, a dead-end street that went uphill from Main Street in Wynantskill. The street continued uphill past the house, and the hill continued for another 500 yards or so after the street ended. The bottom of the street made a T-intersection with Main Street. A Gulf station was on the left, going downhill, and a competing Texaco station opposed it on the right. A small grocery store, first called the RKO and later the IGA, was to the left of the Gulf station. Neighbors, most of whom had been at least a half-mile away in Center Brunswick, bordered the Winter property on all sides. People could talk to each other across the street when working in their yards, or from one yard to the next.

The house had a smallish lawn in front with barren spots between two large maple trees. The front lawn stopped abruptly on the downhill side of the house, where a stand of old pine trees and juniper bushes left only a small opening to the larger side and back yards. Breaking free of the natural barrier from the front to the rest of the property provided access to side and back lawns that were bordered by grape arbors, lilies, hydrangeas and annual flowers of Ella's choice. Flower beds and shrubs dominated the sides of the yards, and an unused goldfish pool sat idle on the side lawn. The larger lawn on the downhill side of the house merged with a good-sized backyard that was fenced in by the next door neighbors. Their property also featured a chicken coop in the far back corner abutting the Winter's property. The back side of the house lot was bordered by fences marking the property lines with the houses on the next street. On the uphill side of the driveway that ran alongside the house was a vacant lot that was used as a playing field sometimes, or left unused at others. It was nice to have the lot, but the family never decided on a permanent use for it. An old garage stood at the end of the driveway, about a hundred feet from the street, and attached to it were an old workshop and chicken coop. The workshop and chicken coop were torn down soon after the family arrived, and despite efforts to preserve the garage, Wilson, Skeeter and Ron ultimately tore it down too. Wilson tried hard to renovate the garage to house the family's two cars, but he was never successful. It had two heavy wooden doors that slid horizontally along tracks that long ago became rusted and bent out of shape. The wheels at the top of the doors that ran along the tracks often jumped out of alignment and it was a struggle to get them back in place. For years Wilson tried to find ways to fix the garage, without success.

Wilson and the boys spent long hours working on the garage, but the biggest job during those years involved digging out and modernizing the cellar. It originally had about five feet of headroom, two cisterns where rainwater was stored, and a massive cast iron coal furnace. Wilson wanted a nice basement with a family room, as was very much the rage with the post-World War II ranch house construction of the time. Digging it out was a major undertaking, especially since the renovations to the cellar coincided with extensive renovations to the upstairs. On the first and second floors, wallpaper was removed, walls were built, and floors were first sanded and later covered with carpet or tile. Paint was stripped from old trim and window casings and new paint was applied. The work went on for years. In the cellar the floor was dug up, with the dirt and rocks carried out in buckets that were dumped into an old mason's wheelbarrow that was then pushed to the edge of the lot next door where the debris was dumped and used as fill.

The cisterns were knocked down, and the old coal-burning furnace was replaced with a modern natural gas system with baseboard heating units. A new well was dug when the old one ran dry. Sewer mains were installed on Main Street and connecting side streets throughout much of Wynantskill within a few years, and the house was soon connected to the sewers. Wilson and the boys worked for at least eight years on one project or another, essentially making their mark on the new property. It did change, and was modernized in many ways.

But Ella would later lament that, "I never really felt at home in Wynantskill. I met other mothers, but it was never the same kind of feeling that we had in Center Brunswick, where I knew most of my friends for my entire life. We kept up our friendships in Center Brunswick even though we moved away. Whenever we socialized it was with our old friends not with newer people. We moved to a new home, but our hearts were always in Center Brunswick. I've always regretted that move."

She and Wilson both worked to pay the mortgage, and while they joined new churches—the family attended at least three area churches in the next eight years, eventually settling on the Pawling Avenue Methodist Church—Ella never regained the same sense of friendships that she had in Center Brunswick.

For all the travelling she had done, Ella's home base was the farmhouse in Center Brunswick, and the family made the half-hour trip to see her parents at least twice a week for the next several years. The trips increased in frequency after Christmas Day 1961 when Archie died. Wilson and Ella had visited Archie in the hospital on Christmas Eve.

"He was really talkative," Ella says. "He was complaining about the other man in the room going on and on. I didn't tell him that he was going on and on too."

They returned home, but at 2 a.m., the phone rang and Ella's sister Olive relayed the news that their father had died in his sleep. The adults in the family, both in Wynantskill and Center Brunswick, immediately went to the hospital to attend to Archie's affairs. The next morning when the Winter children bounded down the stairs to see what was waiting for them under the tree, Wilson stopped them with the sobering news.

"Your grandfather died last night." It was a difficult time, with the joy of Christmas offset by Archie's death. Ella absented herself from most of the traditional activities that day, spending time on the phone with Maude or her siblings, making arrangements for Archie's wake and funeral, or just staying in her bedroom. Archie's death was not the first experienced by the youngsters in the Winter family. Uncle Bob's son Paul, who was born with diabetes, died in his mid-twenties, only a year before Archie's death, and his loss was felt deeply. On the day that Paul died Ron entered Wilson and Ella's room in mid-morning, looking for his mother who was conspicuously absent at breakfast. He found her still in her bed, tears streaming down her cheeks. Ron had never seen his mother cry like that before and it was a shocking revelation to him. The loss of close family members was never painless. The family was large and spread over several communities in the Troy area, but emotionally they were close, and losses to any were a loss to all. Several years before Paul died

Maude and Archie's children arranged a 50th wedding anniversary open house party for them at the Grange Hall in Center Brunswick. Relatives, friends and neighbors pitched in with food and desserts. It was advertised by word of mouth, and turned out to be a huge affair with far more people attending than anyone could have imagined. Virtually the entire family was there. People they hadn't seen in decades, including several of the farm hands who worked side by side with the Archie and Maude, and sat at the big oak table in the dining room for countless meals, heard about the event and made sure they stopped by to say hello. At one point in the afternoon Maude was overcome by the turnout, and tears coursed down her cheeks as she greeted friend after friend from the old days. That anniversary celebration was the last major event in their lives, and although no one spoke of it at the time, it also was the last time that the entire family was together in one place. Archie lived a long and active life but his illnesses eventually caught up with him. In his late seventies Archie spent time in the Samaritan Hospital in Troy where his gall bladder was removed. His return home revealed his frailty, and he needed help moving from the car to the house, as well as help moving about the house in the weeks afterward. From that point on, Archie could usually be found sitting on a lawn chair under the maple tree in front of the house on nice days, or lying on the sofa in the living room. Archie was put on a special diet that included a breakfast of bran, raw eggs and prunes. But even though he recovered somewhat from the gall bladder operation, his overall health continued to decline until his death in 1961.

Maude lived for three more years, and in the summer of 1964 came to spend a few days at Ella and Wilson's house. A thorough medical examination only two months earlier revealed no major problems and she was declared fit and sound. But Maude was complaining of intestinal distress, and a further examination was scheduled that revealed inoperable cancer. She was hospitalized, and then taken care of at her home in Center Brunswick, where she died in the summer of 1964. Maude Ann Clarke Brimmer was buried in Mount Ida cemetery in Troy, alongside Archie and not far from her grandson Paul.

Maude was a hard-working no-nonsense woman, who also possessed a finely honed sense of humor as well as human decency. Her passing may not have been noticed by the world at large, but it was certainly felt by her family.

If a person's life is measured by the emptiness felt when they die, then it could be said that Maude and Archie Brimmer lived full lives that touched far more people than they ever supposed. Both of their funerals were large affairs that filled the funeral homes at their wakes, with long lines of cars accompanying the hearse to their graves.

Many felt the loss when they died, but especially Ella. She loved her parents and she had an innate sense of how important they had been to her life. To this day she can sit back and relate the stories of her youth, often with a new twist, a new angle, or a previously unremarked upon factoid that provides even more depth to their lives. And always, when she speaks of those days, and the people who preceded her and raised her, Ella will end her comments looking down slightly, sighing softly, and murmuring, "That was so long ago," leaving listeners with the sense that it also must feel to her as if it were only yesterday.

The Winter family dealt with the deaths of Archie and Maude, as survivors do, never forgetting them, but ultimately moving on. In time the children made their way through grade school at Wynantskill Elementary and then went on to Troy High School. Skeeter graduated in 1964 and made a stab at college, but the Vietnam War was just beginning and Wilson, by now a foreman at the Watervliet Arsenal, intervened and got his son a slot as an apprentice machinist. That job, since it was in a defense plant, was sufficient to keep Skeeter out of the military. Ron graduated from Troy High in 1965 with a partial scholarship to the state university at Albany. But he and Wilson had been on bad terms off and on for several years, and the combination of living at home, working and attending college soon proved to be an impossible situation.

The relationship between Ron and Wilson erupted one day in the old garage where Ron was swinging a sledge hammer, breaking up the cement floor. Wilson was loading the pieces into a wheelbarrow, but despite working in such proximity, neither was speaking to the other. Finally when he decided he'd had enough Wilson brought his fist up from the floor and nailed Ron right on the jaw. But, aside from his head whipping to the right, Ron didn't move or go down. It was clear after that encounter that it was time for Ron to be moving on.

Ron turned eighteen on October 10, 1965 and a week later had an especially intense argument with Wilson. Ron had been discussing the Marine Corps as a career option in previous weeks but that night it was Wilson who brought up the military. "You want to join the Marines? Go ahead! I'll sign the papers."

On Monday Ron went to the Marine Corps recruiting station in the Troy post office and was scheduled to go to Albany on Tuesday for his physical and other tests. Much later, at the end of the day, he took the bus home and exited it at the bottom of the street in Wynantskill. As Ron was walking up the street toward the house Wilson backed his '63 Chevy Impala out of the driveway. It was Monday, and as always he was on his way to go bowling. He pulled over and asked where Ron had been.

"I joined the Marines," Ron told him.

Wilson flipped. "Get up to the house," he yelled.

Wilson's combat experiences were talked about often when the boys were growing up, but never in a negative, or for that matter, a truthful way. He spoke of his time in the water of Leyte Gulf as a rite of passage that was presented as a normal part of becoming a man. But Wilson also had seen how Marines looked after weeks of fighting on the islands that were taken during WWII, and often talked of seeing a hard, tough Marine who had been in fierce fighting, come aboard the Princeton and break down crying when he was given fresh eggs to eat.

"They'll use you for cannon fodder," he kept yelling. Ella was aghast. She had a stunned, frightened look on her face and kept asking, "What's wrong? What's wrong?"

"Go ahead, tell her—go ahead," Wilson yelled.

Ron told her quietly, "I joined the Marines, Mom." Ella didn't say much, but it was obvious that she wasn't taking the news well. The argument with Wilson raged for another few minutes and then he left for his bowling.

It was 3 a.m. when he returned, as announced by the loud slamming of the driver's side door of his car. It wasn't quite 3:01 a.m. when the house was awakened by Wilson's angry tread on the back steps, across the back porch, through the kitchen, dining room, front hall, up the stairs, down the hall toward Ron's room and BAM -- through his bedroom door.

"Wake up! Get up! Get out of that bed."

"Where are those Goddamn papers? Give them to me. I'm ripping them up. You're not going in the Marines. Get downstairs."

The papers were in a manila envelope on a chair in the corner of the room. Wilson grabbed them and ripped them up.

"That's what I think of your Marine Corps!" Wilson was a

picture of white hot fury and he was on a roll. "I had a lousy score tonight because of you."

Despite the argument that raged for another hour, Ron nonetheless went to Albany for his induction physical the next day. But in a twist of fate that neither expected, Ron's enlistment was delayed a couple of months after he failed the first time due to flat feet. But in late fall, Ron asked Wilson if he would help with Ron's college expenses.

"How much do you need?" Wilson asked.

"About $300," Ron answered. "I'm already paying for my tuition and books, plus transportation to and from school every day. But I can't always make my classes on time, especially the 8 a.m., class and the dean said it would be much easier for me if I had a better schedule and lived on campus. The new campus is opening in the fall and it's beautiful. They took us up to see the rooms. But I don't have the extra $300 and I don't have a way of making it. My schedule is packed as it is."

Wilson deliberated for only a mini-second before he gave his one-word reply. "No!" That one word sealed Ron's future, for the next four years, and the rest of his life.

Oddly enough, Ella was never privy to that conversation. When she discussed it with Ron many years later, she said, "You should have asked me. I would have found the money. You weren't asking for that much and we weren't paying any of your expenses as it was."

Just before Christmas the recruiters called again and said Ron might be able to get through the physical if he tried again. The ultimate decision was delayed until after the holidays, but this time Ron and Wilson had a civilized discussion about Ron's future.

"I don't have any other options right now," Ron said. "But if I enlist for four years they'll guarantee me an aviation assignment, and I can attend a technical school."

This time Wilson agreed and immediately after the holidays Ron signed the final papers, raised his hand and swore an oath to uphold and defend the Constitution of the United States of America. On January 12, 1966 he left for Parris Island, South Carolina and Marine training. He ultimately was assigned to a helicopter unit.

Ella felt devastated, and many years later told her son that she never rested easily or slept well for the next four years, especially for the fifteen months when Ron was overseas, most of that time in Vietnam. Whether Ron's decision to join the Marines instead of staying in college was a motivating factor in Wilson's later decisions involving his children was never discussed. But in 1968, when Nancy graduated from Troy High School, Wilson opened up the coffers and financed her education at an exclusive women's college near Boston. Wilson, who in 1967 also refused to include Ron on his automobile insurance coverage—despite Ron offering to pay—even covered the cost of air fare when Nancy wanted to fly home from Boston to Albany for the weekends.

Eventually Ron returned safely after four years in the Marines including his tour in Vietnam, but this still was not a quiet time on the home front. Ella tried to keep it to herself over the years, and even offered numerous explanations, but Wilson's relationship with his family had deteriorated severely. Skeeter had married and had a child, further insulating himself from the draft. He finished two years of community college and called it quits as far as his formal education was concerned. In time, after the draft and the Vietnam War ended, he left the arsenal and moved out of state. Nancy finished one year at the exclusive women's college, but then moved back home with her parents. She finished a second year of undergraduate work at a local business school. Ron never returned to the Troy area from the Marines. Instead he moved to Connecticut where he worked at the Pratt & Whitney Aircraft engine plant, simultaneously enrolling in college. He had married after Vietnam and had a son. Over the next five years Ron earned degrees in Electrical Engineering and then English Literature while working full and part time at a variety of jobs after being caught in layoffs at Pratt & Whitney.

During this period Larry made his way through Wynantskill Elementary School as his older siblings had done, and then entered Troy High School. But formal schooling was not his favorite activity and Larry struggled. Ella later explained, "Larry was exceptionally smart. But he was bored. School just bored him and I couldn't find the formula to get him excited about it, or even serious about graduating. I pleaded with him, urged him to do better, and tried a variety of 'carrot and stick' strategies. Larry enjoyed working with his hands and appeared to be following in Wilson's footsteps, but the real trick was keeping him in school. He just wouldn't stay focused."

Despite his distaste for sitting in classrooms, Larry was nonetheless a very likable young man, who was easy to get along with, and had a large group of friends. The one person he couldn't get along with was Wilson, who at that time didn't seem to be getting along with anyone.

Wilson was no longer fighting with Ron, who lived two hours away and was a decorated war veteran. But he had regular eruptions with the other family members. In late 1972 Ron was on the receiving end of a surprise visit from Larry. Ron got a phone call, alerting him that Larry was at the bus station in downtown Hartford. He drove there and Larry came out of the building, looking a bit sheepish, wearing a lopsided grin.

"What happened?" Ron asked.

"I had another fight with Dad and this time I just took off," Larry responded.

Larry moved in with Ron, but Ron told him pointedly, "You still have to go to school over here. I know people who can help out, and you can go to a technical high school if you want. But you have to graduate."

Larry agreed to the arrangement, but only stayed with his brother for several days until things cooled down, and then decided to return home. Ron later speculated that Larry's girlfriend had much to do with his decision to return to Wynantskill.

This was not an easy time for Ella, nor for her offspring. She was now in her fifties, as was her husband, and Wilson especially was not happy with his advancing age. But life still had some surprises in store for Ella, and one that was lurking on the horizon would bring about the biggest changes in her life—and not for the better. No one saw it coming, not clearly anyway, and virtually everyone else in the family would have done anything in their power to prevent it. But change came suddenly and permanently on May 27, 1973, and no one in the Winter family would ever be the same again.

CHAPTER FOUR

A Death in the Family, and a New Era

One part of the house in Wynantskill, the section called the "back porch," a closed in, but unheated area just off the kitchen, escaped the renovations that swirled around the rest of the house. The kitchen door opened onto the back porch, which itself led to the outside. The porch windows opened in the summer, but it was not insulated and was simply closed off tight in the winter. It had minimal electric service for lighting one light bulb in the center of the ceiling. The porch sported bare ceiling rafters and floor planking. But it had potential.

The priority list for renovations didn't include the back porch even though Ella dreamed of having her own laundry room. In Center Brunswick, Ella used a wringer washer and outside clotheslines every week, following in her mother's tradition. But in Wynantskill, there was no washer, no dryer, and no hookups for them. A washing machine even without a dryer might have been acceptable, since household clothes dryers were still a novelty. Rather, a clothesline ran from the corner of the back porch to the edge of the garage some fifty feet away. But without a washing machine the clothesline was just a reminder of what was missing.

Sewer connections and a natural gas furnace were among the improvements to the basement so extending the plumbing and baseboard heating a few feet further to the back porch would have been relatively straightforward. But they were not even considered until the early 1970's. At some point, Wilson looked around and decided that a laundry room would add immeasurably to the house. This was good for Ella because she wrestled with myriad ways to clean the laundry for years. At times she would bundle it into large cloth bags and baskets, and haul it to self-service Laundromats. Other times she would bundle it into large cloth bags and baskets and take it to laundry services that would wash, dry and fold it for her. Either way, Ella was responsible for getting the laundry together, loading it into her car, driving it somewhere to be cleaned, driving it back and distributing it to Wilson and the children. For years she combined her laundry and grocery shopping duties into one trip, since the Laundromats usually were in the same strip malls as grocery stores.

However it was viewed, this was an arduous task. Sometimes she took one or more of the children to help her, sometimes she went alone. But the laundry was Ella's responsibility and hers alone.

"I dreamed of having my own laundry room," Ella says. "Finishing the back porch would have made my life so much easier, at least for the laundry."

Finally, after nearly fifteen years of lugging clothing back and forth, Wilson decided to renovate the back porch and turn it into a laundry room. It really wasn't a big job, but he took his time and it proceeded slowly. To speed things up a bit he told Larry to expect to help him on a Sunday afternoon in late May. Larry grudgingly acquiesced primarily because he had no choice.

But Sunday, May 27, 1973 turned out to be a big day for Larry's friends. They had plans to attend the races at Lebanon Valley

Dragway in eastern New York. It was a favorite spot for his older brothers when they were still in high school and now Larry and his friends enjoyed going there also. Larry really wanted to go to the races with his friends, especially since his girlfriend was going too.

But Wilson was adamant. "You can go to the races another day. I need help on the porch. You're staying home and we're working on the porch. I don't want to hear another word about it."

Things were tense between them. They began work after lunch, but after an hour or so Wilson's mood began to change. He later confided that he had been out to an evening of dinner and dancing with Ella the previous night. They stayed out later than they intended, Wilson said, and he was not his usual chipper self the next day.

Wilson had a way of letting you know he had changed his mind that was indirect, but nonetheless final. He'd stretch to his full height, look at the job as if he was figuring out a difficult math problem, and then declare that he needed something that was simply unobtainable at the moment.

"Well," he said to Larry, after going through his routine, "it looks like I won't be able to do as much today as I planned. We might as well call it quits 'til later in the week."

Larry needed no prodding and was back in the house in an instant, hoping to catch his friends before they left. But by then the group had already left for the races. There are many versions of exactly what happened that afternoon, but essentially, one story prevails. Larry made a call to one friend who hadn't gone, and convinced him to pick him up and meet up with the others.

As Wilson later related it, "Larry was riding in the passenger side up front. They were late, probably going faster than they should have. The police said they came upon another car that was going slower. Larry's friend swerved around the car in front of him, passing on a slight hill in a no-passing zone. Some people said the car they were passing speeded up on them. Others weren't sure. But a car came over the hill straight at them."

At the last instant, Larry's friend swerved to the left, off of the road into a field, a maneuver that certainly would have resulted in damage to the car, but possibly could have saved them. But the oncoming car swerved too, at exactly the same time. The maneuver left the passenger side, the side Larry was on, directly exposed to the oncoming car. It smashed into their car just in front of the passenger door, and Larry took the full impact head on.

Larry didn't die at the scene. The police and ambulance came, and he was taken to the hospital where he was stabilized on life support equipment. Back in Wynantskill, Wilson, who was feeling guilty about the rough treatment he gave his son earlier in the day, started cooking a steak dinner. It was Larry's favorite meal, and Wilson's way of saying "I'm sorry," two words that practically no one ever heard him utter.

Wilson gave Larry a time by which he was to return home, and despite the flare-ups between them, Larry was good at getting back at the appointed hour. Wilson was sure he would be back on time, and put the steaks on so they would be ready when Larry walked through the door. The steaks cooked, and then overcooked. Wilson was getting irritated. He paced the kitchen, waiting to hear a car pull into the yard, waiting for the door to open.

But instead, the phone rang on the kitchen wall rang. Wilson picked it up, saying gruffly, "Hello. Yes, this is Wilson Winter. Yes, Larry is my son. What's wrong?" The police officer on the other end then delivered the message that no parent ever wants to receive. Wilson's face went hard, frozen, virtually emotionless. His voice softened noticeably. "We'll leave right away." He hung up the phone, nearly in a daze, then reached over and turned off the stove.

Ella was working as a hostess at a beautiful upscale restaurant in North Troy called the Bordale. It was owned and operated by Joe and Helen Mancuso, family friends, and when they offered her a position as hostess it was a natural fit for her outgoing personality.

She left for the Bordale that day before Wilson announced his reprieve from working on the porch. Larry owned a car, she remembered, but it wasn't running and he took a few minutes to work on it before Wilson called him in to begin work.

In the Bordale's kitchen Ella removed a platter of meat and vegetables from the refrigerator for her meal break. The Sunday afternoon late lunch crowd was gone and the evening dinner patrons were an hour away. She sliced some cold roast beef and began assembling a sandwich using the meat, Italian bread, lettuce and tomato. She was standing next to the phone when it rang and she put the sandwich aside for a moment to take the call. "Larry's been in an accident. He's in Albany Medical Center. We have to go there right away," she was told. Helen insisted on driving her home where she met Wilson, got into the car and they drove to the hospital.

"I remember sitting with the other parents. No one was talking. Then I remember being told that Larry had died."

Wilson recounted, in one of the few times that he ever talked about that day again, that "the doctor told me that Larry had suffered severe brain damage. He said Larry was brain dead, and he would never recover. There was not much to say. I told the doctors to pull the plug on the life support equipment." It was over almost immediately. Larry was officially pronounced dead, and with him, a large part of the life of the Winter family died too.

Ella and Wilson went home, and began making arrangements for Larry's funeral. They kept their composure, but preparing for the funeral was a grueling ordeal. They had to make phone calls to friends and relatives, go through Larry's belongings, pick out clothes for him to be buried in, and at every step of the process, face the horrible fact that he was gone and would never be coming back. Dealing with Larry's death was made even worse by the news the day after he died that his friend had died too. The wakes for both boys were held at the same funeral home, and friends by the scores came to say goodbye.

It is unfortunately an all too common experience in modern America to lose a member of a high school class to traffic accidents. On that occasion, two were lost on the same day and it had an obvious impact on their classmates as well as their families. The funerals were staggered, Larry's in the late morning, his friend in the afternoon, and dozens upon dozens of cars, many filled with young classmates, made for especially long funeral processions.

Larry's death had a devastating impact on the entire family. But it was Ella and Wilson who lost a child and neither was ever the same again. Although Ella ended her career with Stanley Home Products a few years earlier, she was still working—first as a receptionist and switchboard operator with local companies including Ludlow Valve, Levonian Brothers meat packers, and at Channel 10, an Albany area television station before she went to the Bordale. The job at the Bordale gave Ella a different type of employment, but she was uniquely suited for it, and enjoyed it immensely. After Larry died it gave her a place where she could temporarily escape from the memories and the pain they brought.

Nonetheless, for years after his death Ella could not speak of Larry without bursting into tears, or coming close to it. Wilson, on the other hand, went silent. All that had been bothering him in the 1960's and early 1970's suddenly came to an end. Within the next two years, he took an early retirement from his job at the Watervliet Arsenal, although he still bowled on Monday nights with his friends.

There was no returning to a normal life for them, and they agreed that the house in Wynantskill held far too many memories. They sold the house, moved to an apartment complex, and within another year moved to Florida. They found a beach front apartment in Cocoa Beach, which they later bought when the building converted to condominiums. It was a five story aqua colored honeycomb building, with balconies facing the ocean, and an exact twin sixty feet away across a grassy lawn dotted with palms and palmettos.

Wilson insisted on a south-facing unit on the third floor with a patio that provided a view of the Atlantic Ocean. In the summer the sun would be high and the overhang on the patio kept the hot glare out of the living room and master bedroom. In the winter when the sun was low in the sky it would flood those rooms with welcome light and warmth.

In many ways their time in Florida was exactly what they needed. They were financially secure and were able to enjoy the retired lifestyle. They made friends easily and Ella became an unofficial entertainment manager for the condos. She organized dinner nights, music and dance nights, and holiday bashes, and she loved it. They walked on the beach nearly every day, and joined the throngs of residents who made a party out of each rocket launch from Cape Kennedy—Canaveral—that was within sight just north of them.

Their children and grandchildren came to visit and enjoy the Florida sunshine, especially in the winter. Eastern Airlines operated regular flights from the north to Florida, often at attractive rates, and knowing there was housing and warmth waiting at the end of the line made Florida vacations a natural choice. Their sons brought their families and the pool at Twin Towers as their condos were known, became a magnet. The balcony chairs were emblazoned with drying beach towels and swimsuits, and flip flops could be found in every room of the house. Ron made a trip in early 1977 that included a visit to Orlando and Disney World. But it was colder than normal in Florida that year and his family, which had left their warmer clothing back at the condo, loaded up on Disney-themed sweatshirts to ward off the chill. Although most of the travel in those years was from north to south, Ella and Wilson made occasional trips north too. Wilson's retirement income was more than sufficient to pay their expenses, and he also began investing in the stock market. In fact, Wilson became quite adept at his investments, and Ella soon joined in with stock purchases of her own. Wilson made it clear from the outset that he wasn't investing for himself, but planned to leave the stocks to his grandchildren. In fact, it was a regular point of conversation with him about the progress of his investments—universally upwards and a source of pride. If he wasn't asked about his stocks soon enough in a conversation to suit him, Wilson would bring the subject up himself. "Well, the market's up again," he'd say with a smile and roll of his eyes. Perusing the business pages of his daily newspaper became an avocation.

Despite living a life that many Americans work and long for, Ella and Wilson both eventually grew weary of Florida. With each passing year the retired lifestyle wore increasingly thin, and after they lived there for nearly five years they decided to return to upstate New York. And although it was rarely mentioned, Larry's death was never that far from their minds. His passing left a void in the lives of every member of the Winter family, and even among some of his closest friends, that would never be filled. In time, the impact of Larry's death receded somewhat, and the lives of their children and grandchildren occupied much of Ella and Wilson's time and attention. But Larry's memory was never that far from the surface. Eventually they decided to sell the condo and move back north, but their house owning days were over. They rented an apartment in Clifton Park, a community midway between Albany and Saratoga, which was especially convenient because they enjoyed going to the horse races at the Saratoga track in August. They were a short distance off the Adirondack Northway which also made for a quick commute to see family. In 1987 they moved one last time, to the Dutch Village apartment complex in Menands, New York to be closer to their daughter Nancy's home. She lived in Saratoga for a time, but ultimately moved to Menands with Ella and Wilson soon following. Their new apartment was only a few minutes away from her home.

Ella and Wilson already were serving as more-than-willing, on-demand baby sitters for Nancy's daughter, Courtney, who was born in 1984. With their new apartment right around the corner from their daughter, Nancy now had the service of on-call babysitters for the next decade and more. Their apartment had a large living room, a good-sized dining area that accommodated gatherings of up to eight people, a small but workable kitchen, and two bedrooms, one of which was converted to a den with a fold-out couch for overnight visitors. A balcony that overlooked a swath of lawn and an undeveloped wooded area was off the living room, with access through a slider.

The walls of the den were decorated on one side with a display case containing Wilson's WWII medals, a photo of the USS Princeton, and other awards. Photos of their grandchildren were displayed on the other. There was one photo of Larry in the apartment, a winsome view of him in the summer, while on vacation with Ella and Wilson at Cape Cod. He is wearing that lopsided grin, and seems to depict a devil-may-care attitude. Aside from that one photo, however, the apartment did not have any other mementos of Larry in evidence.

Much, much later, Ella explained that she had photos of her late son, and would have preferred to keep them on display, but the memories and regrets were still too painful for Wilson. He never got over the death of his son, and the events leading up to that day. He went to his death unable to talk about it except on rare occasions, and for the rest of Wilson's life, most of the photos of Larry, frozen in his youth, were packed away.

With the reminders of Larry packed out of sight, and the emotional space that their years in Florida had given them, Wilson and Ella resumed a more normal life in their apartment. They enjoyed their neighbors, and their freedom. They travelled extensively in the US, and went to Connecticut several times each year to stay with Ron, who had divorced in 1981.

After Ron remarried in 1984 Wilson helped his son and his family build their new house, starting with clearing trees from the house lot. In later years he also was on hand for renovations and updates. They enjoyed going to dinner in Connecticut, from upscale restaurants to pizza houses and their visits to the Nutmeg State were invariably pleasant. But it also was very clear that Nancy's needs pre-empted those of her siblings. If Nancy was travelling or otherwise in need of her parents' baby-sitting services, that need took precedence over anyone else's plans.

Ella never minded baby-sitting her granddaughter; in fact she was happy that she was able to build a close relationship. But Ella also maintains, "Down the road I figured it would come back to me. Not financially, of course, but I thought that all the hours I put in for Nancy and Jim, baby-sitting Courtney at a drop of a hat, would be remembered when I got older and needed some help myself." That belief would come back to haunt her, and she still talks about it today.

In 1989 tragedy again struck when Wilson suffered a brain aneurysm. He had been at his daughter's house, washing his car in their driveway, and as he bent over to rinse the soap off the lower part of the car he was stricken. Typical of Wilson, rather than asking his daughter for help, he first walked inside and poured himself a cup of coffee, then went back to his car and drove home. He entered the apartment, brushing past Ella who knew instantly that something was drastically wrong.

"He just pushed past me, with a determined look on his face, like every step was an effort, but he didn't say anything. He threw his coat over a chair, went straight to the bedroom and collapsed on the bed. I felt his forehead and he was hot, and sweating. So I got him in the car and took him to the doctor and they put him in the ambulance to take him to Albany Medical Center."

His son-in-law James made a call to Connecticut informing Ron that the prognosis was not good and Ron should hurry to New York if there was to be any opportunity to see his father again.

Ron and Jennifer jumped into Ron's pickup truck and made a beeline for Albany. As luck would have it, Wilson was being transferred from the emergency room to intensive care just as Ron and Jennifer entered the same hospital elevator.

Wilson looked up and wisecracked, "What are you doing here?"

"I heard you had a situation going on and I thought I'd come see what was up," Ron responded. "I think I broke every speed limit in Connecticut, Massachusetts and New York getting here," he added. "A two-hour trip in an hour-forty-five. Think you can top that?"

Wilson was his usual self, responding only with an "Ahhhh. What did you do that for?"

The rule of thumb on brain aneurysms is that the longer a victim survives, the better the chance of recovery. Wilson survived that day, that night, the next day, the next night and ultimately recovered. But he was confined in Albany Medical Center for more than a week, and for a significant portion of that time he could not speak with clarity—not meaning his speech was slurred, but that the words had no context, they just came out at random. The doctors said this was a result of the aneurysm and that he might not ever recover.

But Ron and Jennifer drove to New York very early one morning to visit Wilson in the hospital and arrived there before he awoke. They tiptoed into his room—fortunately he was not sharing it with anyone else. Wilson was sound asleep in the hospital bed and the curtain had been drawn back so nurses could see him from the hall. They sat in the two chairs near his bed and conversed quietly for the next hour. Finally, Wilson stirred, opened his eyes, and smiled when he saw he had visitors.

"How long have you been here?" Wilson asked. Ron and Jennifer both were shocked that Wilson was speaking clearly, with no sign at all of struggling with his words.

"When did your speech clear up?" Ron asked.

Wilson looked puzzled, but responded, "I keep telling them I want to go home but no one will listen. I don't need to be here. I want to go home. When your mother gets here, tell her I WANT TO GO HOME."

Ron assured Wilson that his concerns would be addressed as soon as Ella arrived. Wilson was adamant—"I want my clothes, and I want to go home!"

But at 10 a.m. a nurse came to the room, and told Wilson it was time for his medications. She gave him several pills and stood by making sure he took them all. Within fifteen minutes Wilson's speech deteriorated and he could no longer communicate. By the time Ella arrived Wilson was again in the frustrating position of trying to talk with no one able to understand him. But he could write! And Wilson did just that, taking a pen and paper and listing on it exactly what he had told Ron and Jennifer earlier. He finished the note with the statement "I Want To Go Home!!!" However, with Wilson no longer verbally coherent, there was no convincing Ella, the doctors or anyone else that he could leave the hospital. Ron and Jennifer returned to Connecticut late that afternoon, and the next day Ron talked with his own doctor about his observations. He had a list of medications that the doctors were giving his father, including Phenobarbital, which is used for controlling seizures, and has the side affect of inducing drowsiness. Ron's doctor speculated that Wilson's speech difficulties were a result of the medication.

Ron reported to Ella what he had discovered. "I don't know if it is that drug alone, or in combination with something else, but I saw what happened, Mom," Ron told Ella. "When the drugs had worn off Dad could talk just fine. But when they gave him more drugs he went right back to incoherence. You have to tell his doctor what we saw."

Ella did just that and a few days later Ron and Jennifer returned to New York, reinforcing her position with Wilson's doctor. The drug was finally discontinued, with a resultant improvement in Wilson's condition followed by his release from the hospital.

Wilson's recovery continued after he returned home, although Ella says he also slipped on occasion. Within a few months he resumed driving and visiting Connecticut, but Ella maintains that he was never quite the same again. Those who saw him only occasionally did not see what she saw, but Ella was the closest to him and the most aware of his daily actions.

After the aneurysm, life again settled into a routine, but it was a different routine. Ella kept a wary eye on her husband, and confided to Ron and Jennifer on several occasions that even though he was able to get around and seemed to be fine, there were still little differences in his behavior that worried her. Wilson kept regular medical appointments, generally once every three months, and for a time was on a wide range of medications. But bit by bit he dropped most of the pills until he was down to three or less per day. He was happy with his progress and said so often.

There were also changes in Wilson's physical abilities, including an extreme sensitivity to the sun, and he could no longer work outside with Ron without loading up on sunscreen. For much of the time before and after his aneurysm Jennifer tried to convince Wilson to quit smoking, a habit he developed when he was only eleven, living in New York City, and continued right through his adulthood. Eventually he reduced his smoking from more than a pack a day to about a quarter pack, which was a huge leap. But he continued to tell his daughter-in-law that whatever he eventually died from, it would not be cigarettes.

In late 1997 Ron and Jennifer made a life-altering decision, to move to Florida and go into business with Ron's son Kevin, who moved to Florida in 1992 and made it his permanent home. They decided against selling their home in Connecticut, the one Wilson helped build, and instead leased it out as executive housing to a family from overseas that was in America on a work visa. But, remembering his parents' experience in Cocoa Beach, Ron decided to keep his options open.

Wilson enjoyed the combination of nearness to Connecticut and regular visits and wasn't exactly happy about his son and daughter-in-law making the move. "What are you going to do down there that you can't do here," he asked repeatedly.

Ron explained, "The population is shifting that way, especially over on the west coast around Tampa, and there are better business opportunities there than here."

Wilson was not convinced, and continued to grumble about the move. It was obvious that he liked things the way they were and any change would be unwelcome. They enjoyed many holidays together when Ella and Wilson came to Connecticut and there were regular visits in between, both in New York and Connecticut that allowed them to stay close.

Wilson especially got along with Jennifer, Ron's second wife, which actually didn't settle all that well with other family members. Although there were occasional invitations to join his sister's family in New York for the holidays, only one was ever accepted. Ron and Jennifer went to Nancy's home for Thanksgiving in the late 1980's, for what can only be described as the most bizarre holiday meal they had ever experienced. Nancy invited so many people that there was simply no room for them all in the dining room, and the seating was extended, through the use of additional tables hidden by tablecloths, out into the front entrance foyer. Ron and Jennifer were seated literally at the front door, at the furthest end of the table, where conversation with his parents was impossible. When shown to their seats they exchanged a "why exactly did we come here," glance, and the rest of the meal was punctuated by side comments, nudges and occasional gentle kicks under the table. It took so long for the food to work its way down that it was cold by the time they ate. On the upside of the event was the presence of Uncle Vic, next to Ron and Jennifer, who kept up a stream of comedic comments about their status at the end of the table.

"Do you think there'll be any food left for us?" he queried, with a sly grin. Vic is nobody's fool, and he had a comment for virtually every dish.

Ron asked at one point if Vic wanted a bullhorn so he could order some more rolls from the privileged folks at the head of the table, but Vic declined. "I can still make myself heard on my own," he said with a laugh.

The commentary kept up right through dinner and it was obvious that some ofbarbs were heard at the head of the table, but they also were ignored. Ron and Jennifer made the best of the situation, but vowed they would stay in Connecticut for future holidays where they could enjoy themselves in more relaxed circumstances. In later years, Wilson and Ella occasionally enjoyed Christmas or Thanksgiving dinner in Connecticut, either with Ron and Jennifer or with Jennifer's sister and her family, where there were usually plenty of extra guests, but no one was left out. Ron and Jennifer didn't go to New York for a holiday again though.

Holiday gatherings were only one example of the ties between Wilson and Ella and Ron's family in Connecticut. Deciding to join Kevin in Florida was not easy, nor was there disregard for how Wilson felt about the move.

"Your Dad is really going to miss us," Jennifer said on numerous occasions. But the economy in Connecticut was stagnant at best, and declining at worst. Ron was working at a newspaper in eastern Connecticut in a position he thoroughly enjoyed. But there were no raises for years, and to make any extra money required extra work. Ron took on additional duties whenever possible, but even doubling his workload provided only a limited return. There appeared to be significant economic opportunities in Florida, but to be sure Ron and Jennifer made several trips south to explore the possibilities. In the end they decided to go, but made sure they didn't cut their ties to the north, either Connecticut or New York.

And there was one item on Ron's agenda that he attended to virtually as soon as he arrived in Tampa Bay. Wilson was changing, slowly but noticeably. There was a grayness to his skin tone that was not evident even a year earlier and it left him puzzled and concerned. Ella said Wilson was never the same after the aneurysm, but Wilson continued to maintain that he was fit and healthy. Ron wondered if that wasn't more bravado than truth, and whether there was more to his resistance to their move south than he was saying. Even though he growled and grumbled about their move, Wilson never came out and said what was really bothering him. The move went ahead as scheduled, but Ron already decided he would deal with his concerns about his father as soon as they settled in Florida.

CHAPTER FIVE

The Opening Rift

When Ron, Jennifer and Heather arrived in Florida Ron told his son that it might be wise to take a trip north to visit Wilson and Ella as soon as it was convenient. "Dad doesn't look the same," Ron said. "He has a grayness to him. I think you should go see him while you can."

The timing of his advice proved to be fortunate because Kevin was dating a woman, Sharon, who, as he put it later, "is the person I intend to spend the rest of my life with." It was important to him that his grandparents meet her and get to know her. It was equally important to Sharon that Kevin meet her family in New Jersey. They worked out a schedule where they both could travel, and made the trip north together. Kevin went north in October 1998, and it was at that time that the first signs of major family-wide discord arose.

Kevin decided to surprise his grandparents and drop in without calling first, which worked out well, except that Wilson was alone at the apartment when Kevin and Sharon arrived. Ella was out having her hair done, but came home a bit later, and soon after that Nancy dropped in. If Nancy had stopped in to say hello and then left, maybe things would not have developed as they did. But first she stayed, and then invited herself to join the group when Kevin asked his grandparents to go out to lunch.

The tri-city area of Albany, Schenectady and Troy has literally scores of excellent restaurants, ranging from upscale, to chains, to a plethora of neighborhood grills and taverns that serve excellent food. One of these, the Purple Pub in the burg of Cohoes, a twenty-minute drive north of Menands, was long a favorite destination for two generations of the Winter family.

The Purple Pub had, and still has, excellent steamed Little Neck clams, orders of which were invariably accompanied by pizzas—Wilson loved to order a small anchovy pizza for himself because no one else would eat the little fish—and pitchers of ice cold Genesee lager. In what seemed to be a natural choice, Kevin offered to take his grandparents to the Purple Pub. But as Kevin tells it, and as Ella also recalls it, Nancy immediately began pressing him to go elsewhere, giving the distinct impression that the Purple Pub was not up to her discerning standards. She often took her parents to a country club near their home where she and her husband James were members. The atmosphere there was decidedly different than what you would find at the Purple Pub which isn't upscale; it is after all, a neighborhood "pub."

The question she clearly posed by her negative commentary was "Why on earth would Kevin want to take his grandparents and girlfriend to a neighborhood tavern, when there was a perfectly acceptable country club just around the corner?"

But Kevin knows his own mind and persisted in his plans to take his grandparents to a place they would enjoy—and he would too. Kevin says "I told her that if she didn't like the Purple Pub she could go home and let the rest of the family enjoy lunch in peace. She didn't take the hint and instead tagged along, complaining all the way that there were other restaurants that were far better, at least in her viewpoint."

In fact, Kevin says, "The complaining kept up non-stop right through lunch." But that wasn't the only issue that arose. "There were things I wanted to discuss with my grandparents; questions I wanted to ask. But Nancy kept butting in, steering the conversation to 'safe ground.' I really resented her interference. She had some kind of a need to control everything, from who was alone with my grandparents, to where we ate, and even what we talked about. It got so bad," Kevin said, "that I told her if she didn't like it she could go home. She wasn't wanted, she wasn't needed and she was ruining our lunch."

Kevin to this day has not forgotten and is not likely to ever forgive his aunt for inserting herself into a luncheon that turned out to be his final meeting with his grandparents in a setting where they could still appreciate each others' company.

When he arrived back in Florida, Kevin made a point of relating the events as they unfolded in New York. He visited Ron and asked for a few minutes alone out on the patio. When Ron asked how the visit with his parents had gone, Kevin replied, "The time I had with them was fine, but your sister was a royal pain." When Ron inquired further Kevin related the entire story of the lunch at the Purple Pub.

After absorbing that news, Ron asked, "How did Dad look?"

Kevin replied, "Not that good. You were right about his color. He seemed upbeat though. We joked quite a bit and I think he was really happy that we made the visit. He got along well with Sharon too. That part was great, but your sister did everything she could to ruin it."

The next trip north came in stages. On July 16, 1999 Ron travelled to Connecticut. Jennifer and Heather already were there, staying at Jennifer's mother's house. They flew north earlier in July, partly to escape the summer heat in Florida, and also to attend a family wedding. Jennifer's mother, who was widowed several years earlier, had reunited with and was scheduled to marry her high school boyfriend, with Jennifer and Heather attending. The trip was memorable because Ron was flying on the day that John Kennedy Jr., died.

Ron flew in to Providence, R.I., instead of Bradley Airport, and Ron remarked to Jennifer after landing, "The air quality was noticeably worse up here. We were at 30,000 feet over Chesapeake Bay and I could see the surf on the shore. But when we came in off the ocean to land in Rhode Island, I couldn't see the shore at less than 18,000 feet."

At 10 p.m. Ron and Jennifer were sitting on the front porch of her mother's house just enjoying the coolness of the evening. In Florida the nighttime temperatures often stayed in the mid-eighties with high humidity and sitting outside at night was only marginally better than daytime. They stayed outside for another hour, and didn't hear of Kennedy's death until early the next day, July 17th, after they picked up a rental car. They heard the news on the radio as they drove up I-91 to Springfield and from there took the Massachusetts Turnpike to Albany. It was the same route they had taken many times in the past, and they arrived at Ella and Wilson's apartment two hours after they left Connecticut. Wilson answered the door with his usual cheery greeting—"You're late!"

"How can I be late when I never said when I'd get here in the first place?" Ron answered. Despite the bantering, it was immediately apparent that not all was well. Wilson had gone for his three-month checkup, but his color was not good.

"Well, the doctor gave me a clean bill of health," Wilson announced. "He even said I don't have to come in for my September appointment."

But Wilson didn't look healthy, and admitted that he didn't feel well either. His abdomen was distended and he was tired. Ron and Jennifer stayed for two days and then returned to Connecticut where Ron had an annual physical scheduled with his family doctor. Wilson said he was going to another doctor for a second opinion and would be in touch.

Ron returned to Florida on July 21st, and on July 26th Jennifer, who was still in Connecticut, spoke at length on the phone with Wilson about his most recent doctor's appointment. It was with a cancer specialist, Wilson disclosed, and the news was not good.

A biopsy revealed that he had liver cancer. Wilson admitted that he was in significant pain, and was not certain on the next course of treatment. Over the next week Wilson went for another test, with another doctor. When the test results came back Wilson got the news that he would have to begin chemotherapy immediately.

On Aug. 5, 1999 Jennifer spoke with Nancy, Ella and Wilson about Wilson's condition. Jennifer then called Ron.

"It's not good," she said. "The doctor said your father has to start chemotherapy immediately." After Jennifer relayed the bad news to Ron they made plans for Ron and Kevin to leave Florida the next day, August 6, 1999. Ron and Kevin were both working so Ron asked, "can you make the flight arrangements from up there?" Jennifer did and the next morning Kevin picked up Ron, they rode together to Tampa International Airport, and flew to Bradley International Airport in Connecticut. They met Heather and Jennifer at the airport, rented a car again and drove to New York.

Ron and Kevin offered to stay in New York to help Wilson get to and from his first chemo session, scheduled for a Monday morning. Their workout partner in Florida, a strapping twenty-eight-year-old who was one of Kevin's best friends, had gone through radiation therapy the previous year for testicular cancer, and they had seen how badly it had drained his energy.

"It will take two strong people to get Dad back in the house from the car," Ron said. But he met resistance from Nancy, and later from Ella. "How are you going to help Dad if he can't walk?" Ron queried. But he was told repeatedly that neither he nor Kevin should miss work and that everything would be fine in New York. Ron insisted, "Dad might be sick but he still weighs over 150 pounds. If he collapses that is a lot of dead weight. You won't be able to carry him!"

Ron already had noticed that the cancer was sapping Wilson's energy. Wilson was so tired that he asked Jennifer if she could stay for a few weeks to help Ella around the apartment. Ron and Kevin had a full schedule of business issues that kept them working sixteen-hour days throughout July and most of August, so Jennifer lingering to provide assistance in New York made perfect sense.

But Nancy again interceded, making it very clear that if anyone was to help her mother it would be her. "I have things under control here," was the essence of her comments. "I don't need anyone else. I can handle this." It was Wilson who asked Jennifer to stay, however, and she was not about to back off if he wanted her to stay. Nonetheless, the message from Albany was clear. "You are not needed. You are not wanted." Although Wilson made the initial request for Jennifer to stay, in the end he indicated that he was too tired to argue and said that if Ella and Nancy felt they could handle the situation then Jennifer could return to Connecticut.

They had a final lunch with Ella and Wilson on the Saturday before his first chemo session, and after talking at length with Wilson, left for Connecticut so Kevin could make his plane back to Florida the next day. They understood the seriousness of the situation but still were optimistic that Wilson could recover—at least for a while. But Wilson must have had a premonition about his condition. He was reclined on the couch as Ron, Jennifer, Kevin and Heather were preparing to leave. Wilson looked up at Jennifer and joked, "I told you the cigarettes wouldn't get me."

They said their good-byes, not knowing they were the last words they would ever share with Wilson, again received assurance from Ella that she would call if she needed help, and then drove back to Connecticut together. Kevin immediately flew back to Florida, but Ron had applied for emergency family leave and was able to stay until August 17. After he returned to Florida, Ron had one phone conversation with Ella in which she revealed "Your father is in the hospital."

She said the doctors believed that he would be better able to withstand the rigors of chemotherapy if he was hospitalized. There was far more to the story, but Ella didn't reveal it at that time.

"This chemotherapy is really knocking him out," Ella said. When Ron asked if calling his father might boost his spirits Ella told him, "Not right now. He needs as much rest as he can get, especially after his chemo sessions." Ron promised that he would give his father some space, and would call the hospital the next week after Wilson regained some strength. Ron again reminded Ella that before leaving Albany, Jennifer had left instructions with her and Nancy. "Call if you need any help at all."

The call never came.

During the third week in August Ron called Albany Medical Center, asked for his father's room, was put on hold, and then was told by a chirpy, upbeat receptionist, "Mr. Winter isn't here any longer. He has checked out and returned home."

The message was delivered in such an optimistic tone that Ron thought the chemo was working and Wilson was recuperating at home. Again, figuring it would be best to give him a couple of days to get his strength back, Ron put off calling until later in the month.

When he did call his parents' apartment, he was surprised to hear his brother Skeeter answer. When Ron asked his brother why he was in New York, Skeeter replied "He's dying. Mom needs someone to help her!" Ron told his brother that Jennifer was still in Connecticut waiting to help. Skeeter had no information on why she wasn't called, but continued to insist that he was the only person available to help Ella care for Wilson. Skeeter, who lived four hours away in Allentown, Pennsylvania and owned a business there, said he was staying at the apartment because Nancy and her family had gone on vacation, and help was needed. But Jennifer, who was only two hours away, waiting for word that she was needed, never was contacted.

When Ron told Skeeter that he wanted to talk with his father, Skeeter refused, yelling, "You don't understand death! I do!" Whatever that was supposed to mean, Skeeter steadfastly refused to let Ron have a few last words with his dying father. "No! No! You can't talk to him," was repeated several times and Ron finally ended the conversation.

Ron did learn that the local Hospice chapter was on hand helping out, and called their main office to obtain information on his father's condition.

Eventually, in a conversation with James Patrick, Ron learned that Wilson's condition went from bad to worse right from the start. "When they came back from that first session he couldn't walk on his own," James said. "But Nancy and your mother couldn't hold him up." Nancy was unable to support Wilson's weight either by herself or with Ella, and Wilson collapsed onto the floor in the foyer to his apartment house.

"He just went right down to the floor, and we couldn't move him," Ella said much later. "Two men came down from the office and they helped him up to our apartment and onto the couch. After that we took him to the hospital so he could have a bed right there after his chemotherapy." Wilson was admitted to the hospital, but while there, he was injured when he attempted to get out of bed to use the bathroom.

"No one was there and he had to use the bathroom," Ella said. "There was a bed pan, but you know your father. He refused to use it and tried to make it to the bathroom. But he tripped and fell face down on the tile floor."

By August 28, 1999 Nancy was back from vacation, but Ron already called the Hospice headquarters, asking them to intervene so he could talk with his father. Ella later said that Wilson had slipped into a coma while Nancy and her husband James were still away and never spoke to anyone again.

Ron called Jennifer that night and talked about her borrowing her mother's car and driving to New York to help out. But the issue was already moot. James called Ron in Florida the next day—August 29, 1999—with the news that Wilson had died.

The next day Ron called James and they talked for more than a half-hour, during which James relayed the information about the foyer incident and Wilson's injury in the hospital. When Ron asked what was going on in New York and why he hadn't been contacted, James replied that he didn't know but that many negative comments had been made about him in the preceding days.

"You've got a big target on your back," was James' assessment. What he couldn't answer, and the question that has never been answered, is "Why?"

Whether it was the incident with Kevin a year earlier, or some old family grudges that Ron had long ago forgotten, there was definite hostility emanating toward Ron's side of the family during Wilson's final illness.

Only one side knew it existed, and why. But they never explained it.

Ella for her part was totally occupied with caring for her husband, and knew little of the family issues that were swirling around her. "I was exhausted from caring for Wilson," Ella said. "And I guess I just forgot that Jennifer was still in Connecticut. If I had remembered, or if someone had reminded me, I would have made that call in a second." But throughout the month of August 1999, with her husband's prognosis changing from hopeful to hopeless in a matter of weeks, Ella barely knew what day it was.

"It was such a shock to find out it was near the end," Ella said later. "I had hoped he and I would have had time to spend talking and enjoying some things together. When they (the doctors) first told me (that Wilson's condition was terminal) they said perhaps six months; then they changed it to three; and then down to weeks. This was all in about a month's time. I was trying to figure out why he was in such pain right from the beginning."

"I was with him when he died," Ella said. "We had a hospital bed set up in our bedroom. It was at the foot of our bed and his head was near the door, but facing the windows so he could see outside if he was awake. Wilson hadn't spoken to anyone for more than a week before he died. He went into a coma and that was it. The morning he died, I was in the room with him and I went out to the kitchen for a cup of coffee and to sit down for a minute. Nancy came back from vacation the day before, and came over earlier that morning. She was in the kitchen when I came out and then she went into the bedroom. She was gone only for a few seconds and came right back. She said Wilson died in the time I came out for my coffee and the time she went back into the bedroom. He never came out of his coma, and never spoke to anyone again. There were no last words, no deathbed statements, he just stopped breathing and it was over."

Ron and Kevin decided to fly north to link up with Jennifer and Heather at Bradley International Airport on the day of Wilson's wake, August 31, 1999. Jennifer again made the flight arrangements, and Kevin and Ron again linked up for the ride to Tampa International. Unlike the trip in mid-August when they were going north to help out if possible, this time they began "waking" Wilson in Tampa, knowing he would have joined them if he could have. The day began with a Bloody Mary in the airport lounge around 10 a.m.—oddly enough when Ron raised his glass and toasted "to Dad" they suddenly had several fellow travelers for company—and continued with a scotch on the plane. But at the stopover in North Carolina, knowing they would have to drive in a few hours, and feeling that Wilson was appropriately remembered in a style he appreciated, they changed to sodas and water for the remainder of the trip. The plane arrived in Connecticut just after 3 p.m., they again met Jennifer and Heather, picked up the rental car that had been reserved for them and arrived at the funeral home in Troy by late afternoon. The wake was already in progress and they stayed until the end, talking with friends and family members. Wilson had lived a long life—he was eighty three at his death—and the wake was crowded with old friends and former co-workers.

James invited Ron to stand in the receiving line with his brother and sister but Ron declined, preferring instead to greet friends on a less formal setting in other parts of the room. He didn't want to make it obvious, but Ron had no intention of putting on a false face of harmony after the treatment of the past few weeks.

When the wake was over and the rest of the family headed back to Nancy's house, Ron and his family made different plans. Bob

Soloyna, his best friend from grade school and high school days came to pay his respects, and asked about Ron's plans after the wake.

"I haven't committed to anything," Ron answered.

Bob then suggested, "Are you up for a pizza?" Ron said he was and rather than going back to Nancy and James' where the evening was guaranteed not to be pleasant, he, Jennifer, Kevin and Heather instead met Bob for a pizza, talked over old times, and then retired to a motel nearby.

But the most astounding part of the evening from Ron's perspective was what happened just before they left the funeral home. The mourners were gone, except for a handful of family members including Ron, Jennifer, Kevin and Heather, as well as Nancy and her daughter Courtney.

Skeeter and James were taking Ella outside to the car. Ron, Jennifer and Heather walked to Wilson's coffin one last time, and Heather placed a carnation in the coffin, on her grandfather's folded hands.

They turned to leave, but at the main door to the funeral home Jennifer remembered she intended to take a few extra Mass cards to send to her family.

"Wait for me, I'll be right back," she told Ron, who stopped with Heather and Kevin just inside the door. Jennifer went back inside the room where the wake had been held, stepping past Nancy and Courtney who were leaving. The room was now empty, except for Wilson's coffin.

Jennifer retrieved the cards, and took a moment to say a last goodbye to Wilson. But as she approached the coffin her eyes were drawn to a splash of color on the floor underneath. She gasped in utter astonishment, and for a few seconds was frozen where she stood. To her horror, and disgust, she saw the carnation that only a minute before had been left as a tribute to Wilson, thrown on the floor.

She went to the door. "Ron, can you come in here for a minute?"

Ron, Kevin and Heather were the last people in the funeral home, except for the staff, and they walked back inside the room. The lights were turned up after the mourners left and the room was bright. Sprays of flowers surrounded the coffin and the conflicting aromas fought for dominance. Wilson's body was rigid, but his face bore a neutral expression. He looked as he had looked prior to his illness, even to the extent that he could have just been sleeping. The embalmer and the rest of the funeral home staff had done well. Jennifer pointed to the floor under the coffin. A carnation was on the floor, but there was no flower in the coffin.

"Is that the flower Heather just put in with Dad?" Ron asked. Jennifer nodded and he immediately returned to the coffin, picked up the flower and replaced it on his father's body. There was no one else in the room. Taking the flower out of Wilson's coffin was a cheap and classless act. They never found out who did it, but the list of suspects wasn't very long.

In the morning when they returned for Wilson's funeral, the first thing Ron did was check the coffin to make sure that the flower was still there. And he checked right up until the moment the coffin was closed forever to ensure that Heather's flower stayed with Wilson.

The funeral service was straightforward; two ministers spoke of Wilson's history, his service to his country, a brief history of the family. It was obvious that they really didn't know Wilson and were speaking only from the information they were given. The ministers finished, and asked if anyone else wanted to speak about Wilson. Although Ron planned on giving a eulogy for his father, the events of the previous two weeks, and especially the night before, convinced him otherwise. Kevin approached him after the service saying, "I thought you were going to speak about Grandpa!"

Ron responded, "If I had said what I wanted to say, the way I wanted to say it, they would have interrupted and caused a scene. I'm sure of it. We'll do our own memorial for Dad our own way, in our own time. But I'm not about to let them ruin Dad's funeral and then blame it on us."

As they left the funeral home for the journey to Oakwood Cemetery in North Troy a bagpiper wearing Scottish tartans played outside the funeral home. He piped the mourners in, and he piped them out after the service. When they talked on the previous Sunday James asked Ron what songs should be played, and Ron suggested Scotland the Brave, and Bonnie Dundee, referring to his father's birthplace, among several others. The piper also played at the graveside service, standing to the side of the grave in the shade of several oak trees. He played Bonnie Dundee again, and after a few more words from the minister, and a bugler playing taps, the service ended. At Kevin's urging they stopped at a reception following Wilson's burial, and then left for Connecticut. Kevin had to fly back to Florida immediately; Ron went a few days later.

Ron said goodbye to Ella. "I'll keep in touch," he told her. "I'll let you know how things are going with the business." A few days after they returned from New York Ron called Ella, and in that conversation relayed to her what had happened with the carnation.

"I knew something was wrong," Ella said. "Why didn't you tell me then?"

Ron replied, "I didn't want to cause a problem at the funeral. They would have found a way to rewrite history and blame it on me, so I just kept quiet. But what they did was rotten and I won't forget it."

In September Ella sent a letter to Ron, Jennifer and Heather, saying "Thank you for being there and giving me support." Regarding

Wilson's final service she added "I think he had the kind of funeral he wanted, with the bagpipes and taps. He would have been proud." And then, in an especially appreciated sentiment Ella wrote, "Thank you for the lovely flowers, especially you Heather, for the special one you put in with him." Ella also made note of the hostility from Nancy and Skeeter, adding "I wish things could have been more peaceful." Ella's letter was just one of many regular contacts between Ron and his mother in the coming years, but he didn't speak to either his brother or sister again for at least five years. He wouldn't have spoken to them at all except for two important events, his Uncle Bob's 100th birthday and Ella's 90th .

In early 2001 Ron, Jennifer and Heather moved back north. The lease they signed when they left was still in effect and a family was renting their home, so they lived in a small house on a lake in eastern Connecticut for nearly two years until the lease expired. In this period Ron regularly called Ella, often on Sunday afternoons as he sat by the lake fishing or just watching boats sail by and listening to the sounds from the beach a half-mile across the water. During one of these conversations Ella related that Nancy had brought up the events surrounding Wilson's death and funeral in a discussion the previous week, essentially claiming that all the problems were caused by Ron and that neither she (Nancy) nor Skeeter had done anything except support their parents in a difficult time. There was no way anyone could have known it, but this same theme was repeated in Nancy's lawsuit nearly seven years later.

At the time Ron merely responded, "I told you they'd rewrite history," and went on with the conversation. Fortunately, a number of documents that proved his point were still in his files, and after that phone call, they stayed there—just in case. Although he and Ella were in regular contact while Ron waited to move back into their own home, there was no room in the small house for guests, so for this period Ella did not resume her visits to Connecticut. Ron, Jennifer and Heather returned home late in the summer of 2002, and made plans to have Ella come stay with them for a few days as soon as the house was settled, possibly for Thanksgiving.

But on a mid-November morning Ron awoke with a blinding headache and was seeing double. He went to the hospital emergency room in Manchester, Connecticut, arriving at about 10 a.m., and explaining to the nurse on duty, "I woke up with a splitting headache and I'm seeing double. I took a couple of aspirins but it is just getting worse."

The nurse handed him a clipboard containing several forms. "Have a seat in the waiting area and fill these out," she instructed.

Ron took a seat, did as he was told, and watched as other people came in, were treated, and left, while he was kept waiting. After two hours he went back to the desk to ask when he would be seen. "You'll just have to be patient," was the response.

This went on for a total of six hours, and finally Ron was taken to an examination room—where he sat unattended for another hour. Ron finally threw in the towel and left the exam room, walking through the hospital to the front entrance where his car was parked. He walked through wards, examination areas, radiology, cardiology and other "ologies" all of which were off limits. But he was not challenged by anyone, although he did get a few strange looks, finally arriving at the front of the hospital. He walked outside, crossed the street to the parking lot and drove home with one hand over his right eye most of the way. It restricted his vision but eliminated the double vision.

Once back at home Ron called his family doctor. "They wouldn't see me at the emergency room," he reported.

"What do you mean they wouldn't see you?" his doctor asked.

"I mean I sat there from ten in the morning until five in the afternoon and no one would see me. So I left."

The doctor said, "Come in tomorrow morning for an exam."

Ron saw several doctors in the next two months, and was tested for a suspected brain tumor. But an MRI and a CT Scan, both turned up negative. He was given medication for the pain, but nothing changed. His vision was so bad that he had to get rides from friends and family. His doctor suggested that a spinal tap might be in the offing, but Ron rejected it. Finally Jennifer suggested that Ron see his eye doctor. During an examination a year earlier the optometrist noticed a broken blood vessel deep inside Ron's right eye.

He ordered an extensive series of blood tests and determined that Ron had elevated levels of a key enzyme that regulates blood clotting. He turned his findings over to Ron's family doctor with a recommendation that Ron begin taking a daily Vitamin B9—folic acid—supplement.

But Ron's family doctor never acted on the optometrist's recommendation. Ron made an appointment with his optometrist and the first thing he was asked was "Are you still taking the folic acid?"

"I haven't taken it at all. It was never prescribed," he responded.

The optometrist did another examination and determined that Ron's headache and double vision were the result of what amounted to a cramp in the muscles surrounding Cranial Nerve #6, part of the network that passes images from the eye to the brain. It was causing both the headache and the double vision and would take some months to heal.

Ron immediately dropped his long-time family doctor, signed on with another who consulted with his optometrist, and agreed with the diagnosis. Ron was started on the B9 supplements, but it was another six months before he was back to normal.

The timing of his affliction and recovery were important later on when Ella was sued by her daughter. Nancy testified that Ron couldn't be bothered coming to visit Ella in mid-2003 when she had an operation for a prolapsed bowel.

Ella spent four days in the hospital and then finished her recovery at home in her apartment. There was no question that Nancy took care of Ella during the recovery, not staying at the apartment overnight, but stopping in during the day.

"Of course I didn't go to New York," Ron told Ella's lawyer. "I couldn't go. At the time of Mom's operation the doctors thought I had a brain tumor and I certainly couldn't drive in that condition. But I did talk to Mom regularly, and she didn't think the operation was that big a deal. She said Nancy came over to check on her for the next several weeks, but otherwise, she was fine. We spoke on the phone the day before she entered the hospital, and we were in contact afterwards too." But neither Nancy, nor Skeeter, nor Courtney, nor anyone else ever called to update him on Ella's progress. Ella said then, and she says now, that she didn't consider the surgery to be major.

In the end, both Ron and Ella recovered. There was no sign of a brain tumor for Ron, and Ella made a full recovery from her bowel surgery. But the false claim that would later emerge, that Ron didn't care about his mother and his absence when she had an operation was proof of it, was yet another cause of deep resentment from Ron toward his siblings.

Ron and Jennifer resumed their visits to Ella in 2003 when Ron's condition improved, but with the caveat that Nancy stay away so they could enjoy their time with Ella unimpeded. Ron, Jennifer and Heather attended a family reunion in the summer of 2004, and in December of that year the family gathered in Center Brunswick, where Ella and her brother Bob grew up, and where Bob still lived, for Uncle Bob's 100th birthday. To ensure that it was a happy occasion Ron spoke with his siblings but sat with his cousins and friends of his uncle's. The party was held in the community room at the fire house, and it was packed. The state senator for that area attended and spoke on Bob's behalf, and Bob took the mike himself to joke with his friends and family. It was a great party, and there was more than enough insulation to avoid any unpleasantness.

In December 2006 the family gathered again for Ella's 90th birthday. Ella's birthday wasn't until Jan. 4, 2007, but Nancy and her family vacationed in Florida in January, and Nancy determined that the party for Ella's 90th birthday should be held a month early. Although all of Ella's children contributed significantly to her birthday party, including money, Ella later revealed that Nancy took all the credit for the arrangements. Considering what had happened when his father died nearly ten years earlier, and the continuing manipulation that he saw from his sister, it is not surprising that there would be distance between Ron and other members of his family.

Ella resumed visiting Connecticut after Bob's birthday, and Ron drove to New York on several occasions to bring her to his home. He did this on January 3rd, 2007, the day before her 90th birthday.

Two days into that visit Ella revealed that she had injured her leg in a fall shortly before Christmas and that her leg was still bothering her. When Ron and Jennifer looked at it they were appalled to discover that Ella's injury had not been treated, except with an antiseptic. A deep scrape ran from her knee to her ankle and appeared to be badly infected. Ella said she was delivering a Christmas plant to the office staff at the Dutch Village apartments when she tripped.

"There was a space between the steps and as I went to step up my foot only caught the lip of the step. I didn't fall but I scraped my shin on the stone." Ella said the injury occurred "a day or two before Christmas. I've been putting antiseptic on it every day since."

When Ron and Jennifer examined Ella's leg after she arrived in Connecticut nearly two weeks later, they decided that Ella should get medical treatment immediately. They took her to a nearby emergency room where the wound was treated, and Ella was given antibiotics as well as a tetanus shot. The injury responded to the treatment and eventually healed.

In the summer of 2008, they were surprised to receive a call from Nancy who asked if they would drive to New York to stay with Ella. "Mom had an eye operation, and she can't be left alone for a few more days. But Jim and I are going to Rhode Island, so could you stay with her?" Ella needed surgery for advancing glaucoma, and revealed that "It can give me dizziness for a few days, especially if I look down." The operation was on Wednesday and Ella said, "They want someone around me until Sunday or Monday. But don't worry about it if you can't come. I'm doing fine."

Ron, Jennifer and Heather left Connecticut early on Saturday morning, arriving in Albany before 10 a.m. They stayed until noon on Sunday and offered to stay longer. But they had several animals in Connecticut that required food and water, and Ella insisted, "I'm fine. They'll be back (Nancy and James) by one (p.m.) and I certainly can be left by myself for an hour." Years later Nancy testified that Ella had been left alone for several hours—saying that Ron left New York at 10 a.m., supposedly to avoid driving in a rainstorm.

But Ella later confirmed that she was on her own for only about an hour and experienced no difficulties getting around her apartment on her own after the eye surgery. Although there is no question that Nancy bore the brunt of caring for their mother in the years after Wilson's death—at least in those periods when she needed care—

it was not lost on Ron or his family that his mother did not seem especially happy with Nancy—especially in the two years following her 90th birthday.

Ron offered to have Ella move in with his family several times during this period. But Ella always responded that she was happy in her apartment, and while she didn't see her daughter all that often, she had friends who cared for her and looked out for her. Ron didn't agree with Ella's living by herself, but the apartment seemed to have good security and Ella was, and is, very independent. She did not want to rely on someone else and she made that point very clear. Ron left it at that, but made sure Ella knew she always had a home in Connecticut if she needed one.

As Ella moved into and through her 91st birthday it was becoming more and more apparent that her living situation would have to change. In early 2006, again while Nancy was vacationing, Ella had what she calls an "episode" that put her in the hospital briefly, and gave Skeeter and Nancy even more ammunition to put her into an elder care facility.

"I was going out for groceries," Ella says, "and Skeeter was going to drive me to the store. But all of a sudden I felt tired, really tired, and I decided to take a nap instead. I asked Skeeter if he could come back later and he agreed. He had an apartment in Clifton Park back then so he went home and I went to bed. When I woke up I was standing in the dining room, and three people were in my apartment; my friend Hilda from across the hall, and two paramedics."

Ella says Hilda found her walking in the hallway. "Hilda tried to talk with me, but I don't remember that part and she said I wasn't making sense. So she called the paramedics and got me back in the apartment. I 'woke up' when they arrived and were in my apartment talking. They said I should go to the hospital and I went with them to the ambulance. As I was getting in Skeeter came back to take me shopping, and he followed the ambulance to the hospital."

Ella was in the hospital briefly before her primary care physician ordered her released. Ella attributed the episode to taking prescription cold medicine for three days longer than she should have.

"I had been taking that cold medicine for years," Ella maintains, but "they changed the dosage." The new dose was supposed to be discontinued after five days, Ella said, but "I took the pills for at least eight days, and I believe that caused me to get overtired and to sleep walk." But Skeeter, and later Nancy, saw the incident as further proof that Ella should be institutionalized.

Ella is still the independent, feisty woman she was sixty years earlier. "I know that I need some help and that somebody has to be with me. But I still want some independence and I don't want to live in a facility. Needing help from time to time is not the same thing as needing help all the time."

"I needed some help with the finances for a bit after Wilson died. There were so many forms to fill out and changes to make. But once we got through that I was back on solid ground. Except for going into the hospital after my heart attack and again for the operation, I was still able to do most things for myself. As I said, I know I need help from time to time and it is great to have someone stop in, but I don't need to be put into a home."

Ella was hospitalized two other times, once for the bowel operation and once for a mild heart attack. She also lost a significant portion of the sight in her left eye from glaucoma, and received outpatient treatment at her doctor's office to have a small growth removed from her face—a procedure that took less than a half hour.

"I made it through those times without going into a nursing home and I don't need one now. But Skeeter has been saying for years that he wants me in some sort of facility. He took me to a couple of retirement homes, including one where a lot of my friends and acquaintances from Center Brunswick live now. But I had lunch there one day and they didn't like it when I told them the fish didn't taste right. The waitress told me 'a lot of people got up very early this morning to make that lunch for you.' I guess that means I wasn't supposed to complain if the lunch tasted 'fishy.' Maybe I would have felt differently if Wilson and I had gone to one of those places when we came back from Florida. But neither of us wanted that back then, and I still don't want it now. I am not comfortable having my meals in the company of eighty other people. I like my breakfast and coffee on my own time in my own space. One of the places Skeeter took me to was a room that was so small it was more like a hallway. It was just wide enough for a couch and around the corner was a small alcove where a bed would fit. Either you sit in there all cramped up all day, or you spend your day out in the public area. That just isn't my style."

"I never had the kind of money that you need to go to one of those places anyway. The good ones want you to put up as much as $100,000 and that doesn't include your monthly rent. Sooner or later I would be out of money and then they wanted to put me on Medicaid. Wilson set up his retirement insurance so that even if he died first, which we never expected, I would never have to go on Medicaid and there is no reason that should change!"

Ella got along primarily because she hired a service that sent a woman in two mornings a week to help with light housework and shopping. Otherwise, Ella was on her own.

"Nancy came over on Sunday mornings for breakfast, but that wasn't going well, especially in the last few years. Jim would go sit out on the balcony rather than sit in the kitchen because Nancy and I were always arguing. Otherwise, she called most days, but I only saw her once a week other than Sundays, and some weeks not even that." Overall, Ella was still doing well but her needs were increasing, and the willingness of two of her children to attend to those needs was simultaneously diminishing. Eventually the two trends were going to collide, and when they did, it appeared she would be at the mercy of her two offspring who long ago decided between them that Ella should move into a facility, regardless of what she thought of the idea.

PART TWO

En Garde!

<u>*Note To My Readers*</u>

Everything up to this point has been written in the third person, because I wanted you to get to know Ella Winter primarily from her own point of view. The foreword and Part I are the result of interviewing her on a daily basis for more than six months about her early life.

These interviews have been extremely rewarding and I have gotten to know my mother much better as a result. She has lived a long life, and has faced both joys and crushing tragedies. She has travelled throughout the United States, often completely on her own, and has lived a life of effort and reward.

From here on out, the book will change. Although the events following Ella's move to my house on Dec. 22, 2008 were ostensibly aimed only at her, there was plenty of what the military calls "collateral damage." There was no way the attacks on my mother were or could have been precision strikes.

That my entire family would also be affected was a given from the start. So from here on out, I will tell the rest of the story from my vantage point, in the first person.

Everything up until now has been preparatory. This is where the gloves come off. This is where the battle begins.

Ron Winter

CHAPTER SIX

A Brief Agreement

Late on the night of December 13, 2008, Ella was taken by ambulance from her apartment in the Dutch Village complex to Albany Medical Center. She was suffering from disorientation and confusion.

The admission form said her temperature was normal but at some later time that night she was reported to have a high fever—nearly 102 degrees—as well as a high white blood cell count and dehydration.

The doctors who examined her in the emergency room also listed Ella's diagnosis relative to the disorientation as "altered mental status."

She was accompanied in the emergency room by her daughter Nancy and son-in-law James who told the doctors that they had called Ella at her apartment late that night but there was no answer. So they visited her apartment, and there, according to the medical report, they found her in a state of extreme disorientation, and her apartment "ransacked." The ambulance report states that she was transported to the hospital just before 11:30 p.m.

That is about the only thing on which those involved in this story agree.

On Sunday evening, December 14, 2008, my brother Wilson, aka Skeeter, now living in Florida, called me in Connecticut to tell me of Mom's hospitalization. Skeeter maintained that this was the second "episode" Ella had experienced in a two-year time frame and that this time she would have to be committed to an elder care facility.

Ella strongly disputes this contention and maintains that a previous "episode" that also resulted in a hospital stay, was caused by her taking prescription cold medicine for three days longer than she should have—as was related in the previous chapter. That in turn resulted in what Ella maintains was a sleep walking incident.

Although Ella was hospitalized in the 2006 episode, that time, unlike her hospitalization in December, 2008, she remembers virtually everything leading up to, and after, the incident.

Nonetheless, Skeeter said, a family meeting to determine her fate would take place sometime between Christmas and New Year's Day. Skeeter added that he was travelling to the Albany area just after Christmas. "But I have to see my lawyer in Pennsylvania too. I have a legal matter with Brian (his son) involving the Power of Attorney I granted him. I'm meeting the lawyer on December 29, so our meeting will have to be after that." In response to a question I asked him, Skeeter said he was returning to Florida on January 4, 2009—Mom's birthday.

So we tentatively agreed that the family meeting could take place on December 30th or 31st. "Just let me know what works best for you, and I'll be there," I told him.

In the meantime my cousin Bob Haber called me. He still lives in the farmhouse we vacated back in 1957, and heard that something had happened to my mother. We also were in touch over our Uncle

Bob's hospitalization too. Cousin Bob was curious as to what had happened to Mom, since Uncle Bob had just died, and suddenly, even before our uncle was buried, Mom was in the hospital too.

I emailed Bob with the following message:

From: Ron Winter
To: Bob Haber
Subject: I'll call
Date: Tue, 16 Dec 2008 03:04:07 +0000

Bob

Mom had some kind of a seizure or stroke or something. Jennifer and I were thinking that she may have taken some cold medication that conflicted with whatever else she may be taking. But we don't know.

Mom said - last time, not this time cause I haven't spoken with her - that she went to take a nap and next thing she knew she was out in the hall in front of her apartment. The lady across the hall called an ambulance.

This time Nancy and Jim went over after she didn't answer the phone and she was all out of sorts, didn't know where she was and all. So she is in Albany Medical Center. Skeeter called from Florida yesterday and said they were giving her a spinal tap! Said it might be meningitis!

Oh, and I am supposed to come over after Christmas for a "family meeting" to decide where she is going to be 'placed.'

I'll call tomorrow.

Ron

Mom was admitted to Albany Med late Saturday night,

December 13th, and the following Wednesday, the 17th, after receiving treatment for potassium deficiency, a condition that can cause confusion and disorientation, she was declared ready for discharge from the hospital.

However, by that time, Nancy, who had Power of Attorney over Mom's affairs, had already made arrangements to sign her into the Hawthorne Ridge elder facility across the Hudson River in East Greenbush, New York. But prior to finalizing the move, Nancy's husband, James, made a phone call to me, alerting me of the pending change in status. "If you want any input on this, call before 3:30 today," he said.

I received the message on my voice mail shortly after noon, and immediately returned the call to James. My message, in essence, was "don't put Mom in a nursing home, bring her here. We can care for her and she'll be with family."

James was somewhat skeptical at first, asking how we would manage with another adult in the house. "We had four people living in this house when it was built," I explained. "In fact, it's only been since Kevin moved to Florida that we've only had three people here. Besides, Jennifer and I have been homeschooling Heather for the past four years. She's fourteen now, and we've had it set up like this since she was ten. I moved my office here, into what had been Kevin's bedroom, and Jennifer works only five minutes down the road. She also has flex hours so if I have to go out on a client meeting, she comes home, and goes back to work when I return. We have six hospitals within twenty to forty minutes, excellent doctors only ten minutes away in one direction and a fully staffed emergency room ten minutes the other way. It is open 24/7 and has a helipad too."

I told James that moving Mom into our household in Connecticut would constitute a major change, but it would be manageable under the existing arrangement. "I'll have to move the office from the first floor up to the second floor temporarily," I told him. "But in the spring I can put an addition on and give Mom her own bedroom and sitting room so she can have her privacy. I can't do it now with the ground frozen but we should be able to start in March. Then I'll just put the office back as it was."

James and I had a frank discussion about the cost of such an addition, with James revealing that Mom had saved some money she could contribute, but not nearly enough to cover the complete cost of the project. "Well we can both contribute," I said. "Between us we should be able to put up a suitable addition, and Mom will have her own space when she wants privacy but immediate access to the rest of the house too. Besides, it's better for her to spend some of her money on staying out of a nursing home, rather than putting her in one where they'll go through everything she has in a matter of months."

Even with her Social Security and pension income Ella would have only enough money to pay for elder care for about six to nine months, depending on the rates charged, and after that would have to go on Medicaid, a move that Ella strongly opposed—feared even.

"Mom will be far better off living with us instead of sitting around a nursing home all day," I said. "Besides, once Mom's savings are gone she'll be put on Medicaid or moved to a state approved facility. She'll have no say over her own life."

James agreed with my assessment, and told me that he would call back at 3:30 p.m., the designated time for a conference with medical personnel and social workers. "I'll put my phone on speaker so you can hear everything and join in," he said.

But the conference never took place. Instead, James called at 3:25 p.m., and announced that the proposal to move Ella to Connecticut was "a done deal." The only question he had was when the move would be convenient.

"When can you bring her?" I asked.

"How about this afternoon?" James replied.

"Well, I can't do it today," I said. "I have to completely rearrange the office into a bedroom and my bedroom into an office. I can have it all ready by Friday or Saturday." Thus, Saturday, December 20 became the target date for the move.

James also queried whether Ella should be told immediately that the move was permanent, or simply told that she was coming for a visit, and later informed that she would not be going home.

"We should tell her up front what's going on," I insisted. "She should know what is happening. There's no way I'm going to have her here thinking it's just for a visit and then drop a bomb on her in a week or two that she'll never be going home again." My point was simple: Mom should know what was going on and agree to it beforehand.

James agreed and told me during the second phone conversation that Mom was fully informed. "There are no false pretenses," he said. In fact, since Mom was right there with James when he made that call, I heard him ask her again, "Are you OK with going to Ron's?" Mom answered in the affirmative, and as far as I was concerned from that point on, Ella's move was voluntary, and made with her full knowledge and consent.

I was not about to have Mom in my home, thinking she was just visiting, only to find out that she wasn't going back to her own home, when her own home no longer existed.

There also was a bit of a fly in the ointment. Ella was ready for discharge from the hospital, but for reasons that were never fully explained, Nancy and James did not want her returning to her apartment.

A suggestion that Ella could stay a few days with Nancy was also rejected, partly because the bedrooms in the Patrick household are on the second floor, and reached only via a winding, carpeted staircase that would pose a major problem for a nonagenarian. There also was another issue; the relationship between Ella and Nancy.

"They're like oil and water," James confided, adding that they couldn't co-exist in the same room.

This did not come as a surprise to me, or to other family members who had witnessed the interaction between Ella and Nancy over the previous few years. I remembered all too well the Sunday morning breakfast in Mom's apartment a year earlier attended by the Patricks, and I did not want to go through that experience again.

"She (Nancy) still reminds me of one of those border collies," I confided to my wife after talking with James. "She nipped and barked at Mom then and she still treats Mom like she's herding sheep."

Ella herself would later complain that her traditional Sunday morning breakfasts with family had become a major chore, and her daughter had steadily eroded Ella's participation. "First she wouldn't let me cook the eggs, and then it was the bacon," Mom said. "Eventually, all I could do was the toast and juice."

This situation left the Patrick's with a dilemma, that being, how to care for Ella from Wednesday, December 17, 2008, through Saturday, December 20, 2008. James said he was going to try to convince Albany Medical Center personnel not to discharge her on Wednesday, but rather to keep her for two more days to perform neurological diagnoses, to determine if her disorientation had more than one cause.

Her original discharge form said she suffered from Hypokalemia—potassium deficiency—and that her confusion also could have been caused by senile dementia or even the result of other factors related to being in the hospital. The only condition that was reported to have been treated, however, was the low potassium, which especially in conjunction with the dehydration could cause all of Ella's symptoms.

There was no further diagnosis provided to us in the days leading up to Ella's move to Connecticut, other than the dehydration, fever and infection that were found when she was admitted to Albany Med. We also were not apprised of any further diagnosis after her extended stay at the hospital for neurological testing. An attending physician had recommended that she have follow up care in the coming weeks. Nothing more.

If there were other factors that were involved in Ella's episode, Nancy Patrick certainly would have been the person to know about them. At least, that is the position taken by her lawyer, who claimed in writing that Nancy provided daily care for Ella, including taking control of her finances and virtually all other aspects of her life, from the time Dad died in 1999, right up until her move to Connecticut on December 22, 2008. This care was alleged to be on a daily basis after Ella's operation in 2003.

Nancy's lawyer? Oh yes, a lawyer was quickly on the scene. In fact, several lawyers appeared on the scene, including the two that Ella retained, one in Connecticut, another in New York, to protect herself, as well as an "evaluator" appointed by the judge.

But that was after Ella moved to Connecticut and found to her delight that with some extended sleep, much needed alterations to her diet, and considerable distance between her and Nancy, she was soon very much her old self. She later told the judge that she decided she would stay in Connecticut permanently by the second day after she arrived at our home.

The judge? Oh yes, there was a judge, a couple of them in fact.

And they were on the scene quite quickly too. Because even though the move to Connecticut was originally approved by all involved, and especially by Mom, the feeling of euphoria lasted only three days.

Then matters in New York began to intrude on our life in Connecticut. Then Ella decided to take control of her own life back from her daughter. Then all hell broke loose.

CHAPTER SEVEN

Check (Book) Please

In the early days of December 2008, Mom was not really looking forward to Christmas. This was unusual for her because she is a holiday person. She loves dressing up and going to church on Easter Sunday, she loves Thanksgiving, Fourth of July, Memorial Day, you name it.

But that year she did not even consider putting up lights and the miniature Christmas tree that long ago took the place of the real trees she loved in earlier times. Her disinterest in one of her favorite holidays was a certain sign that all was not well.

But there was more to signal the oncoming storm. Mom and her oldest brother, Bob Mandeville, spent Thanksgiving dinner at her daughter Nancy's house. Three days later, on a Sunday morning, a family member visited Uncle Bob at his home, where he lived alone, and found him to be incoherent and severely dehydrated. Uncle Bob was only a week shy of his 104th birthday.

Several hours of in-home treatment gradually brought Uncle Bob back to a semblance of normality and he stayed in his home in Center Brunswick overnight. But the following day he complained of shortness of breath and fatigue.

As luck would have it, Nancy Patrick took that moment to visit Uncle Bob at his house, about fifteen miles and a half-hour from her home. Ella told us that her brother "was already on the phone calling the ambulance. But Nancy and James had been handling his finances and Nancy went to the hospital too and stayed with him while he was admitted."

Mom said Nancy had a "premonition" about Bob, and based on that decided to drive to his house to look in on him.

Bob was still in the Samaritan Hospital in Troy, New York, on December 4, 2008, his 104th birthday, but several family members—his nephews Floyd and Bob Haber, as well as Floyd's wife Kay and Janet, Floyd and Kay's daughter—went to his room and held an impromptu birthday party with him and hospital staff. This group did not include the Patricks, nor Mom, who had visited him the previous day.

"I thought I was going over to see him on his birthday," Mom said many times in the months since. "But Nancy and James came to my apartment and told me they were going to Boston to visit Courtney, not to the hospital. Courtney had bought a new condo and they made a point that they were visiting her, but they didn't tell me until they got to the apartment. I still don't know why they couldn't take a half-hour to ride me to the hospital. Someone would have given me a ride home. I would have called Kay and Floyd for a ride but it was too late. I really wanted to see Bob. But Nancy got upset with me and then they left."

This turn of events continues to plague Mom, since she never saw her brother again. In the weeks after moving to Connecticut Mom often recounted her disappointment at not seeing her brother on his birthday, especially with regards to what happened next.

By all accounts of those who saw him on December 4th, Uncle Bob had recovered remarkably well and was anxious to leave the hospital and return home.

But by Sunday he was in "distress," and between Sunday night and Monday morning, December 8, Uncle Bob died.

His passing was a terrible blow to Mom. She intended to attend his wake on December 14 and his funeral on December 15. But in the week that it took the Patricks to finalize his funeral services, Mom was hospitalized too, late on Saturday, December, 13th, also suffering from dehydration and disorientation, as noted previously. She too was taken to the hospital by ambulance after an unscheduled visit from Nancy.

I talked with Mom on the phone on the Friday after Bob's death—two days before she was hospitalized—and although she was understandably despondent about her brother's death, and the length of time between his passing and the scheduled funeral, she otherwise sounded normal. It was during this conversation that she said she wasn't interested in decorating for Christmas.

Which is why, after all that occurred in the next ten days, culminating in her move to Connecticut on December 22, she had such a look of surprise and excitement on her face Christmas morning when she entered our living room and saw that Christmas had nonetheless arrived overnight. In addition to the tree and decorations that were in place when she arrived, Christmas came replete with stockings hung by the chimney with care, and of course, presents, including an electronic keyboard for her.

Mom played piano and organ most of her life, but she was complaining of stiff and painful fingers when she arrived in Connecticut. She also said she was suffering from arthritis in her legs and she walked with a noticeable limp. Mom said the condition began more than a year prior to her move, and the pain in her fingers prevented her from playing the piano or her beloved organ. The keyboard, with its significantly lighter touch, enabled her to play music again, especially the hymns she loved.

Mom made the journey from New York to Connecticut with relative ease, once the journey actually started. The target date for her arrival, Saturday, December 20, was pushed back due to a winter storm that cancelled her travel plans on both that day and the next.

Mom returned to her own apartment on Friday night, December 19th, after being discharged from Albany Medical Center, and she said Nancy, James and Courtney Patrick rotated sleeping over at the apartment. Mom was somewhat bemused, she later told me, that her apartment didn't look as though it had been ransacked, although she acknowledged that it could easily have been straightened up while she was hospitalized.

James Patrick told me, and Nancy repeated to Mom, that she—Mom—in the hours before she was hospitalized shattered a glass centerpiece that sat on her dining room table. James also told me that Mom was so agitated that she had to be restrained at the hospital.

But Mom said that when she returned to her apartment the centerpiece was still there with only a hairline crack around the rim. The description of "shattered" did not hold up, nor did the commentary about restraints in the hospital, which the medical records show were used only to keep Mom from getting out of bed to use the restroom after a catheter was employed—several hours after she was admitted.

By all accounts the three days from December 19 to December 22 were uneventful—except for some very strange dreams that Mom later recounted—and Mom was bundled up and trundled off to Connecticut by late in the morning on Monday, the 22nd. It was a beautiful, sunny day, and the Patricks, their car laden to the gunnels with Mom's possessions, arrived in Connecticut at 2 p.m.

The car was unloaded swiftly, and Mom was shown her new bedroom and bathroom, which she already was familiar with due to previous visits to our home. Nancy and Courtney had a brief crying scene in the kitchen while James and I discussed the placement and dimensions of the planned addition to our house.

Then James played with our dog and waited impatiently to leave. All in all, the scene was benign enough, with the exception of two comments from Nancy.

As Nancy and Courtney were exiting the kitchen after their last goodbye, Nancy turned to my wife Jennifer and me, commenting,

"You have no idea what you're in for." We both were shocked at the comment especially since Mom was standing right next to Nancy when she said it, and we interpreted it to be related to the ongoing tension between them.

A few minutes later, as the Patricks were exiting the house, Nancy turned quickly and said, "Mom will be looking for her checkbook. But I have Power of Attorney. If she needs any money, let me know and I'll send it."

If anything was a harbinger of problems to come, that comment wrapped it all very nicely in one package.

Soon enough they were gone and Mom began unpacking suitcase after suitcase of clothes, with substantial help from my daughter Heather, while other possessions and mementos were arranged in her room. It was quickly apparent that Mom was exhausted and was in need of extended sleep. That part came quickly and Mom napped within an hour of the Patricks' leaving.

Another issue that arose within hours was her diet. At dinner Mom wanted a cup of coffee, which would not have been an issue if she had consumed decaf, but for someone who was suffering from extreme dehydration only a few days earlier it was a signal of potential problems.

When asked if she drank coffee at dinner every night, Mom answered, "Sure, unless I have tea." She further remarked that she often stayed up late at night and woke often during the night, which raised immediate concerns about sleep deprivation, in addition to dehydration.

The first change in her diet was swift, with decaf coffee taking the place of regular coffee and herbal tea substituting for the caffeinated variety from lunch onward. She still drinks one or two cups of coffee in the morning, but within a day this small change resulted in an astounding increase in Mom's ability to sleep long hours without interruption.

It also revealed, within seventy-two hours, a much more alert, aware and focused Ella Winter. It was during the period after opening presents and before eating brunch on Christmas Day that the newly alert Mom discovered her checkbook was missing.

She went looking for it because she wanted to write a check to her granddaughter, Heather, as a Christmas present. She was not satisfied with one check to the Winter family that Nancy Patrick had filled out, and she wanted to let Heather know that there was a present specifically for her.

"Where's my checkbook," Mom asked, benignly enough at first.

"Nancy has it," I replied.

"Why does Nancy have it?" Ella inquired.

"I don't know Mom. She said she has Power of Attorney and that she'll send you money as needed. But she definitely said she is keeping it with her."

Upon being told that Nancy mentioned having Power of Attorney, she responded "That's only if I'm incapacitated."

Nancy called later that day and Mom told her directly, "I want my checkbook back." Something else was said on the other end, presumably a refusal because Mom's next comment was "Why not?"

Mom was obviously displeased and questioned several times that day and in the following days as well, why Nancy took her checkbook. Another phone conversation took place between Mom and Nancy on December 27, and again Mom told Nancy to return her checkbook. Again, Nancy refused.

At this point Mom brought up the issue of Power of Attorney. I told her I wasn't familiar with all of its technicalities, but I knew some lawyers who could help if she wanted. She said she did and late that day I emailed my friend Tom Sousa, a retired US Army Lt. Colonel, who worked in a law firm in Norwich Connecticut.

From: Ron Winter
To: Tom Sousa
Sent: Saturday, December 27, 2008 10:58 PM
Subject: info

Hello Tom,

My mother has permanently moved in with us and I need to find out some info on power of attorney and similar issues. Is this in your area of expertise?

Ron Winter

I knew Tom from our local veterans' community, and was impressed with his willingness to pitch in and get things done at our VFW post, as well as his enthusiasm for taking on other responsibilities in the community. He is a dedicated family man, a genuinely decent human being, and I was certain he would be able to help Mom.

We talked the next day and I explained the situation. "Mom moved in with us three days before Christmas. She was hospitalized for nearly a week, with dehydration and potassium deficiency, and my sister Nancy was going to place her in a nursing home. But we offered to bring her to our house. My family agreed but when they brought Mom over, my sister kept her checkbook. Mom found out on Christmas Day when she wanted to write a check. They've been arguing about it ever since, and Mom wants her checkbook back. Nancy won't give it up though, and now Mom wants to know if she can take away the Power of Attorney designation."

Tom told me that rescinding Power of Attorney is literally as simple as saying "I don't want you to be my Power of Attorney," but with a little paperwork too.

I told Tom I'd explain the situation to Mom, but added, "let's give them a couple of days to see if they can work it out between them." Ultimately, I said, Mom was going to have her checkbook back. There was no reason for her not to have it, especially since she was more in control of her herself with each passing day. Mom told me that Nancy's leaving her without access to her own funds made her feel that she was "standing out in a huge snow-covered field, with no landmarks and no idea where I was or where to go."

"I always felt secure, even after Wilson died, as long as I have my checkbook and my bank accounts. That way," she said, "I know I'll never be stranded or helpless." But denying her access to her money had an immediate and extraordinarily negative affect on Ella.

Tom explained that if Mom decided to revoke Nancy's Power of Attorney, he could provide the forms, and I would need at least one non-family witness to be present at an interview with Mom to ensure that she was acting on her own accord.

"I'll explain it to Mom," I told him, "and get back to you in a day or so."

My brother arrived in New York a day earlier, and was coming to Connecticut on the 30th with more of Mom's belongings, I explained, and Mom asked that he bring the checkbook with him. I added that I would communicate the seriousness of the issue to my sister and hopefully it would be resolved without any further ado.

No such luck.

I sent an email to my brother-in-law asking that he pass it on to Skeeter before he left for Connecticut. I listed the things that Mom needed, and focused three times on the checkbook, partly to keep the conversation light, and partly to underscore the urgency that Mom felt about being back in control of her own finances.

From: Ron Winter

Sent: Monday, December 29, 2008 2:21 PM

To: James Patrick

Subject: Stuff for Mom Importance: High

James, can you pass this list on to Skeeter for things to bring over tomorrow?

Thanks

1) Ottoman

2) Bathroom scale

3) Large kitchen clock

4) Sneakers if she has them; any type of exercise outfit if she has one.

5) Her checkbook. She really, really, really, really, really wants her checkbook.

6) Her jewelry. Earrings, necklaces etc.

7) Income tax payment information so she knows due date etc. It needs to be paid.

8) Dentist telephone number and name so we can transfer records.

9) Same info for eye doctor and physicians. Do we have a final analysis from Albany Medical about her recent episode and what they found? Any treatment suggestions the doctor may have had?

10) Her checkbook. She really, really, really, really, really wants her checkbook.

11) Did I mention she wants her checkbook? Nancy told me Mom would be missing it and she is.

12) Is the apartment completely cleaned out? If so, we should cancel the cable, phone and electricity so Mom won't be charged for January when she isn't there. The phone and cable definitely should be cancelled; I don't know the policy with electricity, but it should be taken out of Mom's name ASAP.

FYI, we have reduced the amount of caffeine she is drinking by changing her dinner and after dinner drinks to herbal tea and decaf coffee. As a result she is sleeping a lot more, and I mean a LOT more. Apparently she may have been suffering from sleep deprivation as well as dehydration. She was very afraid of her upstairs neighbor and whether it was valid or not, she believed it was, so in her mind it was valid. She wasn't sleeping well at night at the apartment and was up a lot which I attribute both to too much caffeine and the fear of the man upstairs.

The only guy directly upstairs now is Max the wonder dog and he doesn't scare her or vice versa. Anyway she is going to bed earlier, sleeping later, and taking naps in the afternoon and it appears her awareness is increasing daily. She seems to be getting sharply aware of things and is far less forgetful.

Ron

I quickly received the following email, reproduced in part, which basically showed that no one in New York had a sense of humor, and that they were tenaciously holding on to Mom's money. Mom was outraged when she read the emails from the Patricks, and if

I was to pinpoint a time when the checkbook became an issue, it was at 3:53 p.m., on December 29 when Nancy sent the following email in response to mine.

> *From: Nancy Patrick*
> *To: Ron Winter*
> *Sent: Monday, December 29, 2008 3:53 PM*
> *Subject: Mom's stuff*

I have already put a box together for Mom of things I knew she would be missing. Skeeter will bring them tomorrow. The apartment is not completely cleaned out because it has 22 years worth of stuff for me to sort through. By law there had to be 30 days notice given to Dutch Village in writing, which I have done. I have also paid her rent, cancelled her lifeline, cable, transferred telephone calls to our house (so people don't think she fell off the face of the earth). The power will be turned off when Skeeter leaves, so he doesn't freeze while he is there.

As for the checkbook, the only way Mom will get a checkbook is to open an account at your bank in Hebron. I have been taking care of Mom's checkbook for the last four years, because she was incapable of balancing it. I have power of attorney and all of her checks have my name on them along with hers, so that I was able to pay her bills.

I... will send monthly the amount she feel(sic) she would like to live on as well as the amount you feel that it is costing you for her to live there.

As for doctors, I am totally exhausted from trying to vacate her apartment. I don't have time before tomorrow to get all that information, but will do so soon.

If she can hang on with the cash she has and her credit card until we get back on the 12th, I can then figure out how much she has left to send. (She wrote 3 checks without putting down amounts or to whom which is adding to the confusion, and why you might understand why I have taken the bill paying over.

Nancy

Now, it might seem that was an effort to be helpful and cooperative, but there are a number of factors that arose from this email. First, Mom was ticked when she saw that Nancy was claiming she couldn't balance her checkbook. And when she saw the part about opening a bank account in Hebron, she immediately asked what it would take to accomplish that.

"You'll have to talk with social security and your pension fund office and transfer your deposit here. But that is after we open a new account for you in a bank here. But you have to decide what to do about the Power of Attorney first." At this point I had no idea where Mom did her banking, how much money there was, in what form, or what she would have to do to regain control of it.

Also, although Nancy claimed that Mom had a joint checking account with her, the checks did not bear both of their names. (Mom had given out checks as Christmas presents, so we knew what they looked like.)

This email also proved a point that later would be in contention—that Mom's move was considered to be permanent. If not, why would we have needed detailed medical and dental records, and why would Nancy have promised to get them to us as soon as she could?

More to the point, everything that came next could have been easily resolved if Nancy was not so insistent that only she would have control over Mom's finances. Considering that we were poised to begin the preliminary work on an addition to accommodate

Mom and her belongings, it would have been unwieldy at best and impossible at worst to have Nancy continue to dictate how much of her own money Mom could have, and when it would be available.

I didn't have any estimates on the cost of the addition yet, but based on the basic floor plan square footage, and the prevailing cost per square foot of building in our area, I knew she didn't have enough to fund it herself. My plan was simple: share the cost and give Mom the best possible living quarters she could have, since she would be spending the rest of her life here.

I sent an email to a former client who was a building contractor, both as a Christmas greeting and to apprise him that some work was pending. I didn't realize it at the time, but the message on Christmas Day also proves the point that we considered Mom's move to be permanent and there would have to be some changes to our home and lifestyle as a result.

From: Ron Winter
To: xxxxxxx
Sent: Thursday, December 25, 2008 12:12 PM
Subject: Greetings

Hi Joe,

Just taking a minute to wish you a Merry Christmas and Happy New Year.

Let's hope the New Year brings ... new opportunities for us all.

My mother has moved in as of Monday afternoon and this spring we will be building an addition so we should be seeing a lot of each other.

Ron

Within a couple of weeks Nancy and other family members were floating the claim that Mom had come to our house only for a visit. There never was such a discussion, at least one involving me.

From the very first, I maintained that it would be cruel to have Mom come to our house believing anything other than that it was a permanent move. Nancy's email, despite its harsh tone, nonetheless made the point that within one day of Mom moving to Connecticut, her apartment was being emptied, utilities shut off, and my requests for Mom's legal papers and doctors' information were being attended to.

I foolishly believed at that point, that as long as I didn't ask my sister or brother for any money to help fund Mom's new life in our home, it would not be a problem. I figured, again foolishly, that since we were going to provide around-the-clock care for Mom for the rest of her life, and would be taking all of the responsibility for her, that my siblings would be happy as clams.

"Foolishly believed" is the operative phrase here. I had no idea that my sister was controlling my mother's finances for years as she claimed, and in fact Mom disagrees with that statement. Yet it soon became clear that even my mother didn't know everything about her own money, how much she had, where it was, or who had control.

On December 30, 2008 my brother Skeeter arrived in Connecticut, again with a car full of my mother's belongings—but not her checkbook. He brought a couple of Christmas cards, syrupy sentimental things that basically said "Life will never be the same. How sad it is."

The intent I surmised was to make Mom cry and she obliged. Then she asked for her checkbook. It was not produced. She stopped crying.

After talking in the kitchen for nearly an hour my brother invited us to go to lunch and Jennifer and I agreed to accompany him and Mom to a local restaurant. It actually was tolerable. I say that because there have been more than a few incidents in the past two decades—some alluded to in earlier chapters—which can easily put a damper on any interaction between my brother and me.

But this was for Mom so I put on my happy face and enjoyed lunch. We returned home, and my brother soon made ready to depart for New York. On the way out he gave me one piece of sage advice concerning my mother's care: "Make sure she gets a pedicure. I paid for three of them for her, but she hasn't used them." I assured Skeeter that Mom's toenails would be tended to posthaste.

That was it. That was the only communication from my brother and sister, brother-in-law, nieces or anyone else regarding my mother's medical and mental condition. Even though I asked about her diagnosis I was told only that she suffered from dehydration, confusion and disorientation.

No one said anything like "Oh, by the way, Mom has been suffering from dementia and early onset Alzheimer's for years now so you may want to lock all the doors to discourage wandering." Nor were there any warnings such as, "She forgets who she is, where she is, what she was doing, and balancing her checkbook. Oh, and she can't bathe, brush her teeth or tend to her basic needs on her own."

Not a word. Want to know why? Because while Mom was exhausted when she first arrived in Connecticut, she was acutely aware of what was going on around her. She was never treated for Alzheimer's or dementia, even though my brother and sister were telling her doctors that she was deteriorating mentally for at least three years. But the doctors found no evidence of their claims as I was to discover in the coming weeks.

My mother continued to fret about her checkbook, and grow more agitated about not having it, for the rest of the 30th and throughout the 31st. She enjoyed New Year's Eve with us, but it was on her mind again on New Year's Day.

Around midday Nancy called to say Happy New Year, and again Mom brought up the checkbook. This time the conversation was longer and Mom was firm about wanting her money with her in Connecticut. I gave Mom some space and stayed in the kitchen while she talked on the phone in the adjacent living room. Still, scraps of conversation came my way: "I want that checkbook back; Why not? That's not true. I can do my own calculations." But it was obvious that Nancy adamantly refused to give in, and the phone call ended badly.

Mom was in the living room talking on our cordless kitchen phone, and when she hung up, she stayed were she was, her hand on the back of the couch, just looking down at the floor. She stayed that way, deep in thought, for nearly five minutes, working something out in her mind, and it was upsetting her.

Suddenly, she looked up at me and said, "Let's do this thing."

"What thing?" I asked, although I had a pretty good idea what she meant.

"This Power of Attorney thing. I don't want Nancy to be my Power of Attorney. I told her that was only if I was incapacitated and I am not incapacitated."

"I'll call the lawyer," I told her.

Another great thing about Atty. Thomas Sousa was that he lived in our town, even though he worked more than a half-hour away in Norwich, land of the big casinos. I talked with Tom about Mom's issues once again after our first conversation, and he said he would be happy to see Mom in his office if she needed assistance.

Tom offered to come to our home on New Year's Day so Mom wouldn't have to make the trip, and he also asked, and this is very important, for Mom's full name. Maude Ella Winter I told him. It didn't occur to me until later to tell him that Mom had gone by Ella literally her entire life. But later that day when Tom arrived, with the appropriate forms to rescind my sister's Power of Attorney, and issue new medical and legal POA forms, I realized my error.

Mom spent nearly two hours with Tom, going over the forms and she had some serious issues, especially with the medical POA forms and she wanted those issues resolved before she would sign.

Tom agreed to rewrite that form, and we went ahead with the signing of the legal POA form. Mom again balked because under the line where she was supposed to sign it said, "Maude Ella Winter."

"I never go by Maude," Mom said. We talked it over and Tom noted that she could sign the forms as they were for the time being, and he would make sure to use M. Ella Winter on the revised medical Power of Attorney and any future forms. Since her legal name still is Maude Ella Winter, her signature would be legal. Mom agreed and that is the way it was done.

In addition to Tom's signature, my friend John Tuttle, who was soon to retire after more than four decades in law enforcement, three of which were as a federal investigator, was on hand to sign as a witness, as well as my wife Jennifer. All in all Mom had more than two hours of conversations with the people who were helping her make the change to her new home and new life.

In all of that time no one saw or heard a single thing to make them feel that perhaps Mom was not aware of what she was doing. In fact, everyone there said just the opposite.

Mom discussed her condition with all of us, and ultimately decided that while she no longer wanted Nancy dictating her affairs, she did need someone to have Power of Attorney, in case she was again hospitalized or otherwise incapacitated. She asked me to take over that responsibility and I agreed.

There was a major difference between how I viewed this change in circumstances, and how my sister viewed it, as I later related to Nancy.

To me, the key word was Attorney, defined by Webster's as "One who is legally appointed to transact business on another's behalf." I told Mom, and I later told Nancy too, that I saw Mom's request as a major responsibility, to be there for Mom when she needed me, to protect her from those who would do her harm, but to act more as a benign associate, rather than some form of overlord.

Nancy on the other hand, believed Power was the key word. Webster's defines Power in part as "Possession of control, authority, or influence over others." Mom said that Nancy used her status as Power of Attorney to dictate to Mom how she would live, and what she would do.

Mom didn't agree with that concept, and once the forms were signed there was a complete change in attitude, as well as individuals.

We sat around the table and talked a while more before Tom and John left. Mom spent a good part of that evening reviewing the forms she had signed.

"I never sign anything I don't read," she assured me. That was evident from the way Mom asked that Tom go over the POA forms, explaining every facet of both, and how the new status applied in both Connecticut and New York. Tom even told Mom that she could keep Nancy on as POA in New York and have me perform those duties in Connecticut if she wanted, but Mom was having none of that.

She wanted control over her own finances, and as much of her life as possible, but we were soon to learn that the clash she had with Nancy over her checkbook was literally the tip of the iceberg.

The POA forms were signed in the early evening of Jan. 1, 2009, a Thursday. We discussed calling Nancy to tell her of the change of status immediately, but Mom asked that we hold off. She wanted to talk with Nancy herself, Mom said, and she wanted to do it after Nancy returned from vacation.

It has been my sister's habit for a number of years to go to Florida right after New Year's, and Mom's world in New York revolved around that vacation—so much so that my sister convinced Mom to have her ninetieth birthday party in early December instead of on January 4, the actual birth date, so it wouldn't conflict with Nancy's vacation.

This year was no different and Nancy was set to leave for Florida Saturday morning. Mom said she'd call Nancy in the following week to discuss things with her. In the meantime I prepared a registered letter outlining the change and what I would need in Connecticut.

Changing the Power Of Attorney to Connecticut involved more than just signing some forms. There were myriad details to attend to, the first of which was setting Mom up with a new bank account. Mom already filled out a permanent change of address form on December 29, 2008, so she considered herself a permanent Connecticut resident.

I promised Mom that we would visit a local bank first thing on Monday morning and set up her new accounts. There was more to do, and much of it would have to be done by Mom. The federal government, for instance, does not recognize Power of Attorney and any changes to those federal accounts would have to come directly from Mom.

Nonetheless, for the moment, Mom was happy with taking the first step toward regaining her independence. But as she got up from the table to go to bed, Mom stopped for a moment, turned to me, and said, "She's not going to like this."

That turned out to be a classic understatement.

CHAPTER EIGHT

Power of Attorney

Mom intended to wait until Nancy returned from her Florida vacation to discuss the Power of Attorney issue with her. Knowing that Nancy would be angry with her did not deter Mom from retaking control of her finances.

When Nancy left our house, with the flippant comment "Mom will be looking for her checkbook, but I have Power of Attorney," I figured there would be discussions and some changes—down the road a few months. Nancy exerted a tacit influence over Mom's affairs for the past several years, but even when she was the most involved in Mom's life they did not live together and Nancy was not responsible for week by week, nor day by day, and certainly not minute by minute decisions.

Nancy's concerns, whether she wanted to admit it or not, were basically centered on how much of her own life she gave up to deal with Mom's issues. It looked great to say she had once spent several weeks checking on Mom's condition every day after an operation. But that was a one-time occurrence that came and went several years ago. And in those intervening years, Mom was essentially on her own. When she moved in with us, there was a major rearrangement of our lifestyle, both in terms of space and in dealing with the myriad needs of an older relative. This is not a complaint; it is just a truthful review of what happens when another person permanently moves into a household.

I knew we couldn't begin adding space to our home until March at the earliest, when the ground thawed and construction equipment could begin the foundation. But that was nearly four months in the future from the time Mom moved in, and I figured there would be plenty of time to sort out the finances. What I really was concerned about was Mom's mental faculties, and whether we could provide everything she would need to be comfortable and secure.

I knew I'd have to deal with the Power of Attorney issue, but I didn't expect it to be a priority for several months. I was wrong.

On January 4, 2009, Mom's ninety-second birthday, we threw a surprise party for her. Nancy and her family vacation in Florida on Mom's birthday and have for years, leaving Mom without much of a celebration. But Mom lived in Connecticut now, and we decided to do up her birthday in style. We invited friends and neighbors, and our state representative came and served Mom her first piece of birthday cake—a white cake with strawberry frosting and sliced strawberries for garnishment.

We later discovered that her granddaughter, Courtney, had called at 11 a.m., but Ella was showering and we were outside shoveling snow and letting our dogs get plenty of exercise so they would be calm when the guests arrived, thus the call went to voice mail. I didn't check the phone for messages because it didn't occur to me, and besides, we had party preparations to contend with—without Mom knowing what was going on—as well as a cake to bake. Jennifer and I worked the kitchen while Heather kept Mom busy in the living room playing tunes on the keyboard we gave Mom for Christmas.

The guests began arriving at 1 p.m., to Mom's total surprise and appreciation, and the house quickly filled. We enjoyed food, stories, and Mom even made a dynamic speech before she blew out the candles.

The party continued until about 4:30 p.m. After everyone left, Mom went to her room to take a nap. Jennifer and Heather went to Heather's room where they closed the door and listened to music on Heather's computer. Heather has a cell phone, and uses it to talk with friends and family. She also uses instant messaging on her computer to stay in touch with her friends. She doesn't have a house phone in her room because she doesn't need one there. None of this should matter, but it does.

I went to the living room and turned on the Lions' football game. I lasted about fifteen minutes or so before I fell fast asleep on the couch sometime after 5 p.m. I woke at about 7:30 p.m., hearing the last rings of the kitchen phone. The phone has various loudness settings. I have it set to audible, but not shrill. That also shouldn't matter, but it does.

I sat up, realized the game was long over, and listened to see if anyone else was moving around. I heard laughter coming from Heather's room upstairs, but there was no sound in Mom's room which is just off the living room. I went to the phone and dialed in the code to retrieve messages. It was then that I discovered that Courtney called in the morning. In addition Nancy and James called sometime after 5:30, then Courtney called again, then my brother Skeeter, then Nancy and Jim again, then my cousin and his wife. I sat down at the table and made a list of everyone who had called, and their phone numbers, to give to Mom when she awoke. It was a great day, and I was basking in the glow of knowing we did a good deed for Mom. She really enjoyed the party, she enjoyed being the belle of the ball, and best of all she was taken completely by surprise. We cleaned the kitchen just after everyone left, so I was feeling pretty serene. There was no work to do, except maybe to grab another slice of cake. Overall it was a great day and a nice way to welcome Mom to her new neighborhood.

Mom came out to the kitchen shortly before 8 p.m. She sat down and said "Is there any more of that cake left?" I gave her a piece with a cup of coffee (decaf). I gave her the list of callers and she looked it over while she snacked. I didn't tell her but the messages from Nancy and Courtney had quickly gone from pleasant to demanding, insistent even. "We've been calling all day, why haven't you returned our calls? Where are you? What are you doing? Why didn't you call us back? We have been calling all day."

Obviously no one had been calling all day, and except for the morning call from Courtney, all the calls had come in over a less than two-hour period while Mom was napping. Even if I hadn't fallen asleep watching the game, I would not have awakened Mom to answer the phone. She was still only two weeks from being in the hospital and she needed her sleep. We discovered almost immediately that Mom is much more alert and aware if she takes an afternoon nap.

Mom nibbled her cake, savoring each bite, and sipped her coffee. She looked over the list, but her attention was still on her birthday party and I answered numerous questions about her guests as she worked to get them all straight in her mind. Mom took the last bites of her cake, sipped the last of her coffee and delicately dabbed at her mouth with her napkin. "I believe I have had a genteel sufficiency," she declared—one of her favorite comments at the end of a meal which I'll explain in detail later. She picked up the cordless phone, perused the list of callers and began returning the calls, starting with Courtney. But instead of getting a 'Happy Birthday' greeting,

Courtney started the conversation demanding to know why Mom hadn't returned her call more promptly.

Mom tried to give her granddaughter an upbeat review of her day, but Courtney was having none of that. She demanded to know why Mom hadn't immediately returned her first call, or her second call. When Ella said she had just retrieved the messages and that she had been involved in her birthday party, and napping later, the response was, "A party? Why wasn't I invited?"

Courtney lives in Massachusetts approximately two hours from Ella's new home in Connecticut. Since she was directly involved in moving her grandmother from New York to Connecticut only a week earlier, it simply hadn't occurred to me or anyone else in our family to invite out-of-state relatives. We also had no idea whether Courtney accompanied her parents to Florida for vacation. The whole point of throwing a party for Mom was to mark her special day, and to welcome her to the community. New York was behind her, and regardless of what anyone who still lived there may think about it, if Mom was going to be happy in her new home she would have to meet people and begin accumulating new experiences, new friendships and new memories. We didn't exclude anyone in the family; we simply didn't think they would be willing to take time away from their lives to attend a small afternoon birthday party in Connecticut.

Besides, not only did Nancy and her family regularly vacation in Florida on Mom's birthday, we never heard of anyone taking the time to do something for Mom on that day while she lived in New York—unless we drove to Mom's or brought her to Connecticut.

Ella was a full five minutes into the conversation with her granddaughter before Courtney thought to say "Happy Birthday." But matters were about to quickly go from bad to worse.

Although I cleared the messages before Mom started making her calls, I noticed the message light was blinking again when she hung up after talking with Courtney. In the ten to fifteen minutes that Mom was on the phone trying to soothe Courtney's ruffled feelings Nancy called again, and her message went from the insistent and demanding tone of the earlier messages to shrill.

"Where are you? Why haven't you returned our calls? We're worried about you! We've been calling you all day! Why haven't you called?"

That was bad enough, but while Nancy was calling on one phone, her husband Jim was calling on another phone, with another message, expressing "concern" and wanting to know that Ella was all right.

Ella called Nancy next, and again, rather than a "Happy Birthday," she was immediately subjected to a barrage of questions and again the allegation was raised that the phone had been ringing all day and no one was answering it or returning messages.

Again, Mom tried to talk about the excitement of her birthday, what with the party and the food, and all the people who had come to wish her Happy Birthday. Again, the mention of a party resulted in an outburst—"A party? Why weren't we invited?"

When Ella responded, "Well Nancy, you're in Florida," Nancy answered, "We'd have come back."

When one considers the fact that Nancy and her family left for Florida on Friday, the thought of them flying back to Bradley Airport, an hour from our home, on Sunday, attending a three hour party and then turning around to fly back to Florida again is simply ludicrous.

Before I gave Mom the phone to begin her calls I turned up the speaker volume so she could hear better, which also resulted in my hearing both sides of the conversation clearly, since Mom had the phone away from her ear as Nancy badgered her. Most of Mom's responses were along the lines of "Nancy, you're in Florida. Nancy, no one left you out. Nancy, you wouldn't have come back even if someone had invited you. Nancy, it was just a party, and it was for me!" Nancy was doing her best to ruin what had been a wonderful day up until that point. But we soon realized that Ella had long experience with Nancy and guilt trips and wasn't buying it. Again, it was well into the conversation, in fact nearly to the end, before Mom heard the words Happy Birthday from her daughter, and then it was almost an afterthought.

Finally, Mom ended the encounter with Nancy, and took a half-hour break to fill us in on the conversation, most of which we heard. "She was upset that we didn't invite her," Mom said with a look of incredulity. "She even said she would have flown back from Florida to come to the party. I wonder why she never cared about what I did on my birthday in all these other years she's been gone?" Mom obviously wanted to share what was said to her, and get it out of her system. But she was exhausted from dealing with her daughter and granddaughter and needed a mental break before she made any more calls.

Finally, with a sigh, she made another call. "Let me call Skeets. Maybe he'll just say Happy Birthday without yelling at me." By now it was about 9:30 p.m. Fortunately for her, the conversation this time was quick and straightforward. Skeeter wished her Happy Birthday, said it was nice that she had a party and was off in a matter of minutes.

Oddly enough, within another month, when Nancy had filed suit against Ella, and Skeeter joined his sister in attempting to have Mom declared incompetent, one of the issues he brought up was the lateness of the hour before Mom returned his call that day. She actually got back to him in pretty reasonable time, but that was not what Skeeter told the court.

Mom had one last call to make—to her nephew Floyd and his wife Kay—but after the battering she took from the other members of her family, she decided to wait until the next day to make that call. At least she knew that call would be pleasant.

Mom was feeling tired and simultaneously very grateful that we planned and executed a surprise party for her. As Mom entered her room for the night, she stopped, turned to us with a big smile on her face, and thanked us once again for the wonderful party. She hadn't expected it, and it really had buoyed her spirits.

But the reception she received from Nancy and Courtney was weighing heavily on her. There simply was no expression of care or concern or goodwill for Mom on her ninety-second birthday from the people who had been the closest to her, at least physically, for the past decade. Instead she was subjected to obnoxious, self-centered abuse that put the onus on her to cater to the psyches of her daughter and granddaughter, rather than any effort on their part to add to, rather than detract from, what otherwise was a wonderful day for Ella.

Considering the abuse she suffered on her birthday, Mom was in no mood to discuss the Power of Attorney issue with Nancy until she came home from Florida.

Mom compiled a list of people and government offices to contact to ensure that her mail, phone messages and other affairs were resolved. She was permanently settled in Connecticut and over the next several days she concentrated on arranging her affairs.

In reviewing the emails that came in December we realized that when Nancy shut off Mom's phone she forwarded all the calls to Nancy's house, which made no sense since Nancy wasn't even there. We also discovered that although Mom filled out a change of address form in Connecticut, Nancy did the same thing in New York too, also sending Mom's mail to her house.

Mom contacted the post office and phone company and corrected the call and mail forwarding.

Then we faxed a letter to First Niagara Bank in New York, explaining the situation:

Jan. 6, 2009

First Niagara Bank
475 Albany Shaker Rd.
Loudonville, NY 12211

Dear Sir or Madam:

Your customer, M. Ella Winter, my mother, has permanently moved to my home in Connecticut.

She has changed her address, opened new bank accounts here and is closing her account(s) with First Niagara Bank.

The Power of Attorney status she conveyed upon Nancy Patrick while she was a New York resident has been rescinded and a new Power of Attorney form has been executed in my name.

My mother is no longer writing any checks from her account in your bank. She intends to close the account as soon as all checks have cleared. Online access if it exists should be terminated immediately.

Please send us the current status of all accounts she has with your bank. Regarding Acct. # xxxxxxxxxx we need to know the checks that have cleared, and the account balance.

We also need copies of all account statements for the past year. I would appreciate it if the statements can be sent electronically via email, although faxing them also is acceptable.

Thank you for your assistance.

Ronald Winter
72 West St.
Hebron, CT 06248

I also wrote a letter to Nancy detailing what Mom had done regarding the Power of Attorney, why she had done it, and asking that Nancy help her through the transition period by providing her with documents and records that had been left behind in New York. I sent the letter by registered mail, signature required.

January 5, 2009

Nancy Patrick
37 Folmsbee Dr.
Menands, NY 12204

Re: Power of Attorney for M. Ella Winter (Mom)

Dear Nancy,

Due to her wish to take an active role in her affairs Mom has decided that Power of Attorney authorization is best executed here in Connecticut rather than with you in New York.

Mom has executed a new Power of Attorney and a new Living Will in my name effective January 1, and revoked the previous POA.

Mom has shown an ever increasing awareness since she moved to Connecticut, is sleeping far better and her diet has improved. She also feels much more secure than she did in her apartment in New York. Obviously, having suffered two hospitalizations and four serious falls in New York she needs someone to be with her all day, every day.

A daily phone call to inquire about her condition will not suffice, nor will occasional visits from family members or paid attendants. Mom now is in the company of a family member twenty-four hours a day.

Mom has opened new bank accounts in Connecticut, and is transferring her assets to those accounts, where I will monitor her expenditures to ensure that all stays in order. She has had a dental exam, a physical, and is scheduled for an eye exam Monday, Jan. 12, 2009.

To facilitate this process please forward to me: A list of all financial institutions where Mom has accounts, Certificates of Deposit, etc., and the account numbers so I can help her complete the transfers to Connecticut accounts; a copy of her will; location of safe deposit box (es) if any; stock transfer data; and any other pertinent documents or information that will help me keep track of her affairs.

Mom executed a permanent change of address form on Dec. 29, 2008, so mail should automatically be sent here. However, please forward any important mail that was left at her old address or forwarded to your address, including bills so I can ensure they are paid.

Do not make any future appointments for her in New York as I do not believe that extended travel, especially in winter weather, is good for her health. I will tend to her medical needs in Connecticut and if consultation with her former medical professionals is necessary I will arrange it from here.

Thank you for your cooperation,

Ronald Winter

When Nancy returned from Florida she refused to accept the letter. Nonetheless, Mom wanted control of the situation and she was even more determined to master her own affairs after the confrontations she endured on her birthday.

But Mom never got the opportunity to handle things the way she wanted, due to a phone call from Nancy to Mom on the evening of January 7. By that time Mom's new bank account was open, she spoke with representatives from Social Security and her federal pension, changed her insurance address, contacted one of her banks in New York, and basically reestablished herself in Connecticut.

She was happy, too. She could sit down with Jennifer and go through her finances to determine where she stood, virtually any time she wanted. The difficulties Mom experienced with her checkbook had nothing to do with her mental faculties as Nancy claimed. Ella experienced some difficulties only because she couldn't see the entries. The ledger was too small and with her glaucoma it was impossible to read.

So Jennifer rectified the situation in a manner that was possible anywhere—including New York years earlier. She took the ledger pages to the office copier enlarging them so Ella could see better, then sat down with Ella, going through the deposits and debits together.

To everyone's surprise Ella was faster with math in her head than most people are with typing the numbers into a calculator. In short, there simply was nothing wrong with her mind.

But that isn't what she heard from Nancy on the night of January 7, 2009. Nancy started the inquiry by questioning why Ella visited the dentist the previous day. "I went to the dentist for the same reason I went to the doctor, and I am going to the eye doctor," Mom answered. "I live in Connecticut now, and Ron and Jennifer want to know what kind of shape I'm in." Mom was right about that. Considering her recent medical history, we scheduled a series of appointments to determine the current state of her health across the board.

We sent medical information release forms to Ella's myriad doctors in New York, but in the meantime, we also deemed it prudent to have her examined by a new group of physicians. She missed an appointment for her semi-annual teeth cleaning in December before moving to Connecticut, so Jennifer scheduled a new appointment with our family dentist to make up for the one missed in New York as well as for a general examination.

"How are you going to pay for that," Nancy demanded. "What exactly are you doing there?" By now Nancy was all but shrieking at her mother, repeating, "How are you going to pay for this? Where are you getting the money?"

In addition to keeping Mom's checkbook, Nancy also gave Mom a cash allowance of a couple hundred dollars on the day she moved in with us. Otherwise, Nancy had total control over Mom's bank accounts in New York, and was not planning to give her any more of her own money until they returned from Florida.

Nancy's voice was so loud over the phone that even though I was sitting across the kitchen table from Mom I could clearly make out what Nancy was saying. Mom said quite calmly, "I opened a new bank account here, and I transferred my Blue Cross and Medicare to Connecticut."

Nancy by now was apoplectic, wailing at Ella, "What are you doing?" Nancy continued to press Mom on exactly what she had been doing for the past several days and Ella, in exasperation, finally told her that she had moved all of her affairs to Connecticut. "You said the only way I was going to have my own checkbook again is if I opened an account over here. So I opened an account over here."

Nancy brought up her Power of Attorney status—which actually didn't prohibit Ella from doing whatever she wanted with her own money, regardless of what Nancy had been telling her—and demanded to know how Ella had been able to change her bank accounts and Social Security deposits without consulting her.

Ella calmly replied that she had rescinded Nancy's Power of Attorney and she didn't need Nancy's permission to manage her own affairs. "That was only supposed to be if I was incapacitated," Ella averred.

Nancy, however, went ballistic. Upon being told that the lawyer came to our house and helped Ella with her affairs Nancy exploded, "He's got all your money!"

She was referring to me, not the lawyer. (I should point out here, that Mom's vast "fortune" was sufficient for her to live in a nursing home only for about five months, at the average national rate for such facilities. In other words, it was not much. Mom is still bemused over her daughter's focus on her savings, and often commented, "I wonder what would have happened if I had a million dollars?")

Unquestionably, Mom was the calm and composed one in this ongoing conversation, and she repeatedly attempted to get it through to Nancy that she knew what she was doing, but Nancy wasn't accepting anything Ella told her. She continued to ask about Mom's medical appointments and when Mom said she had another doctor's appointment the following week, Nancy screamed, "He's taking you to find out what's wrong with your head!"

Ella's attempts to reason with Nancy were unsuccessful and she glanced at me with a pleading look. "Let me talk to her," I said to Mom. Mom handed me the phone and as soon as I greeted my sister she hissed, "Did you take Mom to a lawyer to change the Power of Attorney?"

"Why no," I responded. "The lawyer came here."

The next line set the stage for everything that has happened since. "You're a thief!" Nancy shrieked. "You're lining your pockets with Mom's money."

To which I responded, "You're an asshole." And I hung up.

About twenty minutes later the phone rang and it was Skeeter calling from Florida. He obviously was briefed by Nancy and immediately demanded to talk with Mom. She told him what she had told his sister, but again, she was subjected to an avalanche of badgering.

Again, Mom handed the phone to me, and again I was subjected to non-stop invective. I attempted to tell my brother that the decision to rescind Nancy's Power of Attorney was Mom's and hers alone, the direct result of Nancy taking Mom's checkbook from her, and that it obviously was an ongoing issue that had its roots back in New York, not something that just popped up in Connecticut.

But, Nancy did her job of briefing my brother, and he wasn't inclined to believe anything I had to say anyway.

"You called Nancy an asshole!" Skeeter shouted.

"That's because she called me a thief and said I was lining my pockets with the vast Ella Winter fortune," I responded.

"Don't you shout at me," Skeeter replied. I tried to interject that he was the one who was shouting, not I, but my words were drowned out by his.

"Who the hell do you think you are? You hung up on Nancy, too!"

"Did it sound like this?" I asked. CLICK. (We really like comedian Jeff Dunham in this house.)

If, in the next twenty-four hours, my siblings had slept, kept their mouths shut and counted to ten, I wouldn't be writing this. But that is not human nature, or at least not the nature of my siblings.

In the next day, and the days after, Mom talked with Nancy a couple of times, and each time tried to tell her daughter that she was very happy in Connecticut, was being well taken care of, and was grateful that we opened our house to her instead of placing her in a nursing home. Interestingly, no one at this point disputed the words "nursing home." Nancy and Skeeter were trying to commit Mom to some type of elder facility for several years previously, but never convinced her doctors to agree with their assessments of her faculties. In fact, the doctors consistently disagreed with them.

Skeeter was both bombastic and smug when he yelled at me on January 7; that if Mom had gone into a retirement home when he said she should, none of this would be happening. He also claimed that since Mom was twice hospitalized for disorientation and confusion, there was no place for her now but a nursing home with Alzheimer's capabilities. Of course, if Mom had Alzheimer's she would not be allowed to stay in a retirement home that didn't have the capabilities to care for Alzheimer's patients anyway.

But Mom doesn't have Alzheimer's, or dementia. She was diagnosed with dehydration and potassium deficiency, either of which can cause symptoms that appear similar to Alzheimer's. A cursory review of real Alzheimer's symptoms and a close examination of Mom's daily activities showed an ocean of difference between her condition and Alzheimer's.

That close examination did not take place in New York—at least by Mom's children. But it was ongoing in Connecticut and the diagnoses from Mom's new doctors, and those rendered by her family in New York were worlds apart.

Mom told us during numerous dinner time discussions that "I never wanted to go into one of those places. (Nursing home, retirement home call it what you like.) I like my own life at my own pace, and I don't like having my morning coffee with eighty other people."

She described one such place, where many of her old friends from Center Brunswick lived, that offered her a "room" that was little more than an extended closet. It was more of an L-shaped hallway, Mom said, wide enough at the end for a small couch, with room for a bed around the corner. There also was a spot to place a coffee maker, but that was about it.

Everything else that would have been her life was to take place in community settings.

For the next two weeks Mom tried hard to reconcile with Nancy and Skeeter. She had conversations with both of them, and each time told them how happy she was in Connecticut and was doing well, both physically and mentally.

But she also told us in private that she didn't trust Nancy, and was "waiting for the other shoe to drop."

When Skeeter talked with Mom on the night of Jan. 7, his last words to her were "This isn't over."

Mom asked him several times to explain what he meant, but he would only repeat, "This isn't over."

Later in the month Skeeter, who testified in March that he was retired, but actually is running a horse ranch in Ocala, Florida, went on a horse buying/selling trip to Kentucky.

He and Ella talked about his trip after he returned, which was notable because he also later testified that he wasn't allowed to talk to Mom after January 7. That was a lie, as was much else that was said in the future.

Skeeter didn't bring up his threat again, and when he returned from his unsuccessful horse selling venture, he talked with Mom as if nothing had happened. But Mom is not unaware, and she was cautious, while also trying to find out what her children had in store for her.

I did my best to reassure Mom that she was safe in Connecticut, and that no one could force her to live somewhere else if she was happy with us. But Mom kept saying, "You don't know her (Nancy) as well as I do." I wasn't sure what she meant by that, but I did tell Mom that if there was any issue that could be pursued from New York it would have to revolve around the suitability of our home.

Mom's mental faculties were obviously intact, and even though my sister repeatedly tried to confuse Mom and upset her, there was no sign of Alzheimer's. But the issue of whether we were properly set up to provide a home for Mom was resolved before she came to Connecticut. "Nancy, James and Courtney brought you here,"

I explained to Mom. "Skeeter brought more of your belongings the next week. How can they be so anxious for you to be here in December, and suddenly claim that you aren't well-cared for here in January?"

But Mom believed Nancy was up to something—and she had good reason. Although Mom continued to talk with Nancy, my patience with the invective, threats and abuse ran out early.

On at least two occasions between January 7 and January 20, I was forced to intervene when Mom tried to reason with Nancy but got only abuse in return. But every time Nancy heard my voice on the phone she immediately hung up. When Mom wasn't being badgered by her daughter, she was being badgered by her granddaughter.

She kept trying, but the message from the Patricks never changed—Mom should have taken their advice and moved into Hawthorne Ridge instead of moving to Connecticut. "We had a nice apartment picked out for you," Courtney averred in one of her January conversations.

Mom told me in exasperation that she could not seem to get through to her daughter and granddaughter, no matter how hard she tried, and that she didn't want to live in any kind of facility, regardless of what Nancy, Courtney or Skeeter thought of it. One of Courtney's calls amounted to a crying jag from beginning to end, but it did not have the desired affect on Ella.

"She's a very unhappy girl," Mom said after she hung up. "I guess she takes after her mother."

Mom was not successful in convincing either Nancy or Courtney that the change in her living conditions was what she wanted, and far better than forcing her into a nursing home. It was apparent that Mom's point of view was not what mattered. Her daughter and granddaughter, aided and abetted by Skeeter, had plans for her that began with placing her in a nursing home, nothing more and nothing less. They simply did not want to hear anything from anyone who said otherwise.

By mid-month I discontinued any conversations with them, primarily because they were counter-productive. I did talk with my brother's daughter, Michelle, in January, and even though my contact with her was minimal over the years I thought other members of the extended family should know exactly what was going on with Mom.

One part of that conversation in particular had future significance. I talked with Michelle about what I considered the hypocrisy of Nancy's attacks on Mom and our family, especially since she never made an offer to move Mom into her house.

"Mom told me she can't live in Nancy's house anyway, because all the bedrooms are on the second floor," I told Michelle. The only way up is by a winding, carpeted staircase. Mom said she could navigate the stairs when she had to, but feared that with her advancing age they could become hazardous to her, especially since she fell while in Nancy's company on at least two occasions, and feared falling again.

There is a large den right off of Nancy's kitchen, with an adjoining bathroom, which could have been converted to a bedroom for Mom, but Ella said no one even considered renovating Nancy's house to accommodate her. Mom also spent a couple of weeks in Florida at my brother's horse ranch, but by all accounts that visit did not go smoothly and the possibility of Ella moving to Florida was not even remotely considered.

"Mom says Nancy and Jim are talking about selling their house and downsizing, now that all the kids are gone," I told Michelle. Their 2,900-square-foot house has four bedrooms and two and a half baths, with a finished basement and two-car garage on a half-acre lot with a swimming pool.

"Mom says Nancy wanted to travel more," I added. I also told Michelle that Mom mentioned the trips that Nancy and James made to France in recent years, noting that Nancy wanted to return, although Jim didn't. But trips throughout the US were definitely on the agenda, at least as far as Mom remembered.

Whether that was a definite plan or just speculation didn't really matter. Mom said it had been discussed, and I passed that on to Michelle. There also was the "oil and water" situation between Mom and Nancy, and Mom made the point repeatedly that as far as she was concerned, moving in with Nancy was simply not an option.

As insignificant an issue as it may seem, the question of whether James and Nancy might possibly move into a smaller house or do more travelling soon became significant. It also made the point that we could not talk to anyone in the family with confidence that our words would not be misconstrued, twisted or otherwise used against us.

My conversation with Michelle was the last one I had with anyone who was close to my sister or brother, and soon enough Mom's phone conversations also came to an end.

But that didn't mean there was no communication. The calls from New York to our home that had been infrequent when Mom first moved in with us soon came on a daily basis and on occasion even more often.

They ranged from wheedling and cajoling to abusive, insulting and threatening. But modern technology is on our side. Calls that were left on my voice mail are kept in my computer memory until I decide to erase them.

If I don't want to erase them I can upload them to permanent files in my computer and make copies on disks that can be kept elsewhere for security. That's what I ended up doing. More than a hundred calls came in during the next three months, and nearly fifty of them are stored away for future use.

The first call that I saved set the tone for the situation that unfolded over the next several months.

Lessons Learned

1. Document all phone calls, including time and caller. Take notes, including tone of conversation and any highlights, whether threatening, abusive etc.

2. Trust no one. Even people who support you can make innocent remarks that can be misconstrued. Keep your comments between yourself and your lawyer. The less you say the less can be used against you.

3. Keep phone records, emails, letters and all other correspondence, regardless of how insignificant they may seem at the time.

4. If possible, copy voice mails into computer files and onto disks. There is no such thing as too much backup documentation.

CHAPTER NINE

Wrong Number—Messages (and Threats) from New York

If you call my home and your call goes to voice mail, you will hear me asking that you leave a detailed message.

On January 7, 2009, at 6:18 p.m., a couple of hours after Mom advised Nancy that she had rescinded Power of Attorney, a call came in from Nancy Patrick. It went to voice mail.

"Ron, here's your detailed message." She started out by claiming that Mom hadn't handed me the phone earlier that night because she was upset with Nancy, but rather because Nancy said she wanted to speak with me.

"I didn't go ballistic on Mom."

Now, 'ballistic' is the word I used when I spoke with my brother about my conversation with Nancy. Obviously, Skeeter called Nancy to relate our abbreviated conversation to her. Regardless, I stand by the word ballistic. Nancy went ballistic when Mom told her that she had rescinded her Power of Attorney.

But, I do have to point out that Mom uses a different word when she describes the conversation with her daughter earlier on the night of Jan. 7.

"She was hysterical," is the way Mom describes it.

Also, I was sitting right next to Mom throughout the entire conversation and I saw the look on her face. She was totally exasperated and finally said before she handed me the phone that maybe I could get through to her daughter.

That isn't the big deal of this call though. What came next showed Nancy's true feelings.

"How dare you go behind the family's back and change everything so that you have everything in your little control."

Apparently Nancy had forgotten in less than a week that this all erupted because she refused several times between Christmas Day and New Year's Day to give Mom's checkbook back to her. And I have no idea what "the family" is. As far as I know, there was no committee of family members that had regular meetings to determine the status of Mom's affairs. There was only Nancy, calling the shots and dictating to Ella.

But wait, it gets better. The message continued:

"I am only looking out for Mom's best interests. And here's her best interest! You can keep paying rent on her apartment, 'cause as of tomorrow, she still rents her apartment for as long as her furniture is in it, and I can guarantee you Jim nor I will take another stick of furniture out of her apartment. It's all up to you and we will send the rent bill to you."

That statement revolves around my sister's repeated claims between December 29 and January 7 that she was working herself to exhaustion going through Mom's belongings while cleaning out the apartment. By the way, Nancy never asked Mom if she could start emptying the apartment. She just took it upon herself to do it. Mom still is pretty unhappy about the way that turned out.

Although Nancy, Jim, Skeeter, Courtney and Michelle joined forces in Mom's apartment at various points in the week between

Christmas and New Year's Day, going through all of her papers and her belongings, they succeeded in cleaning out only one small storage closet and removing less than one small truck load of furniture. Months later, I would find that the "exhausting" effort they put in resulted in one kitchen table, four chairs, one couch, one bed, two lamps, one dresser and two end tables making it to the U-Haul storage facility in Albany. That probably explains why they never went into the moving business.

Mom's monthly rental at Dutch Village was just under $1,000, which did not include phone, electric or cable. So, to comprehend Nancy Patrick's mindset merely requires reading the "best interests" paragraph in her phone message to me. Her viewpoint of what constituted my mother's "best interests" was quitting on the job and sticking Mom and me with the bill.

There is another facet of Mom's move to Connecticut that came up in this message and deserves review, and it represents the most hypocritical of all the hypocrisies that we faced in the coming months.

Within days of arriving in Connecticut, Mom sat down with me and explained that she was made to feel that she was a terrible burden on my sister and brother-in-law.

"I know I was a burden to them," Ella said. "Whenever they wanted to travel they had to find someone to look after me first."

Ella also said, however, that she babysat her granddaughter Courtney for Nancy and Jim from the time she was a newborn until she was well into her teens. "Nancy went out to California to be with Jim when Courtney was one-week old," she explained, "and that first night Courtney cried all night. We didn't sleep at all. Wilson and I were up all night walking with her, trying to settle her down."

"We never asked for anything from them, but I always felt that when I got old, she would be there for me in return."

Ella further explained that she had a regular income from Social Security and wanted to pay her way as long as she lived in our house. "I don't want to be a burden here," she maintained. I told Mom that she was not a burden to us and we asked her to move to our home specifically because we did not want to see her in a nursing home.

But Mom insisted that she make a contribution and repeatedly asked me to set a figure on what it would cost for her to live with us. It turned out that there was one major adjustment after Mom moved in that provided me with an opportunity to settle her concerns. We heat our house with a combination of an oil-fired hot air furnace, and wood stoves. There is considerable wood available on our land, and cutting, splitting and stacking is a regular activity with us.

I have a large wood stove in the basement that keeps the floors warm, and a smaller one on a custom built hearth in the living room that heats the upstairs. But we were told before she moved in that Mom was not stable, either physically or mentally, and I decided to shut down the upstairs woodstove to avoid any accidents.

This, however, would mean that our oil consumption would jump drastically, right in the middle of the heating season. We had not budgeted for a huge oil expenditure, so I told Mom that if she wanted to make a contribution, she could purchase a tank or two of oil over the remainder of the winter, depending on how much we used. As it turned out that was a good call for both of us. The winter was colder than forecast, and Mom needed the heat turned up much higher than was the case before she moved in. I anticipated that Mom would need higher temps to be comfortable, because I remembered her mother, in the farmhouse in Center Brunswick, after my aunt and uncle bought it.

My grandparents used coal stoves for heat and cooking throughout the time I lived there, but nearly as soon as we moved out in 1957, my Uncle Floyd began extensive renovations to the old farmhouse, including installing baseboard heating.

Coal stoves emit extraordinary heat, especially when they are right in the room with you, as was the case with the potbellied stove in my grandparents' living room. So over the years they grew used to far more warmth than you can get from baseboard heating, unless you really want to see a spike in the heating bill. I still remember my grandmother turning the thermostat up to the eighties and other family members turning it back down again because the heat was stifling. I anticipated that we might encounter a similar situation with Mom.

I also discovered that Mom was suffering from hypothyroidism, a condition that results from insufficient iodine in the diet, hampering the function of the thyroid gland, which regulates metabolism. People with hypothyroidism have symptoms that include extreme sensitivity to the cold, accompanied by dry, itchy skin, which I observed in Mom. We resolved the medical issue by making sure there was iodized table salt available at mealtime, and adding a multi-vitamin/mineral tablet to her diet that provided the RDA of iodine.

Nonetheless, Mom's sensitivity to the cold made for a heating requirement that we didn't anticipate in the fall. Mom, however, was happy to spring for extra oil, since the amount required for one tank, even if it was monthly, required only a fraction of what she spent for basic necessities in New York.

When Nancy brought Mom to Connecticut, she gave her a paltry "allowance," and said she would consider giving Mom more of her own money once Nancy got back from vacation in Florida. Nancy said this was because she had to pay Mom's final bills at her apartment, which didn't really pass the truth test, because Mom paid the final utility bills herself with checks written on her new account in Connecticut.

Nancy also said that Mom could have a monthly stipend, again, coming from her own income, of approximately four hundred dollars. I passed this on to my brother on January 7, in one of the few parts of our "conversation" where I could get a word in edgewise.

Obviously, he related it to Nancy because the next line in her vitriolic message was:

"I never told Mom that she could only have four-hundred dollars a month. That woman can have as much money as she wants to live on."

Based on that statement, Nancy should have had no problem with Mom moving her income and her checking account to a bank in the state and town where she lives. Considering the difficulty of doing business with someone who is more than a hundred miles away, and may not always be around when they are needed, it also made perfect sense to Mom to change her power of attorney designee.

Nancy didn't see it that way. But the next line in her message would have been hilarious if it hadn't been a precursor to such a serious situation;

"But you know what? She doesn't spend more than forty dollars per week!"

Okay, get yourself a good laugh before we proceed with this.

There are many reasons why this was an incredibly stupid statement, but the one that jumps out at me is that one of the top ten signs of Alzheimer's is a growing unconcern with one's personal appearance.

Yet Ella Winter, and her daughter even testified to this in court, is fastidious about her appearance and goes to her hair appointment every week, religiously. I noted earlier that until the middle of December 2008, Mom took the senior citizen bus from her apartment in Menands to Clifton Park, New York every week for her hair appointment.

Seeking out a replacement hairdresser was one of the first things she did upon arriving in Connecticut. Mom still maintains her routine of having her hair done every single week.

It costs twenty-five dollars plus tip for her weekly hair appointment. Every three months or so Ella makes a longer appointment and gets a permanent. That costs a lot more. So basically, my sister was saying that Mom can live on less than fifteen dollars per week!

Now here is where the hypocrisy really flowers.

"And guess what? None of us, none of us, would take a cent for our mother living with us! Not for utilities, not for the phone, not for food, not for anything."

First off, my siblings obviously could have cared less about Ella's feelings. She may be ninety-two, but Mom still wants to make a contribution to this world. She likes to go out to eat every other week or so—and spring for it—which by the way, she did in New York, treating my sister and her husband to dinner every so often.

And she no longer wants to feel that she is a burden to her family. Nancy definitely impressed Mom with the sense that she was a burden, and Mom did not want that following her to Connecticut. So it became a matter of utmost importance to find a dollar amount that could give Mom the sense that she was making a needed contribution to the ongoing operations of our home, without going overboard.

But more importantly, my sister already made Mom pay for all the "work" that Nancy did taking care of her. You may remember in the early chapters that I spoke of the stocks that Mom and Dad began to accumulate while they lived in Florida in the late 1970's. Well Mom still had her stocks, until May 1, 2008 at least.

But on that day, Nancy convinced Mom to sign her stocks over to her. How much were they worth? Well, certainly not the face value of the stock certificates that Mom had in a box that she kept in her closet—because Mom was reinvesting the dividends all along.

There was one number on the stock certificates listing the amount of shares, but the real value was the number kept in the stock administrator's files that showed how much was paid in dividends, how many new shares those dividends were able to purchase, and how much the stock price had risen over the years. The actual value of the stocks is hard to discern because nearly a year passed by the time Mom revealed that she signed the stocks over to Nancy, and she couldn't remember all the pertinent details.

Were they worth a thousand dollars, or ten thousand? Who knows? Mom said at one point that the number forty-four thousand was sticking in her head, but then she said she couldn't be sure.

The value of the stocks, which were supposed to be split up among Mom's grandchildren, is known only to those who took them from her. It isn't even clear what happened to them. Maybe the stocks helped Nancy finance the lawsuit against her mother. Maybe they are still stored away somewhere.

Regardless, on May 1, 2008 the stocks that Ella was accumulating were turned over to her daughter, and it is Ella's position that Nancy made sure she knew it was in "payment" for all that her daughter did for her.

Ella said that as soon as she signed her name, Nancy began pumping her fist, chanting "Yes! Yes!" Ella recalls Nancy even dancing around Mom's apartment singing "I've got the stocks. I've got the stocks!"

"I had a feeling in the pit of my stomach that I made a mistake," Mom said.

But by January, 2009, Nancy seemed to have forgotten that she "charged" her mother for being a good daughter. And although

Nancy attempted to project an air of superiority as she washed her hands of any further responsibility for Mom's care, she also seems to have forgotten that the money she was still trying to control belonged to Ella Winter, not Nancy Patrick.

"If you need money for Mom to live on, I was more than happy to send you money."

There was more to her message that night, but I think by now you get the drift. Nancy considered Mom's money to be her money, and even though Mom moved lock, stock and barrel to Connecticut, Nancy maintained that she would continue riding herd on Mom's finances.

Oddly enough, even though she threatened to leave the apartment as it was, and stick us with the bill, Nancy continued to use it as leverage over Mom.

Upon receiving that message I immediately made preparations to travel to New York and empty the apartment. But I needed the keys to the U-Haul facility, and I needed to assemble some help.

However, at 10:34 a.m. on January, 14, 2009, another call came from my sister regarding the apartment. Apparently, she had given away or promised to give away, some of Mom's belongings and as an afterthought decided she should speak with Mom about it.

"Ron. It's your sister. I'd like Mom to give me a call. If you don't let her call me back, she won't have a say on some of her personal belongings that I would like her to make a decision on. I'm not her; I can't make a decision on some of the things in her apartment that may be very important to her. But the only way I can make a decision is by talking to her. So have her give me a call on my cell phone. Thank you. Asshole."

The ridiculous part of that message was the concept that began the previous week but grew, much as a rumor does, in the following weeks—that I was controlling Mom's access to the phones. Mom was born before it was common to have a phone in your house, but that was a long time ago and she changed with the times. She knows how to use a telephone.

Mom was around when it was common to make operator-assisted calls, she remembers the old crank style phones, rotary dial phones, and push buttons. She even understands the concept behind cell phones. Mom has a phone in her room, can pick up the phone in the kitchen any time she wants, and in fact places calls to anyone she wishes.

She speaks to her brother Vic, she speaks to her nephew Floyd and his wife Kay, she spoke with the management at Dutch Village apartments, she spoke with friends, and she even spoke to the government, the utilities and the banks.

But the real issue at hand in the January 14 message was the disposition of her belongings. Mom did call back, and after that conversation with Nancy said she was considering going back to New York to look the apartment over herself before anything else was removed. For several days that was a consideration, but other events overtook us and Mom did not return to Dutch Village.

Several months later, when her remaining belongings were retrieved from the various places where they were stored, Mom found to her dismay that many keepsakes and mementoes of her past were gone—along with many pertinent documents.

She didn't care too much that the plush chairs that accompanied her dining room table were given to charity—although the table remained—but she did care that her silver tea service was missing, many of her books were missing, her radio- phonograph-tape player system was gone, many old pictures in valuable frames—her aunts, her parents, even a picture of herself as a young woman—all were gone. Even her datebook containing phone numbers, birthdays and other special events was missing.

Nancy left messages later on that the missing items were packed away and "if somebody would just go through the boxes" they would be found. But after all the boxes were unpacked the items that Nancy claimed were at hand were nowhere to be found.

Perhaps it would have been understandable to keep some of those items if Ella had died, or even if Nancy was successful in placing her in an Alzheimer's ward. But Ella is very much alive and functioning. She never authorized anyone to take those items that held such meaning for her.

Despite the interference and the disappointments Mom suffered, the issue with her apartment actually was resolved very quickly.

First, I called my best friend from my elementary and high school days, Bob Soloyna. I saw him several times in the years after my father's funeral and calling him was a natural action from my standpoint.

I explained to Bob what was happening and he was understandably outraged. He also agreed to help finish the job in Mom's apartment, and to provide a truck so we wouldn't have to rent one.

There was another reason for calling Bob, besides his availability. Bob developed an interest in fitness and fighting in elementary school, and he is a lifelong weightlifter and boxer. He fought successfully as a heavyweight in the US Navy's Pacific Fleet on his numerous tours to Vietnam, and he continues to stay fit and strong. Bob Soloyna was known as "The Rock" since we were in high school, and was well known as such long before the professional wrestler who used that name was even born. Bob was instrumental in getting me involved in weight lifting and martial arts when we were teens, and I also continued on with those activities. I knew that even if it were only Bob and me, we would be able to move anything in my mother's apartment.

Fortunately, our crew was rounded out by another friend from Connecticut, John Tuttle, who soon retired after a forty-year federal law enforcement career. John came to our house with virtually no notice on New Year's Day to witness Mom's signature on her Power of Attorney forms, and attended her birthday party. John spoke with Mom at length on several occasions, and used his considerable investigatory skills to determine for himself that she was competent and knew what was occurring around her. When I asked if he could help resolve the situation concerning Mom's apartment in New York John jumped on board immediately.

On the morning of Friday, January 23, 2009, Jennifer, Heather and I piled into John's car, took Mom to my mother-in-law's house where she had a tremendously enjoyable day, and we took off for Albany.

John, known throughout his professional career as "The Duke," regaled us with stories from his law enforcement days, and the trip went quickly. We arrived in Dutch Village two hours later, retrieved the apartment keys from the office and checked to ensure that the POD storage container we rented was in the apartment parking lot.

We entered Mom's apartment and found the place a mess. Aside from the belongings that came to Connecticut with Ella, only her valuables and the small amount of furniture I mentioned previously were gone.

Each room was strewn with Mom's belongings.

I called Bob Soloyna on his cell phone when we arrived in Menands, and within twenty minutes he pulled into the parking lot. We had our usual joyous reunion and The Rock met The Duke.

If you want to get a difficult job done quickly, and you also want good humored people assisting you, I would be happy to be a representative for The Rock and The Duke. Maybe it's because we all are Vietnam Veterans and shared that common background, and it certainly could be that with Bob being a Navy veteran while John is an Army veteran, it made for a natural tag team against the only Marine in the crowd, namely me.

Regardless, they got along great from the minute they met, and we pitched in immediately, moving Mom's furniture and other belongings with a lot of good natured kidding, and plenty of laughter to make the job easier. Every major piece of furniture in the apartment was either heavy or awkward, but while this may have been a daunting task to the New York side of the family, we saw it as a challenge.

Bob parked his truck at the end of the sidewalk leading from the apartment front door to the parking lot. The POD container was uphill about seventy-five yards or so in another parking lot. So, rather than muscle all that furniture up the hill one piece at a time, we loaded the furniture into Bob's truck, and when it was filled he drove it to the container where we unloaded it and packed it inside.

The job took us two hours to complete. While The Duke, The Rock and I moved out the heavy pieces, Jennifer and Heather moved lighter boxes, pictures and knick knacks. The apartment management required that all nail and screw holes from pictures, shades, curtains and blinds be filled with spackle before we left, so Heather took on that job.

We began the job at about 10:30 a.m. The apartment was empty before noon, and the manager was finished inspecting it by 1 p.m. We locked up the apartment, turned the keys over to the management, and headed out to lunch soon after.

There was one down side to the day, however.

When my brother first arrived in Albany after Christmas, he and my brother-in-law rented a U-Haul truck and a storage unit about a mile from the apartment. They made one trip with the limited amount of furniture, and that was it. My brother bragged when he came to Connecticut for lunch in late December that he even argued with the U-Haul attendant over the price of a quart of gas! No kidding, one quart. That's a dollar even in the worst of times.

Anyway, we planned on emptying out the U-Haul storage unit and putting that furniture in the POD with the rest of Mom's belongings so it would all be in one place. But on Monday, January 19, James Patrick sent me the following email:

From: Jim Patrick
To: Ron Winter
Sent: Monday, January 19, 2009 3:14 PM
Subject: rental on storage unit

I have just informed the storage facility that I am no longer responsible for paying the monthly rental on your Mother's storage unit. The unit is paid for until January 26th.

I am enclosing my bills for the first month rent, etc.; when I receive reimbursement for the $105.23 that I have paid, you will receive the keys for the locks.

Jim Patrick

The next morning I purchased a money order for the $105.23 sent it to Jim by overnight mail and alerted him by email:

From: Ron Winter
To: Jim Patrick
Sent: Tuesday, January 20, 2009 3:49 PM
Subject: storage unit fees and apartment

Jim, A money order for $105.23 is on its way via FedEx. It will arrive at your house in the morning.

Thank you for your efforts on Mom's behalf. I will take over from here. I have a crew coming over at the end of the week to empty the apartment and close it down.

Please leave the apartment keys and the storage unit keys with Joan at the Dutch Village office by tomorrow at the latest.

She has been apprised of the situation and is expecting them. The apartment will be sealed so we don't have to worry about any damage between now and the end of the month. I will schedule an inspection with Joan to insure that the apartment has been left in acceptable condition.

If you have any personal effects in the apartment please have them out by tomorrow at the latest. I will not be responsible for any belongings other than Mom's that are left behind.

I had sent Nancy a registered letter which apparently is not being accepted. In it I mentioned that I will need Mom's personal papers. Mom says many of them are in a metal box (possibly green) that was left in the apartment. Please leave the box and her papers in the apartment where I can retrieve it before we start moving the furniture.

Thank you
Ron

I underlined the sentence above where I left instructions on what to do with the keys for a reason. We needed the keys to get into the U-Haul storage unit. I couldn't have made it any clearer. Leave the apartment keys and the storage unit keys with the manager.

But, that isn't what happened. In an unexpectedly childish response, my brother-in-law sent the following:

From: Jim Patrick
To: 'Ron Winter'
Sent: Thursday, January 22, 2009 10:27 AM
Subject: RE: storage unit fees and apartment

Ron,

I received your money order, and Nancy put the keys and your Mother's new pants from Christmas, in the mail to you.

I also had Nancy give Joan the keys to the apartment, and the apartment storage unit as you requested

Jim Patrick

Let's face it; you'd have to be brain-dead to have misconstrued my message. Jim said he was washing his hands of any involvement with the storage facility and he wanted his hundred bucks back. I gave him the money and said leave the keys with the apartment manager.

The so-called "apartment storage unit" referred to in his email was a closet in the basement. My brother said he already cleaned it out. The apartment key opens it. There was no mistake; sending the U-Haul keys by mail was deliberate and childish. I expected far better from my brother-in-law even if his wife was acting foolishly.

So they dropped the keys in the mail, which meant they were in transit to Connecticut when we were in transit to New York. Which meant that even though I went to the U-Haul facility with The Rock and The Duke, and changed the rental arrangements over to my name instead of my brother-in-law's, I also was informed that unless I had a couple of extra hours to spare—I didn't—and didn't mind paying a locksmith a hundred dollars or so—I did—I wouldn't be able to get into the unit until I had the keys.

Now, I know what you're thinking and you may have a point - for exactly twenty-four hours.

"Why," I bet you are saying, *"didn't you just come back the next week, after the keys had arrived, and empty out the unit and be done with it?"*

Two reasons. First, when you rent a POD storage container you have a specific window of time within which it is delivered to the location where you want to fill it, and then it is retrieved by the company and transported to a warehouse where it is stored until you want it delivered somewhere else.

When we made the arrangements with the folks from the POD company, we agreed that they would retrieve the storage unit from Dutch Village no later than Saturday, January 24. After all, it was sitting in the middle of two parking spaces and the Dutch Village management was very understanding in letting us keep it there for two days already.

We could have arranged for it to be on location longer, but it was in a public spot, and once it was filled we wanted it transported to a secure warehouse as soon as possible.

Also, we didn't know when the keys would arrive in Connecticut so there was no way to accurately predict when we would be able to return. Nonetheless, we may have opted to clean out the U-Haul facility and combine it with the POD unit at a later date, except for what happened next.

Because while we were working to help Mom get settled in Connecticut; to get her belongings in one secure location until we could put the addition onto our house; to get her nutritional and medical needs on an even keel; to help her feel safe, secure and most of all wanted in our home; Nancy Patrick, aided and abetted by her daughter Courtney, and her brother Wilson "Skeeter" Winter had a different agenda.

During the same week that we were making arrangements to close Mom's apartment and save her the rental expense, Nancy Patrick was engaged in the most heinous, despicable, deplorable action that I have ever seen between family members. Her actions that week represent the kind of dirt you read about in cheesy tabloids, or see on television soap operas. I don't believe that my siblings' actions are commonly accepted in polite society and I'm certain that most people don't expect them to erupt in their own families. But erupt they did, and what came next is the reason you are reading this book.

Lessons Learned

1. Acquaint yourself with the financial affairs of family members who may wind up in your care. Learn as much as possible before any need arises. We had three days notice that Mom was on the verge of losing her independence. It would have helped if we had known in advance the status of her finances, and that she was arguing with Nancy over the Power of Attorney issue.

2. Spell out all financial issues, and create a family financial and legal portfolio that outlines what exists while your loved ones are able to assist. Make copies for each family member, unless otherwise directed. Simultaneously create a planner that outlines the roles each family member will play.

3. Expect the unexpected. Don't trust anyone. Nancy went into a fit of pique because her plans were thwarted, so from that point difficulties became the order of the day. Expect them, and work around them. Acknowledge any friction when it begins and expect that it will play a larger role if a loved one is incapacitated, even temporarily.

CHAPTER TEN

The Power of Attorneys—Courting Danger

When we returned from New York on Friday night we gave Mom a rundown on the status of her belongings.

She was understandably disappointed that we were not able to access the U-Haul facility to see what was inside. She continued to ask questions about the apartment throughout the next day, and still was considering taking a ride to New York to open the storage unit.

But as we sat down to dinner Saturday night, headlight beams from a vehicle entering our driveway swept across the kitchen wall. The dogs immediately began barking and Jennifer went to the door, spoke briefly and then called me.

A man with a sheaf of papers was standing on the deck and said to me "I guess you've been expecting this."

"Who are you?" I replied, and, pointing to the papers he held, "What is that?"

"I'm here to serve M. Ella Winter and Ronald Winter," the process server said.

He showed me the papers:

In the Matter of the Application of NANCY WINTER PATRICK for the appointment as Guardian of the Person and the

Property of M. ELLA WINTER, An Alleged Incapacitated person and for Provisional Remedies under Mental Hygiene Law...

Oddly enough, the first thought that went through my mind was, "When did Nancy start using Winter as her middle name?" Her given middle name is Arlene, not Winter.

But my sister's name change was just a minor distraction. The real issue was the contents of the papers I was handed. I was very familiar with court filings since, for most of the two decades of my journalism career, I covered or directed coverage of criminal and civil justice either on police beats or in the courts, ranging from traffic offenses, to misdemeanors, to felonies and eventually federal drug and terrorism cases. Over the years I reviewed hundreds upon hundreds of civil cases, reported on many and even was involved in a few. I know how to read the papers the process server handed to me.

I saw that the case was already received and accepted in New York State Supreme Court in Albany, by Judge Eugene P. Devine. As I read further I also noted that the judge decided without any evidence to appoint a court "Evaluator" on Mom's behalf. That would become a major issue later.

In the meantime I told the process server that I hadn't expected any such thing, but seeing as how it was my sister who initiated it, I guessed I wasn't exactly surprised.

"This is stupid," I told him. "She's going to get her ass kicked. This is frivolous, just frivolous."

He told me that he also was required to personally serve Mom, who was still out in the kitchen at the dinner table. "I'll give them to her," I said.

"I'm sorry," the process server said. "I have to give the papers to her myself, and insure that it's her."

I went to the kitchen where Mom was seated at the table waiting for us to begin dinner. I was trying to figure out a way to sugar coat what was coming, but I couldn't think of any. Mom was required to meet the process server face to face, and accept a sheaf of papers that were intended to force her into an Alzheimer's facility against her will.

I figured it was better to just get it over with.

"Mom. You have to come to the door. Nancy is suing us and the marshal has to give the papers to you personally."

A look of stark terror swept over her face and her skin went chalky white. I tried to be reassuring as I helped her out to the front door, but she was petrified.

The process server was solicitous and apologized profusely for what he was doing. I explained to him that Mom moved in with us the previous month and that my sister was attempting to gain control of her money in New York while Mom wanted it in her own bank.

We talked to Mom a bit as the process server watched and he appeared surprised that she was well aware of her surroundings and understood what was happening. Mom made the point of saying that she was very happy in Connecticut and didn't want to be placed in any facility in New York or elsewhere.

We didn't have to tell this guy any of the background. We didn't have to talk with him at all. But I believe it is human nature that when a stranger shows up at your door in the dark of night, carrying papers that falsely claim you are holding an elderly person against her will and stealing her money, there is a natural inclination to set the record straight, right there on the spot and in the future.

Obviously he at least scanned the contents of the suit, which alleged that Ella was totally incompetent, suffering from Alzheimer's – had in fact been treated for Alzheimer's – that her mind was too far deteriorated for her to understand the case or assist in her defense, that I forged her name on the Power of Attorney documents and was holding her against her will!

I glanced over the first few pages of allegations when he first handed them to me, and they were enough to make my blood boil. But only later, when I read some of the libel that passed for a legal action, did I understand why he was surprised to see that Mom was aware, competent and obviously not under duress.

The process server talked with us for a few more minutes then apologized again for the disruption and left. His reaction to actually meeting and talking to Mom was mirrored by dozens of other people in the coming weeks, especially if they read my sister's complaint or listened to her allegations before meeting Mom.

Ella was, and is, in control of her faculties, occasionally forgetful, but definitely not suffering from Alzheimer's or dementia. In the coming months, the truth about Mom's mental status would be discovered, and the real reason why she suffered episodes of disorientation, that I initially believed were only dietary in nature, would be laid directly at Nancy Patrick's feet.

But on the night of January 24, 2009, we could only shake our heads in amazement as we read the lawsuit. It totaled thirty-eight pages of lies, venomous distortions, fabrications, and libel. Right off the bat, Mom was ticked that throughout the lawsuit, Nancy referred to her as an AIP, Alleged Incapacitated Person, which Ella pronounced APE.

In the following weeks she sat at the kitchen table, night after night, day after day, reading the lawsuit and its allegations and every so often would look up and mutter, "I still can't believe they're calling me an ape now."

One of the primary lies the lawsuit offered was in paragraph 4 under **Alleged Incapacitated Person**, where Nancy claimed that Mom *"went to visit with her son, Ronald Winter ... on or about December 22, 2008, and has not be* (sic) *allowed to return home."*

The hypocrisy of what Nancy was doing literally dripped off that page. The entire matter arose on December 17 when Nancy's husband called to inform me that his wife was in the process of signing Mom into a nursing home. When I offered to have Mom move in with us as an alternative, he not only agreed, he couldn't get her to my home fast enough!

They brought a large amount of Mom's personal belongings with them on December 22, 2008 and the very next day they began emptying Mom's apartment without any consultation. They threw away, gave away or stored her belongings over the next two weeks, and had every intention of finishing the job until Mom put her foot down and said she wanted control of her bank accounts.

Then, suddenly, we get served with a legal action that claims Mom was coming to my home for a visit!? And that I wouldn't allow her to return home? They had taken away any home that Mom had in New York! The only home that would be there for her if she was forced to return to New York was in an Alzheimer's facility!

I cannot think of more suitable words for what my sister and other family members were doing than reprehensible and despicable.

The lies continued as follows:

Paragraph 6; the AIP suffers from dementia and/or Alzheimer's disease, a condition which currently renders her cognitively impaired to a point where she no longer is able to undertake any complex rational reasoning.

Paragraph 8: The AIP's condition is progressive in nature and her recovery is not likely.

Paragraph 9: The AIP's mental condition has progressed to the point where she needs a court appointed Guardian not only to make financial decisions, but to make other personal decisions for her.

When I first read through the lawsuit, I also flipped to the back where the "Exhibits" were listed. Exhibits are supposed to supplement the allegations in the filing. There were four exhibits, but none of them contained the one thing that I believed from the outset were necessary for the suit to proceed -- medical evidence that Mom was ever diagnosed with, or treated for Alzheimer's. The claim that she suffered from Alzheimer's was important because it makes the point that the only type of elder care facility that could accept Mom was a nursing home with staff and facilities capable of providing the special care and environment that Alzheimer's sufferers require. The paragraphs spelling out repeatedly that Mom not only suffered from Alzheimer's, but that her mind was massively and irretrievably deteriorated to the point that she is incapable of any type of independent function, also put to lie Nancy's later and continuing statements that she just wanted Mom in a retirement facility, not a nursing home.

Neither the core of the lawsuit, nor the exhibits contained one shred of evidence that Mom had either Alzheimer's or dementia. Yet the lawsuit was accepted on face value and filed in the New York State Supreme Court in Albany as if its allegations were unassailable gospel.

The body of the lawsuit contained numerous paragraphs claiming that Nancy Patrick was the next best thing to Mother Teresa, and that I was the Great Satan, so obviously the only rational candidate to be Mom's guardian was – you guessed it, Nancy Patrick.

Mom bristled at the concept of having a guardian, and does to this day. She is well aware of who she is and what she is doing. Even talking about having someone appointed to take total control of her really gets her blood boiling.

The vast majority of the verbiage in the lawsuit was not only false, it was irrelevant and seemed to be included only to give Nancy an opportunity to say as many nasty things as she could about me under the guise of a legal document.

In addition to the previous claim of unlawful restraint and kidnapping, she also alleged that I forged Mom's name on the documents Mom filled out changing her address.

But in a later section titled **PERSONAL NEEDS MANAGEMENT**, Nancy got back into her false claims about Mom's mental status.

I said previously that Ella is fastidious about her personal appearance. That not only includes her hair appointments, but also her clothing, her shoes, her teeth, virtually everything about her. She gets up every morning on her own, makes her breakfast on her own, makes her lunch on her own, showers, has her coffee, calls friends, reads the papers, prepares for her appointments and visits, all on her own. Failure to do so could be an indicator of Alzheimer's. But Ella does all of those things virtually every day on her own.

However, Nancy Patrick's lawsuit claimed:

Paragraph 53: In addition to the AIP being physically unable to provide for her personal needs, she is also incapable of making adequate health care decisions ... Since the AIP cannot make complex decisions, she is unable to make adequate personal or health care decisions by herself, ... She cannot adequately understand and appreciate the nature and consequences of her inability to provide necessary services for herself.

Commit that section to memory if you can because it is going to be revealed in all its vileness when we get to Mom's actual testimony, and wonder of wonders, Nancy's testimony in which she flat out contradicted her own lawsuit!

In Paragraph 55 under **PROPERTY NEEDS MANAGEMENT** Nancy claimed that Mom *"is no longer aware of the value or extent of her assets, nor is she able to perform any day to day financial tasks, such as paying her creditors, etc."*

But it was in Paragraph 56 of the section entitled **PROPERTY MANAGEMENT POWERS SOUGHT** that the real nature of Nancy's assault on her mother became abundantly clear:

The powers of the Guardian ... must include ...

Subsection a; Authority to marshal the income and all assets of the AIP of any nature, including but not limited to Social Security, dividends, interest, rent and any pension of the AIP.

And in subsection o; *Authority to close or retitle <u>in the Guardian's name</u> bank time deposits prior to maturity, upon finding by this court that ... the Order Appointing a Guardian shall be deemed a declaration of incompetence ...*

Way back in the early part of the suit, under **Property Powers Sought**, Nancy also wanted authority to *"... establish bank, brokerage and other similar accounts <u>in the name of the Guardian</u> ... and endorse, collect, negotiate and deposit all negotiable instruments ... including but not limited to government entitlement checks."*

Nancy even wanted Mom's life insurance! And in what can only be described as the final indignity, toward the end of the filing Nancy demanded that Mom pay all of the legal bills associated with the case including Nancy's.

What this all boils down to in laymen's terms is that my sister was falsely accusing my mother of complete incompetence in a blatant effort to take control of all of Mom's assets and income and put them in a bank account where Nancy and only Nancy had control over them.

In other words, it was all about money.

Although Mom successfully transferred her checking account, savings account and one Certificate of Deposit to Connecticut, she was unable to get the information on two other CDs and a savings account kept in Key Bank in time to make the transfer before Nancy sued her. The account numbers and bank documents were not brought to Connecticut with Ella, and remained in New York. The bank was uncooperative when we attempted to retrieve the information.

Nancy's lawyer, Richard E. Rowlands of the firm Girvin & Ferlazzo in Albany, succeeded in convincing Key Bank representatives in Menands, where Mom did her banking, to freeze her accounts there based solely on Nancy Patrick's false claim that Ella was incompetent. What was truly amazing about the lawsuit was that Judge Devine accepted it, and Key Bank went along with it, without one shred of medical evidence attached. Now, it is true that the judge, before he was elected to the bench in New York, also worked at Girvin & Ferlazzo, the same firm that employed Rowlands. But I am not saying that affected his decision – far from it. What I am saying is that the judge should have at least questioned the absence of supporting evidence, considering that the ultimate aim of the lawsuit was to deny Mom's rights to life and liberty, and simultaneously "marshal" her income and other assets in the name of her daughter.

I also am saying that the law in America, at least the last time I read the Constitution, guaranteed an accused person the right to an assumption of innocence until guilt is proven. In the same vein, a person who is alleged to be incompetent is assumed to be competent until proven otherwise. Hearsay and opinions do not constitute valid medical diagnoses, and nowhere was there a single statement from a doctor, nor even a copy of a medical record, stating that Ella was suffering from Alzheimer's or otherwise was diagnosed as incompetent.

Oddly enough, included as an exhibit with the legal filing was a copy of the letter I sent to Mom's savings bank, First Niagara in Troy, New York, explaining her move to Connecticut and her wish to transfer her funds to her new bank. That bank called Mom, discussed her options and helped her transfer her funds to Connecticut. I'm not sure what the purpose of that letter was, but there was another bank document submitted as evidence that proved the fallacy of the entire lawsuit.

For reasons that seem inexplicable, Nancy submitted a document from Mom's bank changing the signature card to add Nancy's name. But Mom's signature was also required, and there it was – dated December, 17, 2008. If that date sounds familiar it was when Mom was still in Albany Medical Center, and still considered incapacitated, at least by her daughter. That was the date that Jim Patrick called and said Mom was being committed to Hawthorne Ridge, and if I wanted to have any input I should call before 3:30 p.m. That was the day that Nancy came within two hours of putting Mom in a nursing home.

Here she was, only a little over a month later, now claiming Mom was totally incompetent, and was never going to get better, yet she submitted a document bearing Mom's signature dated during her hospital stay as evidence – presuming that Mom would have known what she was doing when she signed that form. It seems that if Mom was competent enough to sign a bank document and know what she was doing, then she was competent enough to decide whether she wanted to live in her son's home in Connecticut or in an Alzheimer's ward.

Oddly enough, even though it was claimed that Mom was "accepted" into Hawthorne Ridge, there was no document bearing Mom's signature to prove that claim. If she was competent enough to sign a bank document that day, she obviously was competent enough to sign herself into the elder care facility too – or not.

It also seems to me that Judge Devine should have read Nancy Patrick's lawsuit, checked the limited exhibits attached to it, and asked at the top of his lungs, "WHERE'S THE BEEF!?"

But he didn't. Instead, Judge Devine of the New York Supreme Court in Albany accepted it into the court system, it now had a file number, and a return date, and regardless of how unspeakably cruel and vexatious it was, we would have to find a lawyer to fight it.

Once again, my old friends in New York came to the rescue, and walking point was The Rock. I have some great memories of the way Bob Soloyna's Mom made me feel welcome in their home when we were in elementary and high school.

Bob told me how he and other members of his family teamed up to care for his mother in her final years, and I figured that since legal issues invariably arise in those situations, Bob probably knew a lawyer in the area who could help. He did, but he also had quite a surprise in store for me.

Bob said that the lawyer I should contact first was not in the Albany area at all and in fact wasn't even in New York.

Bob said, "Call Rich Rodriguez."

Who is Rich Rodriguez? Well, simply put, Rich is my friend. We became friends in high school, and shared quite a few adventures in the years before I left to join the Marines. Rich lived in Wynantskill and was among our circle of friends during part of our high school years. Rich graduated a year after Bob and me, and went on to become a lawyer.

Rich moved to Southern California many years ago, and I hadn't seen or heard from him since 1965. But Rich never sold the house he grew up in, and rented it out after his mother died. He returns to Wynantskill several times each year.

Bob said that Rich would be the guy to get us the right lawyer, and he gave me Rich's office, home, and cell phone numbers. I called all three. Within a day I received an email, and then we made contact by phone.

A really nice aspect of the friendships we have from those days is that although my conversation with Rich was our first communication in more than forty years, it took up right wherever our last one left off.

I gave Rich a complete rundown on what was going on between my siblings and Mom, and Rich gave me a half-dozen names off the top of his head. First on the list was Atty. John T. Casey, from Troy, New York. Rich told me Casey was smart, tough and would not let Ella be intimidated by the legal system. That, I said, is exactly the type of lawyer we need.

It took a few days to get in touch with 'Jack' Casey as he is known, because he also is the parliamentarian for the New York State Senate which was in session. But I did hear back from him and explained the situation.

Jack's immediate reaction was that the lawsuit was invalid because on December 29, 2008, Mom became a permanent resident of Connecticut. The lawsuit was filed in New York on January 20th, 2009. Thus, he believed the New York courts did not have jurisdiction.

We talked at length about Mom's move, about Nancy, Jim, Courtney and Skeeter being instrumental in relocating her to

Connecticut, and how they now were claiming that she was being held by me against her will. That last part had Jack laughing, a reaction that is common when most people hear of my sister's lawsuit. But I didn't think being charged with kidnapping and unlawful restraint was all that funny.

Jack told me to fax over the lawsuit, which I did. He then went to work on a motion to dismiss on jurisdictional grounds.

We had a ton of evidence from all the business that Mom conducted to establish herself in Connecticut, and Jennifer and I immediately began compiling it. Jack was quite reassuring, and even knew my sister and her husband socially.

But he took their complaint seriously and was well aware of the implications. He also urged us to begin the groundwork for a series of affidavits to support Mom's contention that she knew exactly what she was doing when she changed her address and bank accounts.

In the meantime, Mom kept reading the lawsuit. And the more she read it, the more it angered her.

Time after time she questioned what happened to Nancy to cause her to sue her own mother. And there was one facet of the lawsuit that Ella feared nearly as much as the effort to place her in a nursing home.

Throughout the suit, in the various sections where it listed the powers Nancy was seeking, the phrase *"take actions required to make M. Ella Winter eligible for Medicaid ..."* kept popping up.

Mom despised that phrase as much as she feared what might happen to her.

"Wilson made sure that would never happen to me," she maintained. "Why is Nancy trying to put me on Medicaid?"

I explained to Mom that while she had sufficient income to pay her bills if she lived independently, and way more than enough to pay her expenses while living with us, the average cost of nursing home care in the United States is far, far more than she could afford.

It can cost six thousand dollars per month at a minimum to reside in a quality nursing home, and that was not even close to the cost for what is considered quality care in the northeastern United States. Mom said Nancy and Skeeter repeatedly told her that her assets were more than sufficient for a move into a retirement facility, but that obviously was not the case.

When Nancy's lawyer successfully blocked Mom from accessing her funds in Key Bank he put a hold on about sixty percent of her assets. Mom asserted that she wanted that money as a buffer in case she incurs medical bills that aren't covered by insurance and eventually to use for her funeral expenses.

But access to that money was now blocked by her daughter. The end result was that if committed, Mom soon would not have enough money by a long shot to pay the monthly bills at a quality nursing home, regardless of whether it was Hawthorne Ridge or another facility.

And despite Nancy's sworn assertions in court two months later, that she would never, ever, no way in hell put Mom in a nursing home, the allegations repeated over and over in Nancy's lawsuit claimed that Mom was completely incompetent. Retirement homes and assisted living facilities are not for residents who are incompetent. People who are ruled incompetent must reside in a nursing home if home care is not possible, because the ruling of incompetence means they need twenty-four-hour care. Retirement homes and assisted living facilities are not for people who require twenty-four-hour care.

As defined by the Connecticut Department of Social Services:

Assisted living and nursing home care are designed to meet different needs in a continuum of care. While both offer nursing and personal care services, assisted living communities are generally not appropriate for persons in need of twenty-four-hour skilled nursing and rehabilitative services, extensive nursing assistance or intensive therapies, or who have ongoing complex or unstable medical conditions.

If all of Mom's assets remained intact, she might be able to get by for a year before the money ran out, depending on the facility they placed her in, and its financial requirements. But if Nancy was given control over all her funds, then Ella would be applying for Medicaid in a matter of months.

That scared her and angered her.

"Wilson made sure that I had enough to live on so I would never have to go on welfare. He set that up from the very first paycheck at the Arsenal, and he kept it that way until he retired," she fumed. The very threat of going on Medicaid was never far from Mom's mind and she spoke of it often.

Skeeter and Nancy also filled Mom full of stories about her friends from Center Brunswick and Dutch Village and how they just loved every minute of their lives in various elder care facilities around the Albany area. But Mom's visits to some of those facilities left her with the exact opposite impression. And she wasn't told how much of her friends' savings were being drained every month to keep them in those places.

It was difficult to see how the New York State Supreme Court or anyone else was supposed to accept the claims Nancy made in the lawsuit as truthful, particularly since there was an obvious absence of supporting medical evidence, and especially when balanced against her later testimony. These glaring contradictions serve to point out the hypocrisy that was rife in this case from the outset.

Mom was adamant virtually every single day, and often, several times a day, that we explain just what was going on. She didn't want to enter Hawthorne Ridge or any other facility. She was very clear about that. But she also was very interested in the relationship between her bank account, her income, and the fees charged by the nursing homes.

There was one other element of the case that she wanted explained. With Nancy's name on her bank accounts, there was no guarantee that the money Mom was counting as part of her assets would actually be considered hers. Some of it, possibly most of it, could go to Nancy, which would reduce the length of time that Ella could count on her own money. There also was the question of just what Nancy, Courtney and Skeeter planned to do with her. Courtney told Mom that they really weren't going to put her into a nursing facility, but actually had picked out a beautiful apartment for her. Nancy made a similar claim on one of her phone messages, which flew in the face of Skeeter's assertion that Mom's two hospitalizations proved that she could no longer go anywhere but a full-time nursing facility.

And Nancy's lawsuit declared in writing that Mom was suffering from Alzheimer's. If she was suffering from Alzheimer's then she would be required to live in a secure environment. Hawthorne Ridge advertised on its website that Alzheimer's patients lived in confined areas, and both the indoor and outdoor exercise and socialization areas were closed loops that would prevent issues with patients attempting to leave the facility.

The lawsuit revealed a major contradiction in that Nancy was claiming on one hand that Ella was totally incompetent and couldn't make any decisions for herself, including attending to her basic grooming, but on the other hand she was saying that Mom could go into a more independent assisted living facility, once Nancy gained control of her life.

According to Nancy's lawsuit, Ella Winter could not manage for herself without twenty-four-hour care. Thus, it was obvious that a retirement facility or even assisted living were no longer options for Ella, if the claims in the lawsuit were accurate. It had to be one or the other, it couldn't be both. Nancy filed suit in New York Supreme Court alleging that her mother was suffering from Alzheimer's and dementia. Assisted living was out of the question if that was true. But if it wasn't true, then why had a process server shown up at our door at dinner time on January 24?

And why were we now required to hire lawyers to help us navigate the New York court system? More to the point, as Ella herself expressed it: "If they are just making me go to another apartment, where I can do everything I did at home, that costs so much more than my apartment in Dutch Village, why couldn't I just have stayed in my own home?"

Lessons Learned

1. *Learn the legal terms and definitions of situations that may face you. Power of Attorney grants far fewer and less expansive powers than Guardianship. Power of Attorney can be rescinded, but Guardianship has the power of the courts behind it and is much harder to undo.*

2. *Search for a trusted lawyer or firm long before it becomes necessary to use such services. It is important to build a trusting legal relationship such that you are not reliant on relatives' lawyers who do not know you for legal advice.*

3. *Understand the ramifications of turning control over your affairs to another person, even a family member. Write out specifically what you expect from any decisions you make*

concerning handling your assets and what you expect to occur should you later become incapacitated.

4. Medical experts say that 50 percent of Americans will be diagnosed with Alzheimer's as they age, meaning virtually everyone will have to deal with it in one way or another. Take the time and make the effort to spell out in writing, with witnesses also signing, exactly what you expect in the future even if you can no longer contribute. Preparation is the key.

CHAPTER ELEVEN

A Note from My Doctor

After we went through a series of belly-aching laughs, followed by brain-sizzling outrage over Nancy's lawsuit, we began to parse the allegations one by one.

It was obvious right from the start that the entirety of Nancy's vicious legal assault rested on the court believing that Mom was incompetent; a long-term, and steadily declining Alzheimer's sufferer who was being manipulated at my hands.

That Mom might have been a normally aging nonagenarian who had been bullied by her daughter for the past several years actually did occur to many members of Ella's extended family, but you wouldn't know it from the contents of Nancy's lawsuit, nor the actions of the New York Supreme Court in Albany.

The truth of that statement is contained in the lawsuit itself, where it alleges without proof that Ella was suffering from Alzheimer's, where the ultimate goal was to place her in an elder care facility when she was adamant that she did not want to go to a facility of any kind, and that simultaneous with that goal was the "marshaling" of all of Mom's assets in Nancy's name.

But even more demonstrative of the fragility of the lawsuit was the one-line *Paragraph 62: Petitioner* (Nancy Patrick) *requests that this court dispense with the presence of AIP* (Mom) *at the hearing because she could not meaningfully participate in the proceeding.*

Despite all of Nancy's later protestations that she was looking out for Mom's "best interests" and that she only wanted to place Mom in an "assisted living facility," an apartment that she pre-selected, Nancy swore in her lawsuit that Mom's mind was completely and irretrievably gone. To make this point stick she needed to give the impression that she had an open and shut case and there was no sense in fighting it.

In other words, Nancy needed us to roll over in abject fear of the immense legal sword she was wielding—yes, I'm being sarcastic here—and most important, we should hand Mom over to her, against Mom's will, without her consent, so Nancy could proceed as she had planned. No matter what else transpired between the beginning and end of Nancy's assault on her mother, Mom's ability to stand up and speak up for herself was the key to success or failure—on each side.

What shocked us was that Nancy was so blatant about the need to keep Mom away from the courtroom, and away from the judge. We, meaning me, my family, the various witnesses who stood up for Mom by filing affidavits for her, and Mom's lawyers, all spoke with her at length. We all knew she was aware and more to the point, we knew she was participating in her defense. Yet, Nancy didn't want her in that courtroom; that is clear. But why?

One of the many mysteries of this case revolves around the question of what happened to Ella Winter on December 13, 2008. Nancy states in the lawsuit that she was with her mother in the morning that day, and that she came back to Mom's apartment very late that night after calling and receiving no answer.

But that in itself is odd. I have called Mom many times over the years and had her phone go to the answering machine, even in the mid-afternoon and early evenings. Mom has a tendency to nap, which is crucial for her physical and mental well being, and many times she called me back after I left a message for her.

If I called and there was no answer I assumed that Mom was out shopping or visiting, but often she told me she was napping and didn't hear the phone! So what would possess someone to call her very late at night, after 11 p.m., and assume that something was wrong if she didn't answer? Why would anyone have called that late in the first place? If Nancy had concerns why didn't she just go to Mom's apartment earlier in the evening to check on her? Why wait so long?

Here is another mystery. When Jim Patrick called me on December 17, 2008 to tell me that Nancy was only a couple of hours from committing Mom to a nursing home, he also told me that Mom was violent and disruptive on the night of December 13, when he and Nancy went to her apartment. Jim told me the apartment was "trashed." He told me that furniture was thrown around, papers were strewn throughout the apartment, and most significantly that Mom shattered a glass centerpiece that stood on her dining room table. Shattered. Not broken, or damaged—shattered.

Mom was given the same story, and she brought it up numerous times after she moved to Connecticut. There was a reason why she brought it up—what she saw when she returned to her apartment on December 19 did not jibe with what she was told, nor with what I was told. In fact, when Nancy Patrick testified against her mother on March 27, 2009 she described an entirely different scenario than the one that was given to Mom, to me, and to Albany Medical Center.

Nancy testified that when she entered Mom's apartment late on the night of December 13, 2008, she found all the lights on, the refrigerator door open, a Klondike ice cream bar and towels on the kitchen floor, and the water running in the kitchen sink. She further testified that Mom was trying to push the intercom button on the wall, but she was at the wrong wall, and there was no button.

She didn't mention the centerpiece on the dining room table, or the papers and furniture that supposedly were strewn all over the apartment.

Nancy testified that she took Mom to the hairdresser on a special visit earlier that day, so Mom could have her hair done for my Uncle Bob's wake the next day. When they returned, Nancy testified, Mom said she was freezing cold—likely as a result of the hypothyroidism—so Nancy fixed her a cup of tea and a piece of toast.

Nancy testified that Mom then said she was terribly tired and wanted to sleep. So Nancy—left. According to Mom's medical records this was about 3 p.m., although Nancy testified that she was with Mom in the morning.

Nancy claimed in her testimony to have called Mom at 5 p.m., and although there was no answer, she didn't think anything of it because Mom may not have heard the phone. Apparently that is okay when Nancy wants it to be, but as we have already seen on the numerous calls on Mom's birthday, it is not okay when Nancy wants it to be otherwise.

Regardless, Nancy testified that she called Mom three times, and finally decided to go to Mom's apartment. That was after she and Jim went out to dinner. There is no indication as to why Nancy suddenly decided that something was wrong with Mom after she didn't answer her phone.

Nancy testified that she used her keys to get in. But that doesn't explain why Ella was trying to answer the intercom, even if she was confused about its location.

The ambulance report says they transported Mom to the hospital at approximately 11:30 p.m.

The Emergency Room Admit-Transfer form says that Nancy claimed Mom's apartment was "disheveled." Elsewhere on the form it says the apartment was "ransacked." But it also said that Nancy told the medical personnel that at 3 p.m. Mom was "alert, oriented, her normal baseline self."

That statement conflicts with the testimony that Mom was freezing and exhausted and wanted to sleep. It also ignores Mom's earlier episode that she describes as sleep walking, primarily because Nancy told the emergency room personnel that Mom had been diagnosed with and suffered a TIA—mini-stroke—in 2006.

Mom's doctor did not diagnose her as having suffered a TIA in 2006 and she was not treated for a TIA. It was entirely possible that the same thing that Mom believes happened in 2006—sleep walking—was happening again. Whatever it was, it is a viable question.

Another problem that exists with Nancy's version of the events on the night of December 13, 2008, is that it doesn't agree with the version Jim gave—he said Mom was violent and had to be restrained. But Albany Medical Center admission records don't show Mom as being violent or even out of sorts.

In fact, when I heard Jim say that Mom was violent I couldn't even conjure up an image of what that was like. I simply have no memory of my mother ever being violent. She could be a task master when we were kids, and she was not afraid to dole out punishment, but violent was not a word we would ever use when describing Ella.

The admission forms only mention Mom being restrained several hours after being admitted when she tried to get out of bed to use the ladies room and they wanted her to stay in bed using a catheter instead. Mom was disoriented and confused when she was taken to the hospital and the admissions record says so, and apparently didn't understand the issue with the catheter.

She merely wanted to use the ladies room.

Also, unlike the episode in 2006 when my brother was present, Mom doesn't remember anything about the day or the night of December 13, 2008. Nothing. She vaguely remembers that she went to the hairdresser and that it wasn't her normal day to have her hair done.

When asked about that period she remembers that Nancy and Jim surprised her by not going to the impromptu birthday party at Uncle Bob's room in Samaritan Hospital in Troy, New York, on Thursday, December 4. She clearly remembers that Nancy and Jim left for their daughter Courtney's condo in Massachusetts when it was too late for Ella to get a ride from someone else to see her brother. She remembers her brother dying on December 8, 2008, and it matters greatly to her that she was not there for his birthday, and that she was not able to see him again after his birthday.

She has distinct memories of Nancy and Jim attending to Uncle Bob's Last Will and Testament immediately after his death, and that the wake and funeral were delayed until the following week. Ella remembers much about the days before and after her brother's death, which was a devastating experience for her, but she has only one specific memory of what transpired on December 13. Ella remembers being told that she had <u>shattered</u> the centerpiece on her table.

But on December 19, Mom returned to her apartment even though Nancy did not want her to go back there. Jim made that clear when he asked if I could take Mom into our home immediately on December 17, and then told me they were attempting to convince Albany Medical Center to keep her for three more days of neurological testing.

But Mom ultimately did go back to her apartment, on the 19th. It was cleaned up, which certainly was not unusual, but what she remembers most clearly is the condition of the centerpiece.

It was on the table where it belonged and it had a small crack around the top. It was not shattered. That one piece of information sticks in Mom's mind over and above everything else.

But, there is no way to determine just what happened that day without a clear recollection from Mom. Much of her memory has returned in the months after she moved to Connecticut and it is our hope that at some point there will be a breakthrough. But in December and January Mom simply had no recollection of the events of December 13, 2008.

In the meantime, however, we were required to answer a vexatious lawsuit in New York Supreme Court in Albany. And the validity of that lawsuit hinged entirely on Nancy's false allegation that Mom was suffering from Alzheimer's.

We discussed this at length, with Mom and with her attorneys, and decided that the best thing we could do was have her mental acuity tested. Mom already had a complete physical at an area medical office, and I called the doctor who examined her and asked if it was possible to do a basic mental health screening.

I explained what transpired since Mom saw her for the physical, and that the information needed would have to be suitable to submit as evidence.

Mom's doctor, Kristin Gildersleeve, didn't hesitate. Yes, she said, we can do a preliminary screening that will give us a good idea of your mom's basic mental acuity. If there is an indication that we need to go further, we can schedule further tests after we see the results of the first.

We made an appointment for the morning of February 5. The testing would take a couple of hours.

We explained to Mom what we were doing. Frankly, it worried her.

We hadn't received any information from Albany Medical Center on what examinations were conducted on Mom between

December 17 and December 19. In a later chapter I will address the issue of Albany Med withholding Mom's records for nearly four months, but for the moment it is important to note that we needed to see what they did—even if there was no lawsuit—so we could properly apprise Mom's new doctors of previous diagnoses and treatments. But we were not given any information that would help us, despite Mom asking for it herself.

We did everything we could to reassure Mom that the test was just a straightforward examination of her mental abilities, but by now she was terrified of the lawsuit and the possibility that she would be forced to move to an Alzheimer's facility.

Mom read the lawsuit from cover to cover, several times. Sometimes she would just sit and shake her head at what was written about her. Other times she would become introspective, wondering what had happened to her daughter.

It didn't help that Nancy continued to harp on the "best interests" theme. Everything she was doing was all being done in "Mom's best interests" whether that meant leaving her apartment for us to clean out and not finishing the job she started, or filing a lawsuit against her.

Mom opined that Nancy was suffering from post-menopausal hormone imbalances, which certainly could have been true, exacerbated by her daughter Courtney's decision not to return to the Albany/Troy area after she finished college.

"Nancy always thought that her daughter would come back and they would spend the rest of their lives doing things together as a mother/daughter team," Ella said on several occasions. But that did not happen, and Courtney purchased her condo in Massachusetts the previous summer.

I noted during one of these discussions that since Courtney jumped on board with her mother's lawsuit, at least they were a mother/daughter team, even if they didn't live anywhere near each other any longer.

I used these discussions to reassure Mom that her mental abilities were in fine shape. Nancy's lawsuit alleged that Mom was not capable of complex mental reasoning, but each time Mom worked her way through a problem of this nature, I reminded her that she was engaged in complex reasoning all day long and doing just fine at it. Nonetheless, she was still worried when we left for the doctor's office to do the mental acuity test.

She needn't have worried. The Mini-Mental State Examination is by no means a be-all end-all analysis. But it does give doctors a good baseline to see where a person's abilities lie. It is based on a scale of 30, with the top number meaning no mental difficulties. A score of 21 indicates that there may be mild cognitive impairment. Scores ranging from 10 to 20 indicate moderate cognitive impairment, and scores below 9 indicate severe impairment.

We took Mom to Dr. Gildersleeve's office. It was cold, but clear, and a brisk wind was blowing. Mom was dressed warmly but commented on the strength of the wind as we walked from the parking lot to the front door of the medical center. Inside, as usual, the staff was consummately friendly and professional. They remembered Mom from her physical and made a point of chatting and kidding with her, putting her instantly at ease.

We sat in the waiting room for only about five minutes before being called. A nurse took Mom's blood pressure and temperature, and then weighed her.

Mom is concerned about her weight and she was pleased to find out that she lost a few pounds since her physical. This occurred even though Mom has a balanced breakfast and lunch every day, and we sit down to a full dinner each evening. Mom was worried initially that her new nutrition program would cause her to gain weight.

Her fixation on her weight probably was related to Mom suffering a mild heart attack several years earlier. Later she was given a cholesterol reducing drug, and took it for more than a year. But that drug caused diarrhea for virtually all of the time she took it, and she was taken off it in the spring of 2008. A case could be made that Mom's dehydration issues stemmed from the side affects of the drug.

In fact, when Dr. Gildersleeve gave Mom her physical in January she expressed surprise that such a drug would be prescribed for a woman her age. Nonetheless, Mom was very sensitive about her weight and it put her in a positive frame of mind to find out that she can eat nutritious meals and still not become overweight.

Once the preliminaries were completed Mom was ushered to another room where the test was administered. She sat down and correctly answered the year, season, date, day and month. She correctly answered where she was.

Then she was given a verbal list of three items and told to remember them in the order they were given.

But before she was asked to repeat the items, Mom was given a math test—counting back from 100 by sevens. Mom, whom you may remember was good at math when she went to school in the 1920's and 1930's, was ripping through that one faster than anyone else in the room.

The medical personnel were laughing as they tried to keep up with her. Through learning mathematics many generations before American schoolchildren were dumbed down by the "New Math," Ella developed a life-long facility for numbers that stays strong even into her 90's. Mom was doing the subtraction in her head faster than anyone in the room could type it into a calculator. Maybe she wasn't adept at new electronic devices, but she could do the math without them.

But the best test, at least from the standpoint of pure entertainment, was a series of basic commands to determine whether Ella could understand and follow instructions. She was told to take a blank piece of paper in her right hand. She did. Then she was told to fold it in half. She did. Then she was told to throw it on the floor. Mom did as she was instructed, then looked up and asked, "Do you think I'm stupid?"

Everyone in the room cracked up, and Mom was reassured that the tests were necessary to determine if she was capable of following basic instructions. There were more items on the test, and Mom handled all of them with ease. She didn't, however, remember the correct order of the three items she was told to remember when asked about them again five minutes later.

Mom lost two points on that question, but her final score was 28 out of 30. That meant she had the mental acuity of a high school graduate seventy years her junior.

Dr. Gildersleeve noted on her diagnosis form that Mom is in "excellent health for her age with no evidence of dementia." She added that she would write a letter to that effect for the New York courts.

We were ecstatic. I had no qualms about Mom being tested by anyone, so long as the test was objective—and while I doubted many of the claims we heard from New York the test was actual proof that Mom's mind was still functioning.

But even the doctors in New York were saying that Mom did not have dementia, and as the doctors who had treated her previously began sending us her records going back several years, we found only two patterns—my brother and sister trying to convince Mom's doctors that she had dementia, and the doctors finding what Dr. Gildersleeve found.

There still was work to be done, however. We needed affidavits from her lawyers and others who were involved in helping Mom move to Connecticut. We needed to compile all the forms Mom signed so we could prepare a complete package for Jack Casey. As noted previously Jack was going to argue for dismissal on jurisdictional grounds, but there still was considerable legwork ahead of us before he went to court.

Within a few days I received a call from Dr. Gildersleeve's office that a letter on office stationery was ready for us. I picked it up that day and included with it was the doctor's CV—curriculum vitae—in essence a professional resume that showed where she received her schooling and outlining her medical experience. I was really impressed with Dr. Gildersleeve's credentials, especially noting that she possessed a wealth of experience in family practice. My wife and daughter had been going to her for a couple of years and always spoke highly of Dr. Gildersleeve.

After observing her diagnosing and otherwise treating my mother, I understood their enthusiasm. At that point I believed her thoroughness and professional skills would be deciding factors in proving Mom's competence.

When I initially spoke with Rich Rodriguez and later with Jack Casey, I felt relatively certain that my sister's lawsuit would be dismissed as soon as a competent professional got in front of the judge.

The lawsuit was bogus; anyone who read it and spent a few hours in my mother's company knew that. Rich talked it over with me at length, and when I asked what I should expect in the way of legal bills, he estimated that $3,000 should cover the costs, at most $5,000.

Mom was ripped when she heard that. She couldn't believe that even though she did nothing wrong she now was embroiled in a lawsuit that would cost her thousands of dollars. All she did was avoid commitment to a mental health facility that would have stripped her of all her rights and privileges as an American citizen.

Now, her own daughter, whom she doted on throughout their lives, turned on her, and was attempting to take control over her entire life. The lawsuit may have focused on Ella's mental condition and her finances, but there were numerous other aspects of it that proved troubling to Ella too.

For instance, Nancy was seeking the power to determine who would see her mother, and even who would speak to her mother. If Nancy won the lawsuit, and was named Guardian over Mom's affairs, a judge in another state would effectively be reaching across state lines to take away not only my mother's control over her own affairs, but also her right to have contact with other family members, friends or legal counsel.

We were gravely concerned about what would happen to Mom if she was committed, especially since she made it clear several times a day that she would only go into a facility if she was dragged kicking and screaming. And exactly what had Ella done over the course of her life to deserve such a fate?

She moved into her son's home, at the invitation of her own family members, and was settling in as a welcome and contributing member of the household. She only insisted that she retain the right to control her own finances, which she was doing all along, despite Nancy's claims otherwise.

The problem was, the judge who would decide where and how Mom would spend the rest of her life never spent so much as a second in my mother's company and we were tasked with convincing a man we never met that the allegations contained in Nancy Patrick's lawsuit were spurious. Meanwhile, the lawsuit and the ongoing preparations to fight it were taking a huge toll on Mom.

I sent an email to Jack Casey a week before the hearing on her case explaining that the lawsuit was giving Mom bad dreams about courtrooms and judges. She also felt insulted by the demand that a guardian be appointed over her and wanted Jack to push for Nancy to pay all of the legal fees, including Ella's.

Despite the stress and fear Mom was experiencing, we were amassing a huge amount of evidence to support our position. We had affidavits, letters, testimony and most of all, we had right on our side.

People filing bogus legal claims can say just about anything they want in their pleadings, especially if they don't care if there is a counter-suit. But as murky and complex as the law seems to be at times, generally speaking it is based on common sense. Sooner or later, regardless of the nature of the allegations included in the lawsuit, somebody has to sit in the witness chair, raise his hand, swear an oath to tell the truth, and expose himself to cross examination.

Sooner or later the lies face exposure and the person who tells those lies faces exposure right along with them. We had amassed a mountain of professional evidence to offset the hearsay and lies in Nancy Patrick's lawsuit.

It was our goal to have the truth placed in front of an objective judge where medical and legal evidence could be compared to my sister's allegations.

The legal bills were mounting, and Ella's health and well being were suffering as a result of her daughter's assault against her. From the time she moved in with us Ella was not alone for a single moment of the day or night any longer, and was receiving around-the-clock care and attention. We were doing everything we could to reassure her that the truth would prevail.

But when she looked outward from within our immediate family circle, Mom saw her daughter, her other son, and their offspring aligned against her. Most of them were contributing, directly or indirectly to the effort to institutionalize her against her will, and it was a devastating picture.

We wanted the case in front of a judge, and we wanted it done sooner rather than later.

Lessons Learned

1. *Get a Second Opinion. I cannot stress this enough. Not every opinion is the correct opinion. In Ella's case, the second opinion turned out to be remarkably like the first opinion, but that was not evident when she was facing a trial.*

2. *Do your own research. Do not rely on work that others have done. Double check everything.*

CHAPTER TWELVE

An Error in Judgment

The operative phrase in the preceding chapter was "objective judge."

It's nice to think that every time we go into a courtroom, the judge is just that—objective. He or she should be sitting up there at the judge's bench, all robed up like an ancient Englishman, seeing justice, yet blind to all the little tricks that some lawyers use to press their issues when they know their cases leak like a sieve.

The case of Nancy Patrick against Ella Winter was quite a training ground in the nature of the New York Supreme Court in Albany, and how the concept of objectivity was applied.

This will take a bit, but let me explain how it played out.

We gathered all the affidavits and supporting evidence, including one from Mom herself that was sworn and notarized, and another from Jack Casey, Mom's New York lawyer. Jack called Mom on a Saturday afternoon a week before his motion for dismissal was to be heard and spoke with her on the phone for well over a half-hour.

They chatted about seemingly inconsequential issues, which actually was Jack's way of insuring that Mom had a sound memory, and he used the same tactics to test her awareness as her lawyer in Connecticut.

Jack asked Mom to explain the situation regarding her daughter, and Mom gave him a complete rundown on what was happening, starting with the hospitalization and ending with the current situation on the lawsuit.

The conversation resulted in a multi-page affidavit and also provided the foundation for Jack's motion to throw the case out of court. The motion read as follows:

STATE OF NEW YORK
SUPREME COURT *COUNTY OF ALBANY*

In the Matter of the Application of

NANCY WINTER PATRICK
For the Appointment as Guardian of the Person and the Property of M. ELLA WINTER, An Alleged Incapacitated Person and for Provisional Remedies Under Mental Hygiene Law §81.23(a)

NOTICE OF MOTION TO DISMISS

SIRS or MADAMS:

Please Take Notice that upon the affirmation of JOHN T. CASEY, JR., sworn to February 14, 2009, and upon the affidavits of M. Ella Winter, sworn to February 13, 2009, and of Ronald E. Winter, sworn to February 13, 2009, as well as the affidavits of Thomas J. Sousa, Jr., sworn to February 12, 2009 (Exhibit E), and John Tuttle, sworn to February 12, 2009 (Exhibit F), and the medical evaluation of Kristin S. Gildersleeve, MD date February 6, 2009 (Exhibit G), the purported respondent, MAKING A LIMITED APPEARANCE BEFORE THE COURT to contest this Court's jurisdiction over her person and her property, will move this court at the return date of a certain Order to Show Cause, February 17, 2009, at 50 Chapel Street in the City and County of Albany, at 9:30 a.m., or as soon thereafter as counsel may be heard, for an order dismissing the Petition herein pursuant to and will

A. move to dismiss the special proceeding brought under Mental Hygiene Law §81.23(a), on the following grounds:

1. This Court lacks jurisdiction over the subject matter of the cause of action (CPLR 3211 [a][2]), i.e., her mental capacity given that she is a nonresident of New York State and not present within the state; and further that

2. This Court lacks jurisdiction over the person of M. ELLA WINTER (CPLR 3211 [a][8]), since she was not served in conformity with the Order to Show Cause; and further that

3. The pleading fails to state a cause of action (CPLR 3211 [a][7]), since there are no specific allegations necessary under MHL § 81.08 (a)(4) and (5); and further that

B. the purported respondent will also move to vacate the Temporary Restraining Order that has frozen her bank accounts so that her power of attorney Ronald E. Winter (Exhibit C) can transfer her funds to her bank accounts (Exhibit B) in Connecticut; and

C. For such other and further relief as the Court may seem just and proper, including but not limited to payment of the legal fees for the Court Evaluator (MHL § 81.09 [f]), and for reimbursement of her own attorney (MHL § 81.10 [f]) from petitioner's funds.

Yours, etc.,

JOHN T. CASEY, JR.
Attorney for Mrs. M. Ella Winter
47 Second Street
Troy, NY 12180

I got a kick out of the last paragraph where Jack moved that Nancy should have to pay Mom's legal fees. We didn't really expect the judge to grant us that one, but since Nancy had a line in her lawsuit where she wanted Mom to pay all the legal fees associated with the case, including Nancy's, we figured it was fair to give her a case of indigestion too. Jack also submitted the following affidavit in support of Mom's mental awareness after his lengthy conversation with her:

STATE OF NEW YORK
SUPREME COURT COUNTY OF ALBANY

In the Matter of the Application of
NANCY WINTER PATRICK
For the Appointment as Guardian of the Person and
the Property of M. ELLA WINTER, An Alleged Incapacitated
Person and for Provisional
Remedies Under Mental Hygiene Law §81.23(a)

AFFIRMATION IN SUPPORT OF MOTION TO DISMISS

JOHN T. CASEY, JR., being an attorney duly licensed to practice law in the Courts of the State of New York, herein swears under penalty of perjury:

1. I am retained by M. ELLA WINTER, the alleged incapacitated person ("AIP") herein, and I have discussed the various aspects of this matter, of her move to Connecticut, of her property and its whereabouts, of the power of attorney she executed January 1, 2009, and her intent to transfer her assets over to Connecticut, and I found her to be completely lucid and fully aware of her circumstances, what she has in the way of assets, where they are and where she wants them to be.

2. Mrs. Winter fully understood the import of the pending proceeding. She indicated to me that she had permanently moved to her son Ronald's home in Connecticut, on or about December 22, 2008, and has no plan or desire to return to New York State.

3. About this proceeding, Mrs. Winter told me: "If everybody had acted sensibly, we wouldn't have to have any of this." She wants her money to be moved to Connecticut so, "If I need it, I can get to it and won't have to go to Albany."

4. She clearly understood the function of a power of attorney and informed me that she had named her son Ron her new power of attorney because she was living with him, and this would be more convenient, that she had rescinded the power of attorney in favor of her daughter Nancy because she had left the Capital District. She observed wisely: "The more people you have to take care of it [the money] the more trouble you have."

5. Mrs. Winter strenuously objects to being placed in a nursing home or an assisted living situation. She indicated she is perfectly happy living with Ron, his wife and her granddaughter and is quite comfortable.

6. With this glimpse at the merits of the application, I will now address the procedural and jurisdictional deficiencies.

7. The three grounds for jurisdiction for a Mental Hygiene Law article 81 proceeding are set forth in MHL § 81.04, and petitioner has not demonstrated one. M. Ella Winter is not a resident of the state, she is not a nonresident present in the state, nor has she had a guardian appointed for her elsewhere (see, MHL § 81.18) and respectfully, this Court lacks jurisdiction over the subject matter of her capacity.

8. Without jurisdiction to adjudicate her ability to provide for her personal needs, and to determine whether she can adequately understand and appreciate the nature and consequences of managing her property, the Court cannot therefore interfere with her transfer of those assets to Connecticut and so the restraining order freezing her bank accounts must be vacated.

9. Furthermore, the order to show cause provided that the "AIP" be served personally within the state (see, CPLR 308 [1]). Mrs. Winter has lived in Connecticut since December 22, 2008 and was therefore not served pursuant to the court order. Thus, the Court lacks personal jurisdiction over her. While her bank accounts are still in the Albany area, given that the Court lacks jurisdiction over both the subject matter of her capacity and her person, and given that she has executed a valid power of attorney in favor of her son Ronald E. Winter (with the two witnesses supplying affidavits to this Court as to her capacity to grant those powers), and also given that Court lacks any jurisdiction over her property, again the restraining order granted by Judge Devine must be vacated.

10. Even if there were no jurisdictional impediment, petitioner's papers fail to state sufficient facts even to warrant a hearing. The application is devoid of medical evidence or opinion or any records to support petitioner's lay diagnosis of dementia or Alzheimer's disease. Under the "specific factual allegations" required by MHL § 81.08 (4) and (5), there are no "actual occurrences" set forth in the petition to provide a basis for the provisions of subdivision (4); nor are there any allegations as to what financial perils await Mrs. Winter absent a Court order appointing a guardian. Mrs. Winter has moved in permanently with her son, is watched around the clock by adults, has opened bank accounts, and has visited with an attorney and a doctor, both of whom submit evaluations to this Court.

11. While the petition alleges Mrs. Winter was "placed into Albany Medical Center from December 13, 2008 until December 18, 2008 for diagnosis and treatment of her dementia," no proof is offered in support of this allegation. Indeed, as her son avers in his accompanying affidavit, she suffered from dehydration (Affidavit of Ronald E. Winter, sworn to February 13, 2009 at § 9) which close monitoring of her diet has improved.

12. Even if there were no jurisdictional impediment, the petition fails to state sufficient grounds upon which relief can be granted. The petitioner fails to allege enough under MHL § 81.08 (4) and (5) to require a hearing, apart from the obvious jurisdictional issues. Notably the Court's determination must flow from a "clear and convincing" showing, and all the petition contains is conjecture, surmise and conclusory allegations by a lay person.

13. With respect to Mrs. Winter speaking with petitioner, she told me on the phone that the court proceeding has distressed her, and that she believes it advisable to wait until after it is over to speak with the petitioner so that her words don't get misconstrued.

14. Finally, since this petition is not cognizable under the law and is frivolous and vexatious, Mrs. Winter respectfully requests that the Court deny petitioner's request that attorney's fees be paid out of her money, and instead order payment of the legal fees for the Court Evaluator (MHL § 81.09 [f]), and reimbursement of her own attorney (MHL § 81.10 [f]) from petitioner's funds.

WHEREFORE, Mrs. M. Ella Winter respectfully requests that the Court dismiss the pending petition and vacate the restraining notice.

AFFIRMED AT TROY, NY
FEBRUARY 14, 2009

____

JOHN T. CASEY, JR.

Mom is not the kind of person who would just sit on her hands and let someone else do her fighting for her. In direct contradiction to the allegation in Nancy Patrick's lawsuit against her, that Mom's mental state was too far deteriorated for her to comprehend or assist in the proceedings and therefore she shouldn't go to court, Mom not only was involved in the "hands on" response to the attack on her, she wanted to meet the judge face to face.

Mom enjoyed her conversation with Jack Casey, much as she would later enjoy his courtroom demeanor, which frankly, his legal opponents probably saw as akin to facing down a Rottweiler. Jack was satisfied after talking with Mom that what everyone else was saying was true; she was completely cognizant of her surroundings and the legal issues that were swirling around her.

Following her discussion with Jack, he prepared a first draft of an affidavit to submit to the court. Mom read it, and just like her power of attorney forms that she had signed nearly two months earlier, she had changes and suggestions, which Jack read and incorporated.

The final affidavit read:

STATE OF NEW YORK
SUPREME COURT *COUNTY OF ALBANY*

In the Matter of the Application of

NANCY WINTER PATRICK

For the Appointment as Guardian of the Person and the Property of

M. ELLA WINTER,

An Alleged Incapacitated Person and for Provisional Remedies Under Mental Hygiene Law §81.23(a)

AFFIDAVIT

M. ELLA WINTER, being duly sworn, deposes and says:

1. I am the subject of this proceeding and I make this affidavit in opposition, asking the Court to dismiss the petition and vacate the restraining notice on my bank accounts so that I can transfer my funds to Connecticut.

2. I have retained JOHN T. CASEY, JR., to make a limited appearance to object to the Court's jurisdiction over me and my property, to have the petition dismissed, and to allow me, through a power of attorney granted to my son Ronald E. Winter, to move my funds over to Connecticut where I now reside. I do not submit to the jurisdiction of the Court, having permanently left New York State on or about December 22, 2008. Moreover, the Order to Show Cause was not served upon me in New York, which was required under the service provisions of the order itself, and so procedurally this Court does not have jurisdiction over me or, by deduction, over my property.

3. First of all, I am not incapacitated and I highly resent being called an "AIP," that is, an "alleged incapacitated person." I went to the hospital in December, 2008 for dehydration, and not for dementia.

4. As you will see from the affidavits filed in this application sworn by my Connecticut attorney Thomas J. Sousa, Jr., and his investigator John A. Tuttle, as well as a medical evaluation conducted by Kristin S. Gildersleeve, MD, I am in possession of all of my faculties. I can read and understand legal documents, and I know what funds I have in the bank and I am fully capable of managing them.

5. Just for information, and not in any way to respond to the allegations in the petition, I lived at Dutch Village Apartments in Menands for about 22 years until December 22, 2008. On that date, my daughter Nancy, her husband Jim and my granddaughter Courtney moved myself, my clothes, my shoes, my toiletries, my television set and my coffeemaker, my late husband's medals and American flag from his funeral, one of my favorite paintings (to hang in my new bedroom), towels and bedding including pillows and blankets to the home of my son Ronald ... . The day after I arrived in Connecticut, my daughter, her husband, my granddaughter, and possibly others immediately began cleaning out my apartment ... . They shredded and disposed of documents, made arrangements to store some of my furniture until it could be moved to Connecticut, and disposed of the rest of it. My daughter notified Dutch Village apartments that I would not be returning, and turned off most of the utilities except power. The following week, Dec. 30, 2008, my son Wilson Winter III came to Connecticut with another load of my belongings that I had requested.

6. This was not to be a temporary move, but rather is a permanent move for me. The petition speaks about my not being allowed to return home. There is literally no home for me to return to since, upon information and belief, my apartment has be re-leased, my furniture disposed of or stored, and my daughter has now gone to Court in order to put me in a nursing home.

7. I wish the Court to know that, contrary to the allegations in the petition, I can read fine, and I read the newspaper every day, I read magazines and I read music and play the piano. My eye problems have included cataracts and glaucoma, but I can still see well enough to read, and the problems I had reading in New York were simply that I needed new eyeglasses. My prescription was about 10 years old and had changed over time. That has been rectified and I now have a new pair of glasses.

8. With respect to speaking with my daughter, I have been informed that she has called, but I have chosen not to speak with her due to this court proceeding and her desire to put me in a nursing home.

9. I am now residing with my son, Ronald E. Winter, his wife and daughter, and I am most comfortable and happy with the arrangement. Contrary to the petition indicating that I am not getting care around the clock, Ron works at home and there is always someone here.

10. Rather than travel back to New York State to live in a nursing home, I am far more comfortable and better off living here with Ron and his family, and so I wish to assure the Court that even if there were not a jurisdictional problem, which there is, and the Court were to get to the merits of the application, there simply is no merit to it.

11. All I have left in New York are my various bank accounts, and I want them moved here where I can access and manage them.

ACCORDINGLY, I respectfully request that the Court dismiss the petition, thereby vacating the restraining order on my bank accounts, allowing me to move my funds to Connecticut.

Mom's affidavit also was supported by one from me, in which I took the opportunity to set the record straight on some of the falsehoods my sister had included in hers.

STATE OF NEW YORK
SUPREME COURT *COUNTY OF ALBANY*

In the Matter of the Application of

NANCY WINTER PATRICK AFFIDAVIT

For the Appointment as Guardian of the Person and the Property of

M. ELLA WINTER,

An Alleged Incapacitate Person and for Provisional Remedies Under Mental Hygiene Law §81.23(a)

RONALD E. WINTER, being duly sworn, deposes and says:

1. I am the son of M. Ella Winter, and brother to the petitioner, and I make this affidavit in opposition to the appointment of a guardian for our mother. The "AIP" is not incapacitated in any way, is completely lucid and is quite capable of making her own decisions. Instead of an assisted living facility, she presently resides with family in Connecticut, beyond the jurisdiction of the New York Courts.

2. On December 22, 2008, Jim and Nancy Patrick, along with my niece Courtney, delivered Mom to my home with the intention of her making this move permanent. Contrary to allegations in the petition, there was no secret agenda to bring Mom over here temporarily, only to take her back "home," and the proof of that is that Jim and Nancy moved her belongings from her Dutch Village apartment and canceled the lease. There is literally no "home" for Mom to go back to in New York State, and she is quite comfortable here.

3. M. Ella Winter has lived in my home ... since December 22, 2008, and she is in full possession of her faculties. She changed her address as of December 29, 2008 (Exhibit A). At our home, Ella reads the newspaper and magazines, understands what is going on around her at all times, and reads music and plays our piano.

4. I work from my home office, home school my daughter, and I hereby aver to this Court that an adult is present with Ella around the clock.

5. Since December, Ella has opened a checking account and a savings account .... On January 1, 2009, she executed a new power of attorney form naming me as her power of attorney (Exhibit C), since she is living here in Connecticut, and revoked the former power of attorney she had executed with my sister acting in that capacity (Exhibit D). She instructed me to transfer her funds to Connecticut, and I have tried to comply with that request.

6. These actions were undertaken freely and with full knowledge of their consequences, and the attorney taking her signature, Thomas J. Sousa, Jr. (Exhibit E),submits an affidavit, along with an affidavit from investigator John Tuttle (Exhibit F), as to her mental capacity when they were present at our home.

7. The petitioner makes much about Ella's signature reading "Maude Ella Winter" and not simply "M. Ella Winter." The attorney prepared the documents and then instructed Mom to sign them as the name appeared printed below the signature line. This was not a "forgery," but rather our mother executing a new power of attorney and revoking the old one according to the instructions of her attorney so I can transfer her assets over to Connecticut where she can manage them.

8. Upon receiving the petition, and in case we had to answer the merits of it, I immediately had Ella evaluated by a physician, Kristin S. Gildersleeve, MD, and I submit both her report and her CV to the Court. Dr. Gildersleeve found Mom "quite capable of making her own decisions as far as her health care and living situation, as well as financial decisions" (Exhibit G).

9. Contrary to the allegations, she was not admitted to Albany Medical Center for dementia, but rather for dehydration. Since her move to Connecticut we have been closely monitoring and adjusting my mother's diet. We have drastically reduced her intake of caffeine-laden liquids and foods ... replacing them with non-caffeinated drinks. We have sharply reduced her consumption of other foods containing caffeine including chocolate all of which were contributing to her dehydration. We have noted marked improvements in her general demeanor and alertness. She had complained of a sharp pain in her leg which she had attributed to arthritis. It now appears she was suffering from muscle cramping, which has now abated. She smiles and jokes easily, except for when she dwells on the pending court action which has made her extremely fearful for her future.

10. Aside from all this, however, I have conferred with Mr. John T. Casey, Jr., of Troy, New York about jurisdiction. Mr. Casey informs me that the papers were ordered to be served upon Mom in New York State. They were not. She has not returned to New York since December 22, 2008, and has no plans to do so. Thus, not only does the Court lack jurisdiction over Mom by virtue of her being a resident of Connecticut, the Court lacks personal jurisdiction of her due to failure to serve her as the Court, and indeed as the statute (see, Mental Hygiene Law § 81.04) require.

11. This meritless proceeding has interrupted Mom's life insofar as she is trying to transfer her funds over to her bank accounts in Connecticut. Because the Court lacks jurisdiction of Ella, it cannot reasonably keep her property from her, and so ACCORDINGLY, I respectfully request that the Court dismiss the petition and vacate the Temporary Restraining Order and award costs and attorney's fees for this frivolous action.

In addition to the affidavits from Mom, Jack Casey and me, we had additional evidence to support Ella, including affidavits from John Tuttle and Attorney Tom Sousa. I believed that both men's impressions of Mom were especially valid as evidence due to their professions and experience.

I have noted that John was about to retire after a four-decades-long investigative career in the federal government. His keen powers of observation were key to his success as an investigator and he spent considerable time in Mom's company.

Tom Sousa is not only an attorney; he is active in his community both as a veteran and as a parent, especially as a Boy Scout leader. Tom is not a man who could be compromised on the one hand, and on the other, he had taken a special interest in Elder Law. He spent hours with Ella at various times in the afternoons and evenings, and satisfied himself after myriad questions and answers that Mom was aware and contributing.

Tom Sousa's affidavit referring to their meeting when she executed the new Power of Attorney forms, and revoked Nancy's, said in part:

"It was clear to me that Ms. Winter was acting on her own and without outside influence. Ms. Winter reviewed documents, which she

commented upon, including the correction of some of those documents. Ms. Winter requested that I make several changes to the documents, which I subsequently did. These changes included her preference that I show her name as 'M. Ella Winter' in the future (as opposed to 'Maude Ella Winter' which I'd used on the original documents.)

Over the course of the time I spent with Ms. Winter I took note as to how sharp her mental functioning was. Without hesitation she recited her date of birth and social security number from memory. She asked relevant and penetrating questions about the legal documents I presented to her, and she refused to execute some of the documents until I made the changes to bring them into compliance with her desires. She was aware of the time, date, day of the week, weather conditions, fact that her birthday was approaching, etc."

Noting that he met with Mom on a second occasion to review the changes she required to the legal documents, Atty. Sousa noted, *"Once again I was impressed with her mental alertness and reasoning."*

When Mom executed her Power of Attorney documents, John Tuttle agreed to stop by the house to witness her signature. But, being a long-time investigator, John listened carefully to the discussions she was having with Atty. Sousa.

In February, John also provided an affidavit, noting that he served for more than four decades in law enforcement, and by then had retired from the United States Office of Personnel Management/ Federal Investigative Service Division.

John also stated: *"On January 1, 2009 ... I spent approximately one and one half hours with Ms. Winter, during which time I listened to her express her concerns and desires to Attorney Sousa.*

I have also seen Ms. Winter on three other occasions. On each of those occasions I spent at least one hour with her. At no time have I ever seen anything that would cause me to doubt or question her competency. She is always very well groomed, mentally alert, and very much in touch with her surroundings and the events transpiring around her."

After John's and Tom's affidavit's we applied what I considered to be the icing on the cake—Dr. Gildersleeve's assessment of Mom's capabilities after she took the mini-mental status exam.

Dr. Gildersleeve included the results of the exam which were packaged with documents explaining in detail what each score level meant in terms of abilities or impairment.

Then on her personal office stationery, dated February 6, 2009, Dr. Gildersleeve wrote:

Re: M. Ella Winter DOB 1/4/17

To Whom It May Concern:

On 2/5/09 I did an evaluation of M. Ella Winter and found her to be in excellent health at 92 years of age. Mini-mental status exam revealed a score of 28/30. She was well groomed with normal affect and behavior.

It is my opinion that she is quite capable of making her own decisions as far as her health care and living situation, as well as financial decisions.

Sincerely,
Kristin S. Gildersleeve, M.D.
Board Certified Family Practitioner

After everything was filed, Jack attended a hearing on February 17, 2009. At that hearing, as he later related it, Atty. Rowlands claimed to know Mom—it turns out he was the lawyer who witnessed Mom's signature several years earlier when Nancy had her sign a Power of Attorney form. Rowlands said he had observed Mom's mental state and it was steadily deteriorating.

However, Mom said it must have been an unremarkable meeting because she didn't remember him. And, like so many other allegations that came out of New York, she was not at all happy with someone she really didn't know, claiming that she was incompetent when no one in New York had examined her—except two doctors who had been treating her for years, neither of whom agreed with that assessment.

Regardless, Jack Casey said that Rowlands again failed to present a shred of medical evidence to back up his or Nancy Patrick's claims.

But the judge didn't rule just then. He said he was going to take a couple of weeks and review all the evidence. It shouldn't have been all that difficult, the only real evidence was what we presented, otherwise there was none.

New York Supreme Court Judge John Egan scheduled another court date for March 6, 2009, at which time he would issue a ruling in the case. That meant another three weeks of waiting and worrying for Mom.

Adding to the waiting and worrying was the barrage of phone calls coming from Nancy, Skeeter and Courtney. I told Mom about all of them, and I kept about half of them to use as evidence if needed.

Skeeter's messages were nonsense, and Courtney always had some sort of tragedy to relay to her grandmother—an illness, a bad day at work, something else that went wrong in her life. It seemed that there was a deliberate effort to depress Ella and make her mental outlook even darker than it was, considering what she was going through at the hands of her daughter and other family members.

But the most ridiculous and transparent messages came from Nancy. She was uniformly vitriolic, spouting bile and hatred, alleging that Mom was being kept in the dark.

But the most ludicrous, hypocritical and outright laughable message of them all came on February 15, at noontime. I have to reproduce it for you here, because it is just too good not to share with others.

"Hello Mom, it's Nancy, First of all I have to apologize for all they're putting you through over there. I can't even believe that somebody would make you go through what they're putting you through.

"You have to know and you have to believe I would never, ever put you in a nursing home. We've discussed it before, you knew it was never going to happen, and you knew that we were looking for places for you, where you'd be safe, and happy. And I'm so sorry for what they're doing to you.

"If you can call me, please call me, because I want to talk to you and I want to tell you that it's all a bunch of lies that they're feeding you."

Wait, wait before you start laughing and can't stop. What was it Nancy's lawsuit said under the **PERSONAL POWERS SOUGHT** section?

Yes, right there at paragraph 9 *"arrange for her admission to a skilled nursing facility or residential care facility."*

And as my brother Wilson so helpfully pointed out way back in December, you can't allege that someone has Alzheimer's and think even for a second that they will be allowed to reside in anything except a home with around-the-clock nursing care.

Lies? In Connecticut? No. In New York certainly. In New York constantly. But not in Connecticut.

Can you believe that? Nancy was either totally in denial, or simply unwilling to believe that Mom could sit down at the kitchen table, put on the new pair of glasses we had purchased—the first new pair she had had in years despite several operations on her eyes—and read the lawsuit!

Mom would go back to certain pages over and over, noting that Nancy said she couldn't do her own checkbook; noting that Nancy said her mind was shot and she couldn't understand or participate in the proceedings against her; noting that Nancy wanted to take all of her money and put it into an account bearing only Nancy's name; noting that Nancy falsely claimed she was treated for Alzheimer's and dementia; noting that Nancy wanted to put her on Medicaid; noting that Nancy wanted total control of her "social environment"; noting that Nancy was taking her to court and wanted Ella to pay all of Nancy's legal bills in addition to her own; and most of all noting that Nancy wanted to place her in an Alzheimer's facility against her will.

And Nancy had the unmitigated gall to say she couldn't believe what we were doing to Mom in our house.

Let's see. We helped Mom move into a loving and supportive family environment so she wouldn't have to go into a nursing home. We helped her regain control over a portion of her finances and were fighting to help her regain control of the rest. We significantly reduced her monthly outlay, took her to medical, dental and eye doctor appointments.

We discovered gaps in her nutrition and changed her diet to ensure that she was getting proper nutrients every day. We found issues with her eyesight that were not being addressed and we addressed them; we found issues with her health that were not being addressed and we addressed them. That message as much as anything else showed Nancy Patrick's mental state.

I told Mom about each and every one of these messages, and I could see that it both hurt and angered her. I wrestled with the moral dilemma of not telling Mom, and then having Nancy, her lawyers and Judge Egan accuse me of manipulation.

In the end, I figured it was better that Mom know what was going on, so she could make informed decisions about it. But I didn't like it, and vowed that as soon as the legal issues were resolved we would put an end to the daily harassment from New York, Florida and Boston.

In the meantime we waited for March 6th. It came a day early. Not March 6th, but rather Judge Egan's decision. He ruled against us!

Mom couldn't believe it, Jack Casey couldn't believe it and we couldn't believe it.

Jack said the judge ruled against our mountain of evidence because:

1.) Dr. Gildersleeve's statement on Mom's mental health did not include a document indicating she swore to it, despite it coming over her original signature on her office stationery; and

2.) Even if Mom was competent when she was examined by Dr. Gildersleeve, that didn't prove she was competent when she changed her address in December.

Casey showed convincingly and overwhelmingly that the New York courts had no jurisdiction over Mom one way or the other, that proper procedures were not followed when Mom was served, and that Nancy Patrick and her lawyer did not produce one shred of evidence other than pure hearsay to support the allegations in the suit.

Jack was understandably upset with the outcome of the hearing and told me so. He firmly believed the judge was in error and despite the ruling, that the New York courts did not have jurisdiction over Mom.

He also found it inconceivable that Nancy's lawyers provided no medical evidence whatsoever to back their claims, and yet Judge Egan dismissed the results of Mom's mental test and the letter from Dr. Gildersleeve as irrelevant because the doctor was not sworn in. We believed that her signature on office stationery would be sufficient, and certainly could have had provided a sworn copy.

I wrote in earlier chapters that I spent much of my journalism career involved with the courts, either covering cases or covering the issues that became cases. When I heard the decision I was still shocked, but in my mind we would just have to go to the next step.

Mom said ever since the case was first filed that my sister and brother-in-law were too well known socially in the Albany area and that it was likely Jim Patrick had some kind of an in with the legal system. I agreed that it was likely, but also told Mom that the law is the law and at some point the law and not politics nor socializing would prevail.

She was not convinced.

Nonetheless I told Jack that Egan's decision sounded like that part of the movie ***My Cousin Vinny*** where the actor Joe Pesci, playing the part of defense Atty. Vinny Gambini makes a compelling argument as to why the judge should not allow a surprise expert witness to testify until the defense has been given suitable time to scrutinize his credentials and possible testimony.

The late, great actor Fred Gwinn, playing the part of the judge, leans forward convivially, looks down from the bench and intones, "Mr. Gambini, That is a lucid, intelligent, well-thought-out objection."

"Overruled."

Yeah, I considered Egan's decision to be just that—a throw away laugh line in an old movie.

Egan was supposed to look at all the evidence and first and foremost assign weight to that part of the evidence presented by Nancy Patrick that showed someone, somewhere, with a medical degree and a history of examining Ella Winter, was claiming that she was incompetent.

He was supposed to review the part of the lawsuit that said Mom was diagnosed with Alzheimer's and dementia and compare it to the medical records that would support those claims. He was supposed to give Ella Winter her constitutionally guaranteed presumption of innocence until guilt is proven, or presumption of competence until incompetence is proven.

Instead, he said *Ella Winter* had to prove with a preponderance of the evidence that she was competent not incompetent. And when she did prove it, he found an excuse to throw out that evidence. Casey said Egan claimed he wanted to see Ella himself and judge for himself whether she was competent. You'll have to excuse me for taking the position that the New York State Supreme Court system in Albany showed itself to be totally lacking in objectivity that day. In fact from that point on I considered Judge John Egan to be just another one of the bullies who were tormenting my mother.

Late that night, after we told Mom what transpired, we heard a noise downstairs and went down to investigate. Mom was sitting up in her room at 2 a.m. with the lights on, looking around fearfully at every noise.

"What are you doing up at this hour?" we asked her. Mom said she feared that someone would be breaking in at any minute to force her back to Troy and an Alzheimer's ward. "I told you Jim Patrick had connections," she intoned darkly.

We tried unsuccessfully to convince her to go back to bed, that she was safe. But she wouldn't hear of it.

She looked over her shoulder and said quietly, "I'm waiting for the other shoe to drop."

Lessons Learned

1. Expect setbacks. The American legal system works but it is not perfect. The judge in this case may have believed he had the best interests of Ella Winter at heart, or that he needed to see for himself what she was like. What he couldn't see was the impact his decisions were having on Ella. Until he saw her in person he was dealing in abstracts. His decision was discouraging but we pressed on because we knew we were in the right. Expect setbacks, but don't get discouraged when they occur.

CHAPTER THIRTEEN

A Genteel Sufficiency—Appeal to Common Sense

When Ella first arrived in Connecticut she was very concerned about her diet. She gained weight in her later years, eventually topping the scales in the 140 pounds plus area.

I know, that's not a lot of weight, but remember she also topped out at 4 feet, 11 inches and suffered a minor heart attack in May 2003. Four years later she was put on a cholesterol lowering drug that gave her unwanted side affects, including lowered potassium and other essential nutrients, and also may have contributed to her dehydration. Ella eventually told the doctor, in spring 2008, that she wasn't going to take that medicine any longer. But she still was very concerned about her weight.

In Connecticut one of our first concerns and the focus of our initial efforts was Mom's nutrition. We were told that she suffered from dehydration, and later would find that there was much more to her ailments, but that is where we started.

We monitored her breakfasts, lunches and dinners to insure that they were balanced meals and that she was receiving adequate non-caffeinated liquids. Dinners quickly became a focal point of our day, the one time we all were together in one place.

Ella really enjoys dinner time, as we all do, but she worried that she would see a weight gain again. We impressed upon her that the meals were balanced, her caloric intake was below the amount that would cause a weight increase, and that we could adjust things as necessary.

Only after she visited the doctor several times, weighed in each time, and realized that she initially lost about eight pounds, and then held steady, did Ella begin to relax. But in the meantime, especially at dinner time, when she felt that she had eaten enough, Ella would sit back and state "I believe I have had a genteel sufficiency."

It was an old time phrase (it ends "any more would be superfluity," but Mom stopped using the end of the verse long ago) from the days when a lady would be ever so careful not to overeat, but also was walking a fine line between that extreme and insulting the hostess by not eating enough. "A genteel sufficiency" was the code word that you had eaten enough. That phrase surfaced again a few days after Judge Egan ruled that he would be the ultimate arbitrator of Ella's fate.

She was in a terrible state after receiving the news. Jack Casey was still shaking his head over Egan's decision and told us he believed Egan had far overstepped his bounds as a judge, essentially ignoring the law. Jack asked for permission to appeal Egan's ruling and after several days Ella decided we should.

We talked over the legal issues and especially the absence of any medical information from Nancy's side. Ella spoke often of Jim Patrick's social and business connections in the Albany area and insisted they were a determining factor in the judge's decision.

Jim's family was very well known in Troy where they owned a Chevrolet dealership for at least three generations, and where his father was in banking. Jim started out as the manager of his father's used car lot, but he eventually owned his own dealerships in neighboring communities. In time, Jim left the car business opting instead for a career in professional finance. Mom's certainty that his contacts aided Nancy's attacks arose repeatedly in our conversations. But after she talked about it for several days, slept on it, stayed awake at night chewing it over and worrying about it, her mood changed.

"I can't believe I'm letting her control me like this," Mom finally said, adding, "I believe I've had a genteel sufficiency."

With that she gave approval to Jack's filing an appeal and he went ahead with the preparations.

Within a week of Judge Egan's decision Mom filed a new affidavit with the court stating:

Personally appeared, M. Ella Winter, who having been duly sworn, deposes and says that:

1. I am over the age of eighteen (18) years and believe in the obligation of an oath.

2. I presently live (in) Connecticut, and have lived at this address since December 22, 2008. I moved to Connecticut from New York and intend this move to be permanent. I do not plan to return to New York.

3. On December 29, 2008 I changed my address with the United States Post Office. Attached is a copy of the Official Mail Forwarding Change of Address Order (PS Form 3575).

4. On January 1, 2009 I changed my address with the Department of the Treasury Internal Revenue Service. Attached is a copy of the Change of Address (Form 8822).

5. I changed my address with the United States Office of Personnel Management, attached is a letter dated January 5, 2009 acknowledging the change.

6. I changed my address with the Social Security Administration, attached is a letter dated January 13, 2009 acknowledging the change.

I have opened a local bank account in Connecticut … .

I have changed the address for my (credit) Card. Attached is a copy of the monthly statement that will be due on February 12, 2009.

9. I have registered to vote in Connecticut. Attached is a copy of my State of Connecticut Mail-In Voter Registration form.

10. I have changed my address with my health insurance company. Enclosed is a copy of a statement from Blue Cross that was mailed to me on January 9, 2009.

11. I have moved out of my old apartment in New York. Attached is a copy of my final utility bill from NationalGrid for the New York apartment. This bill was mailed to me in Connecticut at my new address.

12. I have obtained new health care providers in Connecticut, to include a family doctor …; a Dentist …; and an optometrist … . Enclosed are registration forms I filled out with these providers. I have also requested that my former health care providers in New York forward my records to Connecticut.

I am 92 years of age and would like the pending legal action to be resolved as soon as possible.

I respectfully request that the Court grant a preference, so my appeal of Judge Egan's decision and order can be brought on expeditiously, in order that I might avoid any more unnecessary expenses.

M. Ella Winter

Subscribed and sworn to before me this 12th day of March, 2009.

At this juncture the issue of legal fees became of primary importance. We had anticipated spending several thousand dollars, perhaps five thousand at the utmost, but with Judge Egan's ruling going against us, a whole new world of billing opened up.

First, instead of receiving notice that Nancy Patrick's lawsuit was dismissed and the issue was resolved, at least in New York, we were now facing further legal action on that front, simultaneous with an appeal of that decision.

Jack Casey was proceeding on both fronts, each of which would require research, court costs and naturally additional billing.

But Nancy also was demanding that Mom pay her legal bills, as well as those of the court evaluator. We were now facing an enormous legal expense, which we did not anticipate.

When we offered to have Mom move in with us rather than being forced into a nursing home, we hadn't anticipated any expense for legal work. I honestly believed that as long as I didn't ask my brother or sister for any money, which I never did, they would be happy that Mom had a home with family and would not have to be placed in a nursing home.

With Judge Egan's ruling going against us, and no objective standard by which to understand his decision we had no way of knowing how long the case would progress or how far we would have to appeal before Mom finally got justice. In a letter to Mom after all was said and done, Nancy claimed that Judge Egan had voiced suspicion about the quickness with which Mom's accounts were transferred to Connecticut. The judge never said that to us, and Jack Casey never related anything like that to us. According to Nancy, the movements were swift and the judge was suspicious she said. Actually, that was her comment to the court evaluator, and we were never told of any questions or suspicions emanating from Judge Egan.

Apparently my sister also thought she possessed some form of mental telepathy such that when she had a thought, it was instantaneously transmitted to Judge Egan's brain.

When Mom transferred her accounts to Connecticut, she didn't think it was done quickly at all.

There is an old adage that time is relative and a minute of passion goes by in a blink, while a minute standing barefoot on a hot stove feels like an eternity. I use that adage because when Mom talked to the court evaluator she told him and he reported, that she felt as though she was on a hot stove.

Nearly a month passed from the time Mom arrived in Connecticut until the money that had been in her New York checking account was finally available to her in Connecticut. Mom spent the month standing barefoot on a stove. Nancy's refusal to return her checkbook to her occupied Mom's every waking moment and conversation from Christmas to New Year's Day. She talked about it often; she brought it up morning, noon and night. By the time I first sent an email to Atty. Tom Sousa asking him if he could help Mom on the Power of Attorney issue, and sent another email to my brother-in-law asking that my brother bring Mom's checkbook to Connecticut with him, I had been hearing about it nonstop for nearly a week.

If I had had enough of the subject, you can only imagine how it was affecting Ella. It was her checkbook, her money, and her control over her own life. To Ella, this was not a speedy process at all, but one that was dragging on interminably.

That Nancy accused us out of the blue of some alternative agenda only served to make me suspicious of her motives. My suspicions were initiated by, and bolstered by, the various claims in Nancy's lawsuit — starting with the lie that Ella had been treated for Alzheimer's. Her claims progressed to the numerous paragraphs where Nancy was petitioning to take all of Mom's assets and put them in Nancy's name and only Nancy's name, in conjunction with the final indignity, the demand that Mom pay all of the legal bills associated with the case.

But in both the long and short term, the fact that we moved immediately to get Mom's bank accounts back in her control ***after*** she rescinded Nancy's Power of Attorney, proved to be the saving factor in her ability to defend herself against the assault from New York.

Mom worked primarily with two banks in New York—First Niagara in Troy, and Key Bank in Menands.

First Niagara proved to be the quintessential professionally run bank. I sent them a letter on Mom's behalf, they called Mom and confirmed that she was not only aware of, but in agreement with the effort to transfer her funds to her new bank in Connecticut. (This included asking Mom a series of security questions which, of course, she answered correctly.)

Once the identity and security issues were resolved, First Niagara Bank personnel moved decisively to help Mom transfer her funds to her new bank. But even then, Mom's money was not available to her until late January—in fact, until after Nancy filed suit and we were served.

The first issue that was discussed after we absorbed the myriad allegations in the lawsuit was the question of how we would pay the legal bills. As I pointed out earlier, I had contacted Bob Soloyna, and on his advice contacted Rich Rodriguez.

Rich and I discussed the lawsuit in depth, and he believed, as did every single objective attorney I ever discussed it with, that the suit would be thrown out as meritless. Based on that belief, we also believed we could successfully fight it for the previously mentioned $5,000 or less.

Thus, we discussed and dismissed the concept of taking out a loan. It was a possibility we kept as an option, but personal loans carry very high interest rates, and the last thing we wanted to do in the middle of a terrible economy was to encumber additional debt.

But once again, Ella stepped up, showing that combination of feistiness, determination and independence that has marked her entire life. Once she had control over her own finances, Ella pointed out that she had more than enough to pay her own way in the legal arena, since her monthly outlay was far less than what she had been spending in New York. By the time we contacted Jack, sent him a copy of the lawsuit, and he had decided what he would need as a retainer, Ella was comfortable that she could hold her own.

In retrospect, Ella's regaining control over her finances was the key to her ability to fight the courts and her family in New York. If she had not moved her money when she did, she would have been at their mercy.

Not only was this the key to fighting against her daughter on an equal footing in the Supreme Court, but her financial independence also gave Ella the ability to take the fight to the Appellate Court.

Jack set to work on the appeal immediately, first filing notice of our intent, and then going to work on the actual appeal. Jack was again confident of our legal footing, and felt that he could successfully argue the law, which in the Appellate Court is supposed to trump emotion.

We now were well into March and Judge Egan set March 27 as a date for a formal hearing on my sister's petition to be named Guardian over Mom. We still were getting daily messages from New York, and Boston, and I was still keeping the best of them for evidence.

For example, on March 11, Nancy called, and after noting the day and time of the call—don't tell me these weren't being recorded on the other end too, please—she went into the usual song and dance ***"I'm sorry you're being so controlled, but I know eventually, you'll be able to get through to me. I love you Mom."***

As usual, I passed the message on to Mom and as usual, she couldn't believe the level of manipulation behind it. Here she was, fighting for her very life, perfectly capable of making a phone call anytime she wanted, and in fact, *making* calls whenever she wanted. But she wasn't calling those who were involved in the lawsuit against her, regardless of how directly or indirectly, and Nancy's messages were a perfect example of why Mom felt that way.

Again on March 16, Nancy called after a barrage of calls the preceding days from both her and Courtney to tell Mom that Courtney was sick. The messages were passed on, and Mom sent out a get well card to her granddaughter, a reasonable compromise when you consider that in less than two weeks, her granddaughter would be driving to Albany to testify against her grandmother.

This again was a classic: ***Hi Mom, It's Nancy, it's about 10 after 9 on Monday. We're back home now.***

We went over and cooked about a week's worth of meals for Courtney yesterday. She's starting to feel a little better, she's going to try to go to work today.

Michelle called her and did know the remedy she was looking for from you and she was disappointed that her grandmother couldn't call her with it, but we understand that you're not able to act like an adult over there and you have to be told what to do. I'm sorry and as I said, we're going to straighten it out as soon as we can.

The remedy my sister was making such a big deal about was combining a teaspoon of honey and a teaspoon of lemon to make a sore throat feel better. Courtney left a message asking what it was—***"something about honey and lemon?"***

Mom's response was, "Well if she knows that much, then she has the recipe." But it really wasn't about the recipe, it was about control and manipulation and Mom was just too smart for the lot of them.

Also, if you are a member of the electronic generation that we hear so much about, and you are a college graduate who studied abroad, you presumably have the ability to turn on your computer, link to the Internet and do a search for a honey and lemon sore throat recipe. I did, and here's what I found:

Web Search Results

1 - 10 of about 18,200 for honey and lemon sore throat recipe.

Yeah, that's right! A couple of clicks on the computer and I found 18,200 returns for a honey and lemon sore throat recipe. The third one on the first page was a video that even showed how to make it, with sound and everything! What a breakthrough!

What was especially hilarious about this period was that after Courtney received the get well card from Mom, which Mom signed *Grandma Ella*, Nancy called and criticized Ella's signature! Nancy claimed that Courtney was *"concerned"* about Mom's signature, and *"she thinks it's really disrespectful. I agree with her."* There was no way to please that group, but on the other hand, no one in Connecticut was the least bit interested in pleasing them anyway. It worked out very well that way.

As the planning and execution of the appeal was progressing, there was one nagging issue that continued to confound Ella. I have mentioned that approximately sixty percent of her savings were in the Key Bank, and that Ella dealt with the Menands, New York branch. We sent inquiries to Key Bank in Menands at the same time that we sent inquiries and documentation to First Niagara Bank.

Unlike the professional response from First Niagara, Mom started getting a ration of disrespect from Key Bank nearly immediately. Mom asked me to handle the transfer of her funds in Key Bank to her Connecticut accounts, the same as First Niagara, but right off the bat Key Bank told me they wouldn't accept a Power of Attorney form that was sent by fax—after they gave me the fax number and said to send it over that way.

Then they said they wanted original forms. This meant that Mom had to get new forms from Tom Sousa, sign them, and have them notarized. We ended up doing several sets of the forms just in case any other organizations or institutions decided to follow Key Bank's lead.

All this time we were dealing with the manager and assistant manager at the Key Bank Menands branch.

Then we were told that the funds couldn't be released because Judge Devine ordered them frozen, which really stunned me because there was no evidence or testimony of any kind, and how a judge could just freeze someone's bank accounts on the say so of someone else was appalling. They claimed there was a Temporary Restraining Order on Mom's accounts.

But when Judge Egan issued his ruling on March 5, he said that Mom's accounts were not legally frozen, that Judge Devine had not made any such order and he ruled that Key Bank should release her money immediately.

Key Bank refused. We called Jack Casey, he called Key Bank's lawyer, and their lawyer agreed that Mom's money should be released. Jack said the Menands Branch manager and assistant manager were told to release Mom's funds.

Then they refused to talk with us. I called, Mom called. I talked and the assistant manager said she couldn't talk about Mom's accounts. I told her she didn't have to say anything, just release the money as she was told.

Mom talked to the branch manager and got the same run-around. Then they sent us to customer service who said Mom should be able to access her accounts no problem. We called back to Menands, and they referred us back to customer service, refusing meanwhile to even speak with us other than to say they were sending us to customer service.

Oh, and the really great one. The Key Bank Menands branch sent Mom a letter in March back-dated to January saying they were freezing her funds and if she wanted any more information on what was happening to her money to call — Atty. Richard Rowlands, Nancy Patrick's lawyer!

And when Mom called them to ask the meaning of that, they told her to call Rowlands!

Unfortunately, Mom never got control of the money in Key Bank while the legal issues remained. It was not for lack of trying. We dealt with an array of people going all the way to the corporate offices in Ohio, and the end result was a continual runaround.

I emailed Jack Casey telling him I had called Key Bank to transfer my mother's funds to her Connecticut bank, but when I got through to the office of the woman who was his contact at the corporate level—shortly before 3 p.m.—I was told she had left for the day.

So I called first thing the next morning. The representative I spoke with said she had no knowledge of Jack speaking with Key Bank's lawyers in New York, adding that she still had not received notification from the Menands branch that I was legitimately Power of Attorney for Mom. I told her, for the second time, that Key Bank's Customer Service section had me in their computers as of Tuesday as POA.

But the rep said her computers don't talk to the rest of the computers in the system so she had to get confirmation from—you guessed it—Menands. But she said Menands wasn't forthcoming so she was "reaching out" to someone at the district level, whatever that means.

Even though she had been working on Mom's case for three days, the Menands branch refused to confirm that they have an original POA form, signed and notarized, as well as the letter rescinding POA for Nancy Patrick, going all the way back to Jan. 15, 2009, again signed and notarized.

Jack went the extra mile in trying to loosen Key Bank's grip on Mom's money. He was on them as continually, much the same as he was on Albany Medical Center, which, like Key Bank, went the extra mile to deny my mother what was rightfully hers—in the case of Albany Med, her own records.

But Key Bank just sent us around in unending circles, and even gave no heed to directives from Supreme Court judges in New York. The hassles with Key Bank and Albany Medical Center were unnecessary obstacles to Mom winning her freedom, and as the letter from Key Bank showed, Nancy Patrick and her lawyer were at the core.

Nonetheless, while the legal and financial issues continued unresolved, we did make several attempts to cut straight to the heart of the lawsuit and resolve it as quickly as possible to spare Mom the continual stress.

Jack Casey relayed to us on several occasions going back into February that Judge Egan wasn't satisfied with claims of Mom's competency because he personally had not seen or interviewed her. We were told that the law doesn't require the judge to examine Mom; it requires petitioners like Nancy Patrick to provide evidence that proves, or at least supports the claim, of her incompetence. But Judge Egan was calling the shots and pulling the strings and I made several offers to resolve his uncertainty.

In the meantime, Judge Devine had appointed a court "evaluator" to the case, who also was making representations that he wanted to interview Mom.

I suggested early on that we would be more than happy to bring Mom to New York where the judge and the evaluator could both have their interviews—on two conditions: the first was that Jack be with Mom in both instances so she would have legal representation; and, two, that the New York courts guarantee Mom's safe passage back to Connecticut once the interviews were over.

But despite all the posturing and representations of acting in Mom's best interests, we could not get a guarantee of safe passage. This became even more of an issue for us after Judge Egan ruled that he had jurisdiction, because to put it bluntly, not one lawyer I spoke with agreed with him.

Also, on two occasions Nancy and Courtney tried to arrange a "meeting" with Mom where they would take her out of Connecticut to be in their company for several days.

Nancy said she wanted to take Mom to say goodbye to the doctor who had been treating her glaucoma. Why on earth she would have to do that is anyone's guess, but the claim that it would take three days was ridiculous.

If you recall, Nancy neither offered to have Mom move in with her, nor had a place for Mom to stay, except for upstairs bedrooms that would have been next to impossible for Mom to access. So if Mom was going to New York for three days, in the company of my sister who was suing to force her into an Alzheimer's home, just where was Mom supposed to stay? I have my suspicions and they don't include my sister's house.

After that plan fell through, Nancy's daughter Courtney called and left a message that she wanted Mom to accompany her and Nancy to Pennsylvania for a few days in February to attend my niece's birthday. I had the distinct feeling that if I had a complete brain meltdown and agreed to that idea, the road from Connecticut to Pennsylvania would run right through Albany. We didn't agree to either proposal, but we were highly suspicious of any overtures that involved my sister taking custody of Mom and driving away. It simply was not going to happen.

Thus, the judge's ruling on the jurisdiction and improper service issues just heightened our fears that something was amiss in Albany. I believed that if Mom was able to sit down with the judge and the evaluator one-on-one, they would have no recourse but to declare her competent and dismiss my sister's lawsuit.

There was another reason why we offered to bring Mom to Albany for an evaluation by the judge. Money.

Every facet of the case my sister brought against Mom was causing unforeseen difficulties, and dealing with them was running up the legal bill. We also did not have a ruling on Nancy's effort to make Mom pay her legal fees and the court evaluator's fees. The bill was already far more than we expected, and an appeal was pending. We were hoping to avoid the hearing that Judge Egan scheduled for the end of March, and Jack was still working to that end too.

We didn't fear Mom meeting and talking with the judge and in fact were encouraging it. But a day in court is a huge expense, and by now we were looking at a bill that was fast approaching $10,000.

Driving to New York and meeting with the judge and court evaluator would save Mom thousands of dollars. We were confident of the outcome if we could convince them to agree to the arrangements.

Toward the end of March we received a message from Nancy's lawyer that had been passed through Jack. If we agreed to come to

New York they would agree not to ***serve*** her while she was there! Wow! What an offer!

We looked at each other and just broke out laughing at that one. Mom ***already*** was served. We weren't worried about her being ***served***; we were worried about her being taken into custody by the Albany New York Supreme Court system.

We were worried about court officials or thugs spiriting her away to an Alzheimer's facility where it is a safe bet she would have stayed no matter what we did to free her. I guess I should be royally offended that Nancy and her legal team thought they were so smart, and we were so stupid, that they could try to parse words that way and sucker us in. I haven't lost any sleep over their arrogance though. All along I've just considered the source.

Suddenly, two issues arose simultaneously, almost as if the principals in New York had been talking with each other, which brought an end to the impasse.

We received word that the appeals court judge agreed to hear Jack's appeal on Mom's behalf. But he wouldn't hear it until two months after the March 27 date for Mom's scheduled hearing before Judge Egan, and he would not order a stay— postponement—of the hearing.

And, at virtually the same time, we received an email from Jack, telling us that Atty. Chad Balzer, the court evaluator, was threatening that if we didn't allow him to come to Connecticut to interview Mom, he would get an order forcing the visit on us.

I did not and do not understand why it had to be done that way—except that the court evaluator charged us $300 per hour for nearly four hours of driving on the scenic Massachusetts Turnpike and associated highways in Connecticut. Not bad work if you can get it.

Naturally we agreed, but once again we believed that the Albany New York Supreme Court system was stacking the deck against Mom.

Lessons Learned

1. Maintain control over your finances. Keep a separate account if necessary just in case of emergencies — such as unanticipated legal issues. And don't shortchange yourself. Legal fees mount quickly and the initial stages of a case may not go your way.

2. Don't expect help from places that have a stake in your case. They may have policies that require them to do nothing until they get new orders, or they may just have an attitude. Either way, you won't be helped until new and final orders arrive from someone in a high enough post to make the new orders stick. Press your case, but expect delays where there should be none, and expect no help where help should be given.

3. Conserve. Try to find ways to keep the costs down. If you can drive to the lawyer do it, rather than the other way around; if you can do research, do it; if it is not an emergency use mails rather than faxing; use the Internet and email if possible. Think conservatively.

CHAPTER FOURTEEN

The Evaluator

The evaluator assigned to Mom's case by New York Supreme Court Judge Eugene Devine was a young and personable lawyer named Chad Balzer.

Jack Casey spoke with him several times, but we had no direct contact with him in January, February and most of March.

On Saturday, March 21, Atty. Balzer called us in Connecticut and said he wanted to interview Mom the following day in our home. I told him we had no problem with that and asked him what time he would be coming over. I also pointed out that we offered to have a meeting with him in New York several times over the previous month with no response. After discussing the length of the trip from Albany to where we live in Connecticut, he said he would leave his office at 1 p.m. and be at our house around 3:30 p.m.

I told Mom that she was going to have a visitor the next day, but didn't play it up much. She was experiencing far too many sleepless nights over the case and I didn't want to cause her any more stress than was absolutely necessary.

I told Atty. Balzer that we were going to brunch Sunday morning, and would be back sometime between noon and 1 p.m. I said we'd expect him at 3:30 p.m.

We went to brunch as planned the next morning, and arrived back at the house at 12:45 p.m. I was shocked to find a message on my voice mail from Atty. Balzer, saying he arrived early and I should contact him on his cell phone. I did, and he told me he was driving around our neighborhood, checking it out. Make what you will of that, I have several theories, but I'm keeping them to myself.

Mom, meanwhile, sat down at the piano to play some of her hymns. Mom's recovery from the aches and pains caused by low potassium in her diet was rapid as soon as her vitamin and mineral intakes were adjusted. Most of what had been considered arthritis turned out to be muscle cramping due to the potassium deficiency she suffered before moving in with us. When we stabilized her diet, the aches and pains disappeared and the first thing she did in response was to begin playing the piano again. She sat down to play most days, and was at it when Atty. Balzer arrived. I met him in the driveway and walked him into the house, bringing him over to the piano where I introduced him to Mom.

She greeted him graciously and we all sat down at the kitchen table. Mom was obviously surprised, a bit concerned, and not exactly her usual confident self. Nonetheless she engaged him willingly, and answered his questions as best as she could.

I realized that Mom was getting some of her dates wrong, and shook my head at it a couple of times. This tendency to become confused was apparent when Mom was under high levels of stress and although she was trying her best to appear relaxed, in truth Mom was wired pretty tight inside.

I realized some months before that Mom was struggling with all the new information she had to process in her new home. Back in New York, Mom lived within a roughly twenty-mile radius of Center Brunswick for about eighty-three of her ninety-two years.

She went to the same doctors, dentists, grocery stores, and hairdresser for years. She could get you from Point A to Point B with relative ease, pretty much anywhere east of Albany. But in Connecticut she had to learn a new address in a community that has three distinct sections, two zip codes and two post offices. For virtually the entirety of the time I lived in Connecticut, either Dad or I drove when they came to visit and we went somewhere. Mom was free to observe the scenery or just talk with Jennifer or my children, without having to know where she was or how to get to and from our homes.

But now Mom was learning by total immersion, and virtually everything around her was new. She had to learn the names of two new medical doctors in addition to their office staff, she also had a glaucoma doctor, a retina specialist, a new dentist, two lawyers, a new drug store, a new grocery store—three of them in fact—and a new hairdresser. She lived in a location that had six other communities within a ten-minute drive in virtually any direction.

She was meeting new people every single day, attempting to remember who they were and how they related to her. In the meantime she was trying to remember every facet of her ninety-two years of life. If Ella was tired, or over-stressed she could become forgetful. But unlike an Alzheimer's patient, she knew if she forgot something and it bothered her. When she did forget something, she would keep working on it until it came back to her.

A classic example involves a friend of mine who attended Mom's birthday on January 4th. He told Mom of his love for riding motorcycles, and offered to give her a ride on his Harley when the weather turned warm. Mom laughed at him, and said she'd take him up on it! Whenever we mentioned his name after that, if she temporarily forgot who we were talking about, we'd merely remind her of his offer to give her a motorcycle ride.

"Oh, now I remember," she'd exclaim, and then add something that showed she knew exactly who we were talking about. She was building bridges in her brain, pathways from a trigger to a memory, and even though it took time, and she wasn't as quick as she had been fifty years earlier, Mom was still getting the job done.

But it was also true that she would sometimes be forgetful, and that usually happened when she was overstressed and/or overtired.

There was one other issue at play when Chad Balzer was questioning Mom, and to this day I don't know if it was on purpose. Back in December, before all the unpleasantness began, I emailed my sister with what I thought she would receive as very good news.

I told her that we found some discrepancies in Mom's diet, particularly the caffeine, and that as a result of reducing the caffeine, Mom was sleeping more, both at night and in taking naps during the day. Nancy responded that Mom taking afternoon naps was nothing new. So she was aware, as was I, that Mom regularly takes a nap after lunch. This happens to many people, especially if they have a high starch intake at lunch. Breads and pasta are sure to bring on the nods for instance.

It was our intention to bring Mom home from brunch in time to take her nap, ensuring that she would be refreshed when Balzer arrived. Changing the time of the appointment without letting us know was certain to have a negative impact on Mom as it would be disrupting her routine and she would be tired.

But there was nothing we could do about it. It wasn't that Mom wasn't aware of what was going on when she was tired, but she wasn't as sharp. Then again, who is? After we were at the table for a half-hour or so, Atty. Balzer asked my wife Jennifer and me to leave! He said he wanted to talk to Mom alone. I wasn't sure about that at all.

I didn't want Mom left alone—especially without legal representation. It was bothering me that we hadn't been notified of the meeting with Atty. Balzer until Saturday afternoon. Both Jack Casey and Tom Sousa were out of town, and now the evaluator shows up two hours early, Mom didn't get her regular nap, and he was telling us that he wanted time with Mom alone.

I looked at Jennifer, and could see the request bothered her too. I weighed whether I should just tell him no, but that also could give the appearance that we didn't trust Mom to speak her own mind when we weren't around.

Balzer was telling us repeatedly that he loves working with the elderly and how much he cares about them, but every step of his visit seemed as though he was putting Mom in the worst possible circumstances under which to conduct his interview.

But I listened to several conversations she had with Nancy and Courtney in which they tried to tell her she didn't know her own mind, and each time Mom held her own. I agreed to the meeting with the evaluator because we didn't have anything to hide, and I was hopeful that if he reported back to the judge that Mom was competent it could spare her a long trip to New York and a hearing.

So, against my better judgment we left the table. In fact, we left the house and went outside for more than a half-hour. We finally ran out of interest in walking around our own yard while a stranger was inside with Mom, and decided the least we could do was wait inside the house for him to finish.

We reentered the house and went upstairs to what had been our bedroom, but now was the combination bedroom and office. It was cramped and crowded and I was anxious to get moving on the addition so Mom could have a proper bedroom and living area outfitted for an elderly person. And I wanted my office back so I could do my work at a regular desk, with things arranged the way I wanted them, not stacked on top of each other. My bedroom by now had double rows of files stacked in front of one of the two desks I used. The copier and fax machine are nearly on top of my keyboard and the phone is in between them.

We waited upstairs for about another half hour and I finally decided enough was enough. Atty. Balzer had been interviewing Mom for about two hours by now, and regardless of what he determined it was time to put an end to the session.

I walked back downstairs and into the kitchen, and heard him telling Mom that Hawthorne Ridge was a great place to live. Why, his own father lived there in the retirement section, Balzer said!

This was a shocker! I say that because I didn't think there should be even the appearance of a conflict on the one hand, and because upon hearing Atty. Balzer's comment we learned that a second member of the Albany legal community had a relationship with Hawthorne Ridge, the other being my sister's lawyer.

In fact, Atty. Tom Sousa filed an affidavit that he sent to Jack Casey, making exactly that point.

His affidavit stated: ***"During the January 28, 2009 telephone conversation, Attorney Rowlands spoke at great length in a very favorable manner about the facility in which they (he and Nancy Patrick) were seeking to have M. Ella Winter committed. Attorney Rowlands told me he had a very close relationship with the facility and mentioned that it is owned or managed by a client of his."***

I could be wrong, but I couldn't help feeling that there was far too close a relationship between the legal entities in the Albany Supreme Court and Hawthorne Ridge.

Atty. Balzer finally said he had one item left on his agenda, and that was a tour of our house. I thought, as did Mom, that he meant he wanted to see Mom's quarters. She told him to hold on a minute while she made sure her room was picked up.

She had been interviewed for more than two hours at this point and excused herself to go to her bedroom before she allowed anyone to view it. She joked with Balzer about this, and he got a laugh out of it too. When Mom emerged from her room, he quickly viewed it, then her bathroom, then the laundry room. Then he said he wanted to see the rest of the house, including the master bedroom!

Again, I felt I was being imposed upon, and I didn't like it one bit. But again, I felt that if I didn't acquiesce it could be viewed as us hiding something, so I brought him upstairs. He eyeballed the room my wife and I use, noted that it was cramped and crowded, said hello to my daughter who was standing in the doorway to her room, but made no effort to view it.

But Balzer had more surprises in store for us. He said that even though a hearing was scheduled for the following Friday in front of Judge Egan, Nancy was now backing off on her intent to put Mom in an Alzheimer's ward, and instead just wanted to place her in an assisted living facility.

I pointed out that Nancy's lawsuit, which is what the judge had to go by, claimed that Mom suffered from Alzheimer's, was treated for Alzheimer's and dementia, and that she would need twenty-hour care, which is not what you get in assisted living. I also pointed out that backing off on the claim that Mom had Alzheimer's meant that there was no merit whatsoever to Nancy's lawsuit, as we had maintained all along.

I later communicated this conversation to Jack Casey and asked why we didn't just get Nancy's lawyer to drop the lawsuit entirely. Apparently, however, there was a disconnect between what Atty. Balzer was told, and what Nancy and her lawyer intended. Saying that Mom did not have Alzheimer's, and admitting that she could exist on her own in an assisted living facility meant that the core of the lawsuit, the claim that Mom was incompetent, was false, and therefore there was no case. That point never made it to the courtroom in Albany until Mom went to trial.

After viewing our bedroom, Atty. Balzer went downstairs, said his goodbyes to Ella, and I walked him out to his car. Atty. Balzer told me then that Mom was obviously competent, even though she was occasionally forgetful. He said she was a delightful woman, and that he would make that point to the judge.

In what I considered another odd question, Balzer then asked me if I would still allow Mom to live in our house if we didn't put the addition on. I answered, "Of course," but questioned why, since I willingly gave Mom a place to stay, and was supporting her in her fight to retain her freedom, should I have to give up my office?

Why should we suffer a major inconvenience, when we had the ability to make the adjustment much more comfortable for everyone with a simple addition? After all, it was our house, in Connecticut, not New York, and none of the participants in the Albany Supreme Court faction live here. We do.

We are providing twenty-hour care for an elderly relative, who has a high degree of independence but also has needs that require someone to be with her at all times. We are happy to be doing this, but it does require a major realignment of our family's activities.

I pointed out that the addition was intended simply to make our home more comfortable for Mom, and give us the room we needed for all of her belongings. And the unasked question was: why did the New York court system give a damn what I did with my house, considering that now we had an official—*New York sanctioned*—opinion of her competence, meaning she had every right to move to Connecticut and stay in Connecticut despite what my sister was saying?

But in what was another shocking moment, Atty. Balzer then suggested that I should be appointed Mom's guardian. I immediately rejected this idea, because it already was brought up more than a month earlier and I already talked it over with Mom.

If I was appointed her guardian it would negate the immediate threat from New York, that much is true. But Mom was adamantly opposed to anyone being named her guardian. She is well aware that guardianship brings with it far more powers for the guardian and far less independence for the individual, than naming someone Power of Attorney. Mom made the point repeatedly that she does not need, does not want, and will not agree to anyone being appointed her guardian. She asked me to take responsibility as Power of Attorney for her medical and legal affairs, and I agreed. But that was as far as she wanted it to go, and I had no reason or inclination to push the issue any further. I told this to Atty. Balzer and he left soon after. He assured me one last time that he found Mom to be competent and there was nothing to worry about.

We gathered inside as soon as he left, and sat down with Mom to discuss his visit. She told us how Atty. Balzer was going on about Hawthorne Ridge and how it was such a great place. But Mom said she told him repeatedly that she wanted no part of any elder facility, regardless of what it was, where it was or how nice it was. Period. She stressed that she was very happy living here in Connecticut.

Apparently he finally got the message.

I told her how he also approached me about being her guardian, and she confirmed that his discussion with her covered that topic too. And she told him the same thing I did—Ella wanted no part of a guardian taking control of her and her affairs. At least he told me that he was going to report Mom as being competent. I relayed this to Jack Casey and we all expressed the hope that with the evaluator's report confirming Mom's competence, we now could put an end to this nonsense for good.

In fact, Jack Casey pushed exactly that angle later in the week, but without the expected results. Once again, Mom and the rest of our family jumped through all the hoops, answered all the questions, opened up our home to an unwanted intrusion and once again the message we were given did not seem to make it to Judge Egan's ears.

We conversed with Jack Casey several more times right up through Thursday, but while the week started out on a positive note, Jack finally told us that it appeared Mom would have to come to New York. The underlying reason was that although Chad Balzer relayed his findings to my sister, as well as his opinion that I should be appointed Mom's guardian, Nancy insisted that everything she said in the lawsuit was accurate. She maintained that the only acceptable outcome was that she should be named Mom's guardian as outlined in her petition.

Travelling to Albany for a hearing again posed a dilemma for us, because we would be required to appear in the courtroom first thing in the morning, but it is at least two hours to Albany, and considerably more when driving in rush hour.

That meant the entire family, but especially Mom, would arise before 6 a.m., and be on the road by 7:30 a.m., at the latest. Or, we could go to New York the night before, rent hotel rooms, and run the risk that Ella wouldn't sleep all night in the unfamiliar surroundings.

Whichever alternative we took, the end result was the same. The petitioner, Nancy Patrick, who lives only twenty minutes or so from the Albany County Courthouse, would have no trouble at all getting there in time to testify against the woman who bore her and raised her, and to a great degree raised her daughter Courtney too.

But the Alleged Incapacitated Person, Ella, who by now had shown the entire free world that she was competent, and who supposedly had the benefit of the law on her side, was several hours away and would have to once again endure a major disruption of her life to satisfy a judge who apparently didn't believe anyone including his own court evaluator! There was not a doubt in my mind that if we were part of the Albany political structure, cesspool-like though that structure may be, we would not have spent more than a week getting Nancy Patrick's case thrown out of court.

We did everything we could in those final days to avoid putting Mom through the ordeal of a court appearance in Albany. She did absolutely nothing wrong. She merely exercised her right as an American citizen when she moved to Connecticut and said she wanted to stay—with control over her own money.

But it was Ella who was being treated like a criminal, simply because her only daughter was playing out the role of a spoiled brat who will stomp her feet and hold her breath until she turns blue if she doesn't get her own way.

We even went so far as to call the state senator from our area, herself an expert in elder law and related legislation. We explained the situation to her several weeks earlier and she promised to help in any way she could.

But she too was rebuffed by the New York courts, and when she made a less than ten-minute call to Chad Balzer, he just added it to his bill.

The evaluator's report went in Mom's favor, just as her mental competency test proved her abilities, just as the interviews by two lawyers and several witnesses proved. But Mom nonetheless was on the docket at the New York Supreme Court in Albany on Friday morning, March 27, 2009.

Jack assured us that the judge assured him that it wouldn't be for a full hearing. He said it would just be for an hour or so in the judge's chambers first thing in the morning. I wanted to believe him. I really did. But by now I had zero faith in the abilities, intent and most especially the word of any official associated with that court.

Lessons Learned

1. Ensure legal redundancy. That means, if your primary lawyer is out of town, be sure he has a backup in case of emergencies. We had no choice but to allow the New York appointed court evaluator to interview Mom in our home. But she should have had legal representation. Mom had one lawyer working for her in New York and another in Connecticut, but we were given literally no notice that the evaluator was coming to our home. In the end, Mom held her own, as we knew she would, but there should have been someone to call to sit with her as she was being questioned.

PART THREE

Blind Justice

CHAPTER FIFTEEN

By Trial and Error

The ride from Connecticut to Albany was mostly quiet, and Ella was at best introspective. She sat in the back seat, flanked by Jennifer and Heather, nodding off occasionally, but commenting too, especially on the extent of damage on the Massachusetts Turnpike from a winter storm that broke thousands of trees like match sticks.

Aside from the concern about the day ahead, it wasn't an especially onerous ride. If we had known what was waiting for us, it would have been much worse.

John Tuttle, the now-retired federal investigator who witnessed Mom's signature when she changed Power of Attorney in January, was keeping close tabs on the case, and offered to go to Albany with us, for support at least, and for testimony if necessary. John visited us numerous times after Mom moved in, and on occasion even sang hymns with her while she played the piano.

John knew as well as anyone that Mom was competent, and he was outraged at the attacks on her from New York.

On the other end, in Albany, Bob Soloyna also waited to let Mom know that she had friends and support, even in New York. Jack Casey told us to arrive as close to 10 a.m. as possible, and gave us the address where Judge Egan's office was located.

According to the game plan in effect when we left Connecticut, we were to meet Jack and he would accompany Mom into a meeting with the judge. Evaluator Chad Balzer might also be there, in addition to my sister's lawyer, but essentially, this was to be a meeting between Mom and the judge to confirm her competence.

John offered to drive and we left our house at about 7:30 a.m. We arose at about 5 a.m., Mom finished showering and dressing by 6 a.m. and she finished breakfast—coffee, a bowl of Cheerios garnished with a banana, orange juice and her daily vitamins, by 6:30 a.m.

We took extra time to go over everything we might need. We spent hours the previous day and night going through the documents that accumulated since Mom moved in on December 22, but we gave it one last review to make sure we weren't leaving anything essential behind.

When we left we had a briefcase full ranging from the lawsuit to Mom's medical records, phone records, emails, you name it.

Until the previous day we hoped that Mom would not have to make this trip and we still didn't understand why we were forced to waken her at such an early hour, hustle through her morning routine, and fight two cities' worth of rush hour traffic—Hartford and Springfield, MA—to be in Albany to prove what was obvious to everyone by now.

Nancy Patrick was backtracking as fast as she could peddle on the claims that Mom was suffering from Alzheimer's, and was trying to make it appear that she only intended for Mom to go into an assisted-living facility rather than an Alzheimer's ward. That isn't what her lawsuit said, however, and not what we got for a response when we suggested that Nancy just drop the legal action. And Nancy Patrick did not have the authority to commit Mom to any facility anywhere, at any time, regardless of what she thought.

Yet, the fact that Mom didn't want to go into an elder facility, and that she repeatedly told family members, lawyers, and doctors that she was very happy living in Connecticut and wanted to stay there apparently didn't enter the equation as far as my sister was concerned.

Nonetheless, if she was now acknowledging that Mom was competent, there simply was nothing left to argue about. If Mom wasn't demented, if she was capable of handling her own affairs in an assisted-living facility, then she obviously was competent and the decisions she made were her own and made with sound mind. Nonetheless, we still were in John's car at 8 a.m. making our way to the Massachusetts Turnpike and on to Albany.

One factor in our favor on the ride was that a portion of Mom's records from Albany Medical Center were now in our possession. Jack Casey finally had enough of the continual stalls, delays and outright lies from Albany Medical Center's records department and the previous Friday sent a paralegal from his office to camp out there until the records were delivered. Even with that, Jack reported that she spent the entire afternoon waiting for the records, and that Albany Medical personnel tried every possible ruse to get her to leave without the documents.

We were told that by law Albany Medical Center had thirty days to deliver the records to us from the time our official request was received. We made the request the first week of January, but the records weren't forthcoming until March 20, nearly ninety days later. They weren't in our hands until the beginning of the next week since the package was so large that Jack had to send them by mail.

In the meantime we received full documentation from Mom's other doctors going back nearly to the time my father died, and we were able to compile a fairly comprehensive overview of Mom's medical history.

Jack's final push to get the records from Albany Medical Center, while successful, did not give us anywhere near enough time to do a comprehensive review of them. There were more than eighty pages from her December hospitalization, and much of that was medical parlance that would require translation by a professional.

Jack recommended that we have them reviewed by a medical/legal professional, which we probably would have done if there was time, despite the extra cost. As we were to learn later, those records held a devastating—to my siblings—revelation concerning Mom's treatment, especially after her initial discharge date of Dec. 17, 2008.

We nonetheless were able to review both the admissions and discharge forms, and the one thing that jumped out from them was that Mom was treated for potassium deficiency and dehydration. There simply was no indication that she was diagnosed with nor treated for Alzheimer's or dementia, only Hypokalemia—potassium deficiency which can cause every one of Mom's symptoms.

We crested the hill on Route 90 in East Greenbush, New York, at 9:30 a.m., and were coming down to the exit for Troy and Rensselaer when I placed a call to Jack to let him know we were twenty minutes out and moving fast. We were rounding the curve after the Troy exit and the tall buildings of downtown Albany were in sight when the boom was lowered.

There was a slight change of plans, Jack said. We needed a new destination address because we wouldn't be meeting the judge at his office, we would be meeting him at the Albany County Courthouse a block away. And Mom's daughter was insisting that Mom endure a full-scale public trial in the county courtroom!

I didn't tell Mom about the change of plans. I figured she was already under enough stress. I got the address and directions from Jack, and just before 10 a.m. we drove onto Chapel Street behind the courthouse, and met Jack who was outside waiting for us.

John parked his car and we made our way up the sidewalk behind the courthouse, around the corner and up a slight hill to the entrance door. A woman was on the sidewalk, apparently waiting for us, and asked Mom if she wanted a wheelchair.

Wrong question! Mom is fiercely independent and responded, "Certainly not!"

I'm not sure who the woman was, or who put her out on the sidewalk, but if the goal was to make Mom look frail and unable to get around on her own, it was a dismal failure.

Inside the door to the courthouse lobby, before we ever got to the guard at the metal detector, a member of my sister's legal team was waiting. He shadowed us as we went through security, and then got on the same elevator that we used, listening in on our conversations as we went up to the courtroom.

Once again it was apparent that Mom's family in New York completely misjudged the situation by assuming that we would be discussing last minute strategy in a public area. The fact was, there was no 'last minute' strategy. The strategy from the beginning was to let Mom speak for herself, and show the judge that she was completely aware of what was going on around her. That was the strategy all along and there was no reason to change it.

The instant Mom walked through the door of the courtroom, Nancy Patrick lost. It would take nearly seven long, tedious hours to prove it, and Nancy Patrick still would never accept that she was wrong, and was wrong from the outset, not just when Mom moved to Connecticut, but for many years before that.

Mom was competent and everyone knew that. But first we had to get through the trial.

As Mom entered the courtroom where my sister, brother, brother-in-law, niece and a woman we didn't know were waiting,

Mom was swarmed by family members, virtually all of whom would soon be testifying against her, but at the moment were trying to suck up to her and put on a show for the judge.

But she was having none of that. "I'm angry with you," she told her son, daughter, granddaughter and everyone else within earshot.

"But, Mom why are you so angry?" they mewled.

"Because we're here, going through this," Mom retorted.

"Go give Mom a hug," my sister instructed her daughter, "She's not herself."

Actually, Mom was herself, and more so than she had been in quite some time. On top of that, Mom was as ticked off as I have ever seen her and was in no mood for any nonsense from my sister, brother or anyone else on their side.

After the fake hugs and expressions of concern, my sister, brother, niece, brother-in-law and the lady we didn't know all took the stand and tried to convince Judge Egan to sentence my mother to life confinement in an Alzheimer's facility.

Nancy approached Mom several more times that day as the trial wore on, primarily during brief breaks, but Mom was having none of it. At one point Nancy was pressuring Mom so intently, with her silent lawyer at her side, that I finally interceded and told him, "Hey counselor, how about getting your client back to your table and away from Mom?" He didn't respond but Jack Casey did, and joined in urging the lawyer to take my sister to her side of the courtroom until the case was over.

The first order of business was a conference with all the lawyers and the judge, the upshot of which was the opinion by everyone involved, except my sister, that the entire case was bogus. Jack asked Mom if she was amenable to some form of settlement, as proposed by my sister, but Mom just laughed that off.

There was no reason to settle a case in which a completely competent person is being falsely accused of incompetence. Mom was competent and a legal declaration of that fact was the only outcome we sought that day. Anything less was unacceptable. We responded that if Nancy was willing to drop her case and have it dismissed by the judge, then we would be happy to go back to Connecticut. Nancy refused.

Jack told us she was pushing to go through a full trial and I looked across the court room at her lawyer, Richard Rowlands, and said as much to him as to Jack, "Let them, they're going to lose anyway." I saw Rowlands' head snap back and he gave me a strange look, and it occurred to me that he had no idea of the true level of Mom's competence.

The judge acknowledged that Nancy would not withdraw her lawsuit and immediately got into testimony. My sister's lawyer called the lady we didn't know who as it turned out was an employee of Albany Medical Center's neurology department, Elizabeth Smith-Boivin. Ms. Smith-Boivin testified that she was the director of the Alzheimer's Resource Program at Albany Medical Center, the section that spent two days examining Mom on December 18th and 19th .

She was there to testify on my sister's behalf about Alzheimer's, and she also stated that she had access to patient records including Mom's, and reviewed Mom's records prior to testifying. In her introductory statements Ms. Smith-Boivin testified that she had a wealth of knowledge about Alzheimer's, and primarily works with the families of people who have Alzheimer's. But she isn't a doctor. In fact, Ms. Smith-Boivin testified that she has advanced degrees in social work, but not medicine, and she helps families construct non-medical treatment programs:

Ms. Smith-Boivin—*"It is my job to counsel both the patients and families on how to live with some of the symptoms of depression. How to make home modifications. How to use compensatory techniques to achieve maximum levels of functioning, despite deficits and those sorts of things."*

In other words, she counsels, but she doesn't diagnose. Ms. Smith-Boivin testified for about an hour, and Jack Casey repeatedly objected to her testimony as being irrelevant and unresponsive. He objected, because Ms. Smith-Boivin wasn't a doctor, and because she never examined Mom! But most of all, Jack repeatedly objected to Ms. Smith-Boivin's testimony because she never even met Ella Winter!

Judge Egan overruled many of Jack's objections and let in everything including the kitchen sink as far as her testimony was concerned. In retrospect, that probably worked in Mom's favor, because after it was all over, no one could say that Nancy didn't get her day in court.

But under cross-examination Ms. Smith-Boivin admitted that of the symptoms described in my sister's lawsuit regarding Mom's condition on the night of December 13, Alzheimer's was only one of sixty-five possible causes. She agreed with Jack when he asked pointedly if that meant there were sixty-four other potential causes of Mom's condition, none of which were Alzheimer's.

Jack also showed her the December 13-17, 2008 admission and discharge forms from Albany Medical Center where it said Ella was treated for potassium deficiency and dehydration. But when he asked if low potassium levels could have caused Mom's disorientation, she responded, "not at that level."

Ms. Smith-Boivin is not a doctor, she can't legally diagnose ailments nor prescribe medications, yet she supposedly knew exactly what potassium level would cause disorientation and confusion in a ninety-two-year-old woman she never met.

But we would learn much later that it wasn't what Ms. Smith-Boivin testified to that was the most relevant to Ella's future. Ms. Smith-Boivin testified that she read Mom's records, and discussed her condition with the attending physician, but she apparently never saw the discharge documents from her own department!

If she had, the case would have ended with her testimony. As it was, the contradictions in her testimony were self-evident and the case moved on to my sister.

We were then treated to enough neuroses to put a newly minted psychiatrist through an entire career.

The essence of Nancy's testimony was that a conspiracy existed prior to Mom's being hospitalized, perpetrated by yours truly. She claimed on the one hand that I was conspicuously absent from my mother's life for the decade since my father died, yet, somehow, I managed to learn about all of Mom's finances, and was just waiting for the right moment to wrest control of Mom and her money away from Nancy. She made a number of claims about how she was a doting daughter, and with the exception of occasional assistance from my brother, Mom simply could not get along without her.

There was another interesting facet of my sister's testimony, and it appeared to form the base of her allegations that I had some long-term strategy to interfere with her plans for Mom. That belief was based on her repeated claim that I initiated the contact with her husband Jim on December 17, and "volunteered" to bring Mom to Connecticut.

But the phone records show that Jim Patrick called my home on the morning of December 17, 2008. He left a message telling me what my sister was up to, adding that if I wanted any input into the matter, I should call before 3:30 p.m. that day.

I was on a client call and returned to my home office just after noon. I retrieved Jim's message, discussed it with my wife and we decided that we should offer to let Mom move in with us immediately. I called Jim back and made my offer, as previously noted. Jim said I should call back at 3:30 p.m., he would put me on speaker phone, and I could take part in the discussion. But Jim called first, at 3:25 p.m., and told me there would be no conference.

"It's a done deal," he said.

But Nancy claimed in her filings and in her testimony that I called out of the blue and threw a monkey wrench into her well-oiled plans—hence the conspiracy theory.

As it turned out, much of my sister's testimony was sheer fantasy or a significant revision of actual facts, such as when she said I did not visit New York to assist with my mother's recovery after an operation for a prolapsed bowel in 2003.

I didn't go to New York then, but there was a reason and a very good one. Set aside the fact that no one ever called me to tell me that Mom had an operation—to this day Ella brushes it off as inconsequential—but if they had, there was nothing I could do. I knew about the operation because Mom and I spoke two days before it was scheduled, and she knew I could not come to New York.

Nonetheless, neither my brother nor my sister gave me as much as a courtesy call.

The reason I could not come to New York was because I was horribly sick at this point in my life, and doctors for a time thought I had a brain tumor. Even if someone bothered to call and tell me what was going on with my mother, I couldn't travel.

Eventually, it was discovered that I didn't have a brain tumor, but instead was suffering from a combination of Vitamin B-9 deficiency and dehydration. That double whammy was causing double vision and blinding headaches, and for several months, including the period when Mom had her operation—she was hospitalized for a couple of days and then recuperated at her apartment—I couldn't drive. For once in my life I was forced to put my own interests first, and as it turned out, both Mom and I recovered completely.

My sister also alleged that I did not speak with or otherwise contact Mom for ten years after my dad's death. This was flat out false. It is true that after their reprehensible behavior while my father was dying, and again at his funeral, I was not interested in any contact with my siblings. But that didn't mean I wasn't contacting Mom. In fact we were in contact with Mom immediately after we returned to Florida, both by phone and by letter, and that contact continued throughout the next decade.

In January 2001 Jennifer, Heather and I returned to Connecticut. But we couldn't move back into the home we built with my father's help because we leased it out when we moved south, and the lease still had about eighteen months left on it.

So we rented a cottage on a lake in rural eastern Connecticut and lived there until the lease was up in the late summer of 2002. The cottage was tiny and there barely was room for us, which meant that our previous practice of inviting Mom over for a few days' visit every so often was put on hold.

I was not interested in going to New York for overnight stays, because to visit Mom almost always meant visiting with Nancy too. I knew that if my sister interrupted a visit with Mom it wouldn't go very well and I didn't think that was fair to Mom.

So I called her, or she called me, and we kept up on what was going on in our lives. Mom was especially interested in what occurred at Dad's funeral and in the months leading up to his death, so I filled her in with the specifics.

I told her about Jennifer waiting in Connecticut for a call to help her that never came—which distressed Mom intensely since for roughly the last two weeks of my father's life he was cared for at home. When Nancy and Jim took a vacation for a large part of that time Mom really needed some extra help, even with my brother Skeeter on the scene. I told her how upset we were at the despicable act of throwing a flower that Heather placed in Dad's coffin onto the floor; how shocked I was to be working in Florida and to find out too late that my siblings kept me in the dark about the seriousness of Dad's illness; about their refusing to let me talk with him; and on and on.

Mom wrote a letter to us a month after Dad's death, stating in part: ***"Thank you for being there, and giving me support. I think he had the kind of funeral he wanted with the bagpipes and Taps. I think he would have been proud."***

She also addressed the issue with the flower: ***"Thank you for the lovely flowers, especially you Heather for the special one you put in with him."***

And Mom also showed that she was aware of what was going on with Nancy and Skeeter, although she didn't mention it at the wake or funeral: ***"I wish things could have been a little more peaceful ..."***

Shortly after we received Mom's letter she called us in Florida to see if we were back to normal. She apologized several times during this conversation for not asking Jennifer to come to New York to help with Dad's care in his final days. She noted that the most difficult time was during the week when Nancy was on vacation, and that she was so exhausted she wasn't thinking straight.

We told her then and many times afterward that we understood what she had been going through and we had no hard feelings about her actions.

Mom addressed that issue best in her letter when she wrote, ***"It was such a shock to find out it was near the end. I had hoped he and I would have time to spend talking and enjoying some things together.***

When they first told me they said perhaps six months, then they changed it to three and then down to weeks. This was all in about a month's time."

Mom said she continually asked Nancy what she (Nancy) had done to create such a gulf between us, but that Nancy repeatedly feigned ignorance of the situation or gave such an unbelievable version of the events that it was nearly laughable.

I clearly remember one phone conversation as I was sitting on the front lawn by the lake on a lazy summer Sunday in 2001, watching boats drifting by, and listening to the sounds from the beach across the water. Mom was relating one of Nancy's explanations about what supposedly transpired in New York two years earlier when Dad was still alive. After Mom finished, I could only reply, "I told you she'd rewrite history."

We moved back to our home in late 2002, and were planning on inviting Mom over for either Thanksgiving or Christmas that year. But I was stricken in mid-November and for the next nine months or so was out of the loop.

In 2004 when I was back on my feet again we resumed our visits with Mom, with the understanding that was reached many months before—that we did not want to visit with Nancy and preferred to come when she would not intrude. On occasion I would pick Mom up and bring her to Connecticut.

It was odd to hear my siblings testify that I had no contact with Mom during this period, especially when my brother drove by in the parking lot at Dutch Village, eyeballing us when I brought Mom back from a visit in the summer.

In 2004 we attended a family reunion on the Mohawk River north of Albany, during which we maintained a polite distance from my sister while enjoying the company of many of our other relatives.

My cousin Floyd and I for instance, along with my daughter Sara, had a great time eating Little Neck clams at the raw bar. My grandson Aidan, who then was two years old, engaged in a food fight with my Uncle Bob, who was only a few months short of his 100th birthday.

We returned to Center Brunswick in December 2004, when my uncle turned 100, and attended a huge party at the Center Brunswick volunteer fire department where Uncle Bob was a member since the late 1940's. Again, we spent most of our time with Mom and our other friends and relatives, avoiding contact with my siblings as much as possible. But we did visit Mom regularly and occasionally brought her to Connecticut.

We enjoyed these visits but we also realized along the way that Mom wasn't getting all the care she deserved from my brother and sister, despite what they claimed.

At one point we brought our floor shampooing equipment and did all the rugs in Mom's apartment. That was my father's chore when he was alive, but it was obvious that it wasn't getting done by my brother and sister.

Likewise, in January 2007, we brought Mom to Connecticut for her real 90th birthday. As I mentioned in an earlier chapter Nancy scheduled her party in early December because a party on Mom's actual birth date would have interfered with Nancy's vacation in Florida.

As an example of the manipulation surrounding Ella in New York, we contributed a third of the cost of the party, at least as it was outlined by my sister. But we found out after Mom moved in with us that Nancy claimed she paid the entire amount and that we only paid for our lunches. My brother's input supposedly was the birthday cake.

We picked Mom up on the afternoon of January 5, 2007 and brought her to Connecticut. Mom didn't say anything to us the first day, but the next morning she was complaining that her leg hurt. We examined it and were shocked to find a viciously infected injury running from her kneecap to her instep.

We asked what happened and Mom said she fell and injured her leg a couple of days before Christmas when she was taking a plant to the office at Dutch Village as a Christmas gift for the management. That was about two weeks previously! She was treating the infection with applications of an antiseptic several times a day.

We took Mom to the local emergency room and doctors immediately gave her a tetanus shot, put her on antibiotics and tended the horribly infected wound. The doctor was curious as to how she went so long without anyone tending to the injury.

It is obvious that we enjoyed plenty of contact with my mother in the previous decade, yet we were forced to sit in Albany Supreme Court listening to my brother and sister testifying under oath that they were Mom's only sources of support. My sister tried to paint a picture of herself as a doting daughter who was always there for our mother while everyone else was off living carefree, irresponsible lives. But later in the trial it was Mom herself who put the lie to that concept.

Mom was asked by Rowlands if she recalled Nancy's testimony where *"she talked about all of the things that she has done for you over the last ten years?"*

Ella: *"You know, I did quite a few things for her too over our lifetime. I'm certainly appreciative of the fact that she did the things that she did, but I don't think that she should have done some of the other things that she did."*

That old adage that lawyers should never ask a question in the courtroom if they don't already know the answer should have applied right here. But Rowlands ignored it and said to Mom, *"May I ask what other things she did to you?"*

Mom, referring to the arguments she had with Nancy over her checkbook replied, *"Well, like the fact that she wouldn't give up the money. She had the money and I asked her to give it to me, and she just wouldn't."*

That was it. That was the case. I told Jack Casey from day one that I had nothing to do with Mom's fighting with Nancy, but Nancy and Skeeter decided between them to continue the ill will that was driving them a decade earlier when Dad died.

They created a conspiracy out of whole cloth, declared Mom incompetent, filed a lawsuit saying so, and demanding that Mom be placed in an Alzheimer's facility. One of the most perplexing stances taken by my siblings was that even though the lawsuit specifically stated that my sister, as guardian, would have the power to place Mom in a nursing home, even without a court order, Nancy kept claiming that she never would do that.

But in contrast, my brother kept claiming that Mom's mind wasn't right, and she couldn't be making decisions on her own. That level of mental deterioration requires twenty-hour care, and that is what is defined as nursing home care.

The two of them couldn't even keep their own stories straight.

Take for instance my brother's testimony about his visit to our house on December 30, and subsequent luncheon at a nearby restaurant. Mom really wanted her checkbook to show up on that visit, and when she learned that my brother did not bring it, she went very quiet.

But that isn't what my brother saw.

Casey: *"As your mother sits here today does she have the right to make her own decisions as to where the money is?"*

Skeeter: *"I would say she did, if she knew where the money was. She doesn't know where the money is."*

Casey: *"So if she executes a power of attorney nothing need be said after that. Right?"*

Skeeter: *"She was not in the right frame of mind."*

Casey: *"Were you there when she executed the power of attorney?"*

Skeeter: *"No. I was not sir."*

Casey: *"So you really don't know whether she was in the right frame of mind, do you?"*

Skeeter: *"I know what frame of mind she was in when we went to lunch on December 30th."*

Casey: *"But she didn't execute the power of attorney there. Did she?"*

Skeeter: *"It was already in the works. It was executed the first of January."*

That statement is not true. As I wrote elsewhere in this book, Mom didn't make the decision to change the power of attorney until the afternoon of January 1, when Nancy refused for the last time to send Mom her checkbook.

Atty. Tom Sousa who came to our house late that day, did so to make it easier on Mom so she wouldn't have to travel to Norwich in the winter. He lives nearby, and the standard Power of Attorney forms don't require much in the way of personalization.

He took a few hours to prepare the forms and came to our home when he was done. While talking with Mom before she signed the new forms Tom even told Mom that she could assign a new Power of Attorney in Connecticut, but still keep Nancy as Power of Attorney in New York if she so desired.

Mom was not the least bit interested in allowing Nancy to have charge of her affairs in New York or anywhere else, and said so. It was as simple as that. No big conspiracy, just the ability to get things done when they needed to be done.

But not having a clue as to what really happened didn't stop Skeeter from pursuing the conspiracy theory, regardless. Continuing his questioning about the Power of Attorney form:

Casey: *"Did she make any reference to it?"*

Skeeter: *"No."*

Casey: *"Did she say: He is forcing me to sign a paper?"*

Skeeter: *"She was not in the right frame of mind when she went to lunch. She couldn't remember things. Jennifer and I had to help her into the restaurant. This was only a few days after she was released from the hospital."*

Actually, it was nearly two weeks from the time Mom was released from Albany Medical Center, and as I have mentioned, she made a stunning recovery once her diet was adjusted and she began to sleep better. But on the 30th of December, 2008, when we went to lunch with Skeeter, what I remember is Mom laughing a lot, but also having quiet moments where it was obvious that something was on her mind.

The really sad aspect of the luncheon with Skeeter on December 30th was that aside from her concerns about the checkbook, Mom had a great time—until Skeeter ultimately ruined it for her. She even said so after Skeeter left to return to New York. He said he was leaving for Florida early in the morning on Mom's birthday, and wasn't coming back north until Memorial Day. (That alone would have made a family meeting in mid-January—as alleged by Nancy—quite difficult, especially since he was on a horse trading trip at that time.)

Mom asked Jennifer and me if we enjoyed ourselves and we all agreed that it was more enjoyable than any of us expected. I guess we all had a good time, except Skeeter, who apparently was taking some kind of mental notes to use against his mother when he testified against her three months later.

But my brother had even more ludicrous testimony to add to the record before he stepped down and shut up.

I noted that my brother talked to Mom after he made his sales trip to Kentucky, mid-January. And Nancy testified that her last conversation with Mom was on January 22nd, two days after she filed the lawsuit against Mom in Albany Supreme Court, and two days before we were served in Connecticut.

But their phone messages, especially Nancy's, were so vitriolic by then that I refused to talk to them and instead let them go to voice mail. Then I retrieved the messages and if they concerned Mom, I told her what was said and let her deal with it if she wished.

On two occasions in the next few months this resulted in direct action: when my brother's grandson broke his ankle and Mom sent him a get well card; and again when Courtney came down sick and Mom sent her a get well card too. At least in the case of Skeeter's grandson he appreciated the card and the reason for it.

But Skeeter, who in January accused me of turning off my kitchen and living room phones, as well as the one in Mom's bedroom, when Mom didn't return the birthday messages fast enough to suit my siblings, had a different tack on my phone system when he testified in March.

Casey: *"If (Ella) decides to live in Connecticut full time she can do it, right?"*

Skeeter: *"Absolutely."*

Casey: *"If she decides not to take your phone calls she can make that call, can't she?"*

Skeeter: *"Yes, she can. If she had a phone. They don't have a land line. They have cell phones."*

Casey: *"She can decide whether or not to take a phone call, right?"*

Skeeter: *"Not if she doesn't get them. If he doesn't give them to her. He has a cell phone. The voice mail is on his cell phone."*

Frankly, I have no idea where he got all that. It isn't true, and it doesn't matter. Mom got all the messages and at times I even told her when Nancy left another insult, or slur, or threat. But I did act as a buffer between the messages we were getting and Mom.

Rowlands obviously bought into the false claim that my sister was constantly in touch with my mother prior to the move to Connecticut, and asked Ella, *"In fact, you talked to your daughter pretty much every day?"*

Mom came right back with, *"Not every day. She was busy. She has a busy life, you know ...?"*

That was another nugget of the reality that was Mom's life prior to December 13, 2008. Nancy claimed she was always there, as claimed in this testimony:

Rowlands: *"Would you describe your relationship with your mother starting from the time that your father passed away?"*

Nancy: *"My Mom has been my best friend for my whole life and until the last three months we have been inseparable."*

But Ella wasn't buying that.

Rowlands pressed Mom about her relationship with her daughter later in the day, *"Didn't she take you to all of your doctors' appointments all these years?"*

Ella: *"Sometimes she did. Towards the last she did more than usual. But I have different people. I took myself in the beginning. Then after I had the accident (2003) I didn't drive anymore, so then I took the senior citizen buses for years to all of the different things that I had to go to. Now Ron and Jennifer take me ...."*

Mom says she saw Nancy maybe once or twice a week, and often those encounters were not pleasant for Mom. I witnessed some and certainly heard what Nancy said to Mom on the telephone after Mom moved to Connecticut. Nancy's husband Jim described their relationship as "oil and water" and he was right.

He saw it, we saw it, other family members saw it, and Mom acknowledged it. Nancy was not trying to drag Mom back to New York because she had a place for her to live or because she missed her. She wanted Mom in a facility, and Mom didn't want to go.

But if Nancy won, regardless of the type of facility Ella was confined in, Nancy would have complete control over her finances and every other aspect of Mom's life.

There were many other inconsistencies in the testimony, primarily showing that while my sister and brother were bent on proving that Mom was incompetent, she actually was acting on her own right up to her hospitalization in December. Nancy testified for instance that Mom voted in the November 2008 presidential election, which would be difficult if she was demented.

She also testified that *"My mom keeps an immaculate apartment. Everything was always perfect."* She later testified that Ella is *"fastidious"* about her appearance.

I agree with that testimony, but it is diametrically opposed to the definition of someone suffering from Alzheimer's where loss of concern with personal neatness is an early sign.

And there is an unspoken element here. One facet of elder

abuse is neglect, which can be manifested by untreated injuries and especially dehydration. Mom had both.

Nancy also claimed, in the pleadings and again on the stand that she took control of Mom's finances immediately after Dad died in 1999, and that Mom couldn't handle the task. But again, Mom was not in agreement.

Rowlands: *"And did she take care of your checkbook?"*

Mom: *"She helped me with it one time when, I guess it was an operation on my eye. I wasn't seeing too good, and I wasn't writing too good so Nancy helped me with it. Ron helped me with it. The woman that came in and cleaned for me, she helped me with it. At that particular time, it was just the fact that I wasn't writing good. I knew what was going on with the checks, but I just couldn't write that well."*

Another element of the conspiracy theory blown to smithereens. You may have noticed by now that another unsubstantiated claim in my sister's lawsuit, that Mom was incapable of complex thought and therefore unable to comprehend or take part in the case, was simply ridiculous. Mom was handling complex thoughts and issues every single time she opened her mouth. And Jack Casey loved it! He was looking over at me, his hand held over his face so the judge couldn't see that he was on the verge of bursting out laughing!

There also was testimony that showed an apparent willingness from a very early date to attribute any normal age-related deterioration on Mom's part to mental rather than dietary or environmental factors.

For instance, regarding the 2003 surgery, Nancy testified that:

"After my mom's surgery I noticed that she wasn't doing well balancing her checkbook, so we sat down one day and looked at it and it had not been balanced actually for eight or nine months."

Nancy went on at length about how after Mom's bowel operation she just couldn't do things the same any longer, and even that she told her husband Jim that Ella just wasn't the same and it was obviously because of the operation.

Oddly enough, Nancy may have been right about the observation, but so wrong about the cause.

One of the most immediate side effects of a bowel operation can be a significantly reduced absorption of potassium—which again can cause all the symptoms that Nancy and Skeeter said they were seeing. But in both cases, they immediately decided that Mom's issues were mental rather than dietary in nature and from that point on they wanted Mom in a home.

Obviously neither looked any further nor did any research on possible side effects. If they had, Mom would not have suffered from dehydration, much less potassium deficiency.

In further remarkable testimony Nancy averred:

"I have watched her eating habits for ten years. I have been watching everything that is in her refrigerator. Everything that she is doing…"

If there is any truth to that statement it would seem plausible that Mom's dehydration, her excessive consumption of caffeine, her reduced intake of potassium that left her disoriented and confused at times, especially if she also was dehydrated, and her untreated injury all can be placed squarely at Nancy's feet.

Nancy testified that she was there all the time that she knew everything that Mom was doing, and even what was in her refrigerator. Yet Mom had periods of confusion and disorientation, and was hospitalized for dehydration and potassium deficiency. So, where should Mom go to file a complaint over her care?

And again, even though Nancy was claiming on one hand that Mom had no choice but to go into a nursing home, and even named the facility of her choice in the lawsuit, she testified just the opposite.

Rowlands: *"Did you ever have any conversation with your mother about putting her in a nursing home?"*

Nancy Patrick: *"I have never even mentioned a nursing home to my mom. The last thing in the world I would do with my mother is ever put my mother in a nursing home. My mom would come and live with me before I would put her in a nursing home. I would do whatever it took not to put her in a nursing home."*

And yet, in all that happened between Dec. 13, 2008, and March 27, 2009, Nancy Patrick never once offered to let Mom move in with her. In all the fallacious, vexatious statements in her lawsuit against her mother, there was not one that even hinted at the possibility of Mom moving in with Nancy.

The reasons were twofold. One, Nancy had no place for Mom to live, and two, neither of them would ever have agreed to that living arrangement.

The number of inconsistencies between Nancy's testimony and reality was incredible. For instance going back to her operation in 2003, Nancy said Mom was apartment-bound and recuperating from her surgery for seven weeks, but she also testified that Mom was cleared to go back to driving after six weeks!

Nancy testified that Mom was very nervous about driving again after her operation, but she did go out driving. Unfortunately, the first time she ventured out after her operation, Mom had a minor rear-ender when a car in front of her began to turn right on red. Mom followed the car in front of her, but as she looked left at the intersection to check for oncoming traffic the car in front stopped suddenly and Mom's car tapped its bumper.

There was little to no damage, but the incident was upsetting and Mom suffered a minor heart attack at the accident scene. She was hospitalized and that was the end of her driving.

Considering Nancy's testimony that she was constantly at Mom's side, constantly monitoring every facet of Mom's life, even to the nature of the food in her refrigerator, it is reasonable to inquire where Nancy was when Mom ventured out on her first time behind the wheel after her surgery.

The answer is—who knows where Nancy was? Because all we know for sure is that she wasn't with Mom. At a point where Ella really needed someone with her, at a time when it made sense to take Mom to an empty parking lot to let her practice before going out on the road again, Nancy was the nowhere woman.

Nancy's testimony was followed by Skeeter's which was good for laughs since he obviously didn't read the lawsuit before he ran his mouth about it, and even got into an argument with Mom's lawyer about his legal standing in the suit.

If Nancy prevailed in that suit and Mom's assets were turned over to her guardian, they would have gone to Nancy and only Nancy. Skeeter didn't seem to understand this, and to this day we strongly suspect that Skeeter didn't realize he would have been left hanging in the wind if Nancy prevailed.

Following Skeeter was Nancy's daughter Courtney who spent at least a half hour on the stand and contributed exactly nothing to the case. Her testimony was notable for one reason and one reason only.

It hurt Ella to the quick to see her granddaughter on the witness stand helping in the effort to institutionalize her. It stunned her that the girl she helped raise sometimes to nearly the level of a surrogate parent, would turn on her and join in an effort to portray her as incompetent and demented.

Ella was hurt and hurt badly by her granddaughter's testimony, not by its lack of validity and relevance, but by its very existence. She commented on more than a few occasions after the trial was over that Courtney was heavily influenced by her mother, and maybe she was.

But Ella also noted that when Courtney took the stand against her, she was twenty-four years old, owned her own condominium in a very expensive Boston suburb, was employed and independent. Ella said that apparent level of independence was not duplicated on the stand. She has never forgotten that her granddaughter testified against her, and it is not likely that she ever will.

There never was an ounce of validity to Nancy Patrick's suit, and many people were irrevocably hurt by it, primarily Ella. Nancy's own testimony that she would never put Ella in a nursing home or Alzheimer's facility, and that she didn't consider Ella demented, only proved the vexatious nature of her lawsuit. Nancy also claimed that she filed the suit only as a way to restore communication between Ella and her children.

But Mom's contact with Skeeter and Nancy continued unabated until the night we were served the lawsuit. And as a reminder, Skeeter threatened on the night of Jan. 7, 2009, when Mom informed Nancy that she rescinded her Power of Attorney, that "this isn't over."

It seems obvious that considering the time it takes to prepare a lawsuit, its genesis was in that conversation, and had nothing to do with how many times Mom talked with them on the phone. Nancy testified to that, as did Skeeter. So Nancy's claim that she filed a lawsuit to open lines of communication with her mother was false because by her own testimony those lines were still open even after Nancy's suit was filed in Albany Supreme Court.

Nancy also testified that the various claims she made in the suit were there only because the law required it. Personally, I would love to see the New York State law that says that before a case can be filed in Supreme Court a petitioner must make false claims of imaginary illnesses, non-existent treatments, and illegal acts including kidnapping, unlawful restraint and forgery.

Nancy even claimed, after the trial was over, that Skeeter and Courtney both testified for reasons other than concern for Mom's welfare.

In a voice mail message left on my computer she claimed:

"You want to know why Courtney came from Boston on the day of the court case? Number one, she came to support her mother, cause she feels so badly for her mother, because her mother has been ripped away from her mother, and number two she came because you know what she thought? She thought if she didn't come to court she might never see her grandmother again.

And when she was trying to say goodbye, you wanted to rip her away and take her to lunch."

I'll get to the lunch issue later because it is too good to miss. But regarding the rest of the message, no one ever said that Mom wasn't going to see her family, and every member of the family was told directly that all they had to do was to give us some advance notice that they wanted to visit and we would work out our schedules accordingly.

But even if we didn't go to that length, since when does going to court to see your grandmother also include testifying against her? Courtney could speak with Mom at any time during any break in the proceedings. But she didn't. Instead of simply sitting in the spectators' section of the court, waiting until it was over to speak with Mom Courtney was sworn in, took the stand and by doing so committed the very individual act of testifying in support of her mother's efforts to institutionalize her grandmother. There is no way around that, and there is no latter day excuse that can ever explain or make up for it.

The hypocrisy and the revisionist history that surround the case of Nancy Patrick vs. M. Ella Winter are thick enough to cut with a knife. Nancy's attempts to rationalize why her daughter testified against Ella are a classic example.

Nancy filed a lawsuit alleging that Mom was incompetent, attempting to have herself named Mom's sole guardian, and in the process taking 100 percent control over all of Mom's assets and the very fabric of her life. She not only sought the power to put Mom into a nursing home, she made sworn statements to the effect that Mom's mental state was deteriorated to the point where that was the ONLY option. And she wanted to use Mom's money to pay all the legal bills associated with the suit!

When we proved time and again that Mom was competent, Nancy changed her story as often as the wind changed direction. And when it suddenly occurred to Nancy that the world sees her as something far less sympathetic than Mother Teresa, she scrambled to find explanations for her behavior. Those explanations were as thin, unbelievable and ridiculous as the lawsuit itself.

The most frustrating and infuriating aspects of this case were that Nancy started out making unfounded allegations claiming I was trying to take Mom's money. That claim right on its face was false since Nancy's lawyer, abetted by Key Bank in Menands, New York, impounded sixty percent of Ella's total assets and Ella had complete control over the remaining forty percent. Also, the court evaluator, according to his report, had the authority the "preserve the property" of Ella Winter, but found no such action was necessary.

Nancy then moved on to claiming that she was driven to initiate her legal assault due to a non-existent ban on communications between her and Mom. Again, by her own testimony, Nancy's last conversation with Mom was on Jan. 22, 2009, two days after she filed suit against Mom!

But in the end, it was not anything that Nancy said, or Courtney said, or Skeeter said that drove a stake through the heart of their case.

At some time after 2 p.m., on March 27, 2009, Ella Winter took the stand in her own defense and in the next hour or so eviscerated the petitioner, the witnesses against her, the opposing counsel, and the entire case.

Mom got up from the defense table, walked with my help to the court clerk who swore her in, then went to the witness stand. Jack Casey questioned her as to her knowledge of who she is, where she was, where she lived, and a litany of similar questions that showed she was in command of her faculties. She talked about her assets and showed she knew what she had and where.

But here is where it got funny, at least as funny as it could get considering the circumstances. Nancy Patrick's lawyer, Richard Rowlands, repeatedly attempted to trip Mom, or catch her off guard. He was unsuccessful.

Nancy testified that Mom didn't know the banks where her accounts were located.

"This is the ... reason I was trying to get her some help," Nancy testified.

Apparently that help included changing the signature cards at Mom's bank, which was done in the case of First Niagara on December 17, 2008 when Mom was in the hospital. And if Nancy needed help, or if Mom needed help determining where her accounts were located, all she had to do was look in Mom's pocketbook. Mom made out a contact card for each person with whom she had financial dealings and she knew exactly where the cards were located. Once again, that wasn't the action of a demented person who could not handle complex thoughts. And issue by issue, Ella Winter cut the legs out from under every point of contention in her daughter's lawsuit.

For instance, Nancy and Courtney claimed that Mom's move to Connecticut was known far and wide to be temporary.

The testimony shows a different story:

Rowlands: *"I think you testified that originally you were a little unsure and were going to go over on a temporary basis, but then decided that you did like it there. Is that true?"*

Ella: *"I didn't hear that it was a temporary basis, I just heard that I was going over to Ron's because I needed a place to stay. That's all."*

Then Rowlands tried to undercut Jack Casey's representation of Mom and her legal issues.

Rowlands: *"Did your attorney tell you that Nancy has tried to settle this case at all? Did he convey any of our proposals to you?"*

Ella: *"Did you?"*

Rowlands: *"No. Your attorney, Mr. Casey. Did he discuss any settlement options of this case?"*

Ella: *"No. But did you give any to him?"*

Rowlands: *"Well yes. Of course."*

Ella: *"Oh. Well, what did you give him?"*

Once again, the woman who was not supposed to be capable of independent or complex thoughts turned the tables on an experienced lawyer and was interrogating him, instead of the reverse.

Rowlands: *"If I told you that Nancy's main concern was that she has been unable to speak to you after years of talking to you every day—"*

Ella: *"Well, my thing is that I heard that you weren't supposed to talk with the enemy."*

It was obvious to virtually everyone in the courtroom, and I believe this includes Nancy Patrick's lawyer, that Mom was not only competent, but was holding her own and better regardless of what was thrown at her.

Getting back to the nursing home issue:

Rowlands: *"That is your concern isn't it? That you don't want to go to a nursing home?"*

Ella: *"No. I do not."*

Rowlands: *"But you really do need help with paying your bills and ..."*

Ella: *"I get all the help I need right in Ron's home."*

Rowlands: *"I understand that. He is helping you, but you do need help?"*

Ella: *"Yeah, well I can still make out my own checks and things like that, but I let them make them because my writing is poor now. Ever since I have had the operation on my eye. My writing is poor and I don't like it. So Ron and Jennifer make out the checks and I always see them. I have my checkbook though. I don't give that up any more at all."*

Rowlands: *"So Ella, if there were a proposal that there would be a guardian appointed to help you ..."*

Ella: *"Do I have to have one?"*

If the banter between Ella and Rowlands was fun at this point, remember, Ella was not supposed to be capable of bantering with anyone, much less an attorney in the middle of a trial. It was about to get better.

It was apparent that Rowlands couldn't break Mom and yet he was still under pressure from Nancy to find something to score on, so he asked Mom for permission to converse with Nancy. (You're actually supposed to ask permission from the judge.) When he returned to the questioning, Rowlands had another issue.

Rowlands: *"A question for you. If Nancy were to withdraw the petition, would you consider having someone independent from your children to oversee your finances for you and help you?"*

Ella: *"Why would I have to do that?"*

Rowlands: *"I'm just asking the question? Would you consider it?"*

Ella: *"Well, I don't see any point to it. I'm still a big girl, and I still have a mind, whether they believe it or not. And I like to do my own thing."*

Rowlands again appeared stumped and again initiated a conversation with Nancy, but the judge was clearly getting impatient.

Nancy took one last shot at Mom, noting that in previous testimony when Mom was being questioned about her six accounts in three different banks Mom said "hundred" when she should have said "thousand." But Mom corrected herself and that ploy went down the drain too.

I thought it was just amazing that my sister was testifying that she didn't want anything bad to happen to Mom, like confinement in a nursing home, yet to the very end she was trying to find some way to prove to the judge that Mom's mind was shot.

After that the judge talked to Mom one-on-one for about twenty minutes, which, if we absolutely positively had to go to New York to prove Mom's competence, this was really all the conversation that was necessary.

Mom and the judge had a nice conversation about Mom's early life, her marriage, her children, World War II years and the present. The judge told Mom to turn and face him, one and one, and just talk, which they did. Mom was completely lucid, aware and in control. Finally, Judge Egan was satisfied and excused Mom.

I then provided brief testimony on two elements that I strongly disputed—the claim that Mom's move was temporary and that no one used the expression "nursing home" when talking about placing her somewhere. I pointed out that Jim Patrick told me there were no "false impressions" as far as Mom being told the truth about her move.

I also pointed out the obvious, that with Nancy bringing most of Mom's belongings to Connecticut and shutting down her apartment, there was nowhere in New York for Mom to live except an elder facility. Then things got really funny—for a courtroom where someone's life is on the line.

I testified that Jim Patrick called me, not vice versa, and told me that Nancy was only a matter of hours from putting Mom into a nursing home. My sister was sitting next to her lawyer, staring down at the table, but at that her head snapped up so violently I thought it was going to fly off and hit the wall in the back of the courtroom.

Nearly simultaneously, my brother-in-law shot up from his seat in the spectator section and flew up to hold a whispered, but intense conversation with Rowlands.

I quickly surmised that if there was a communication breakdown it was between my sister and her husband. He apparently never corrected the false impression that I was the one who initiated the call, and that my conversation with him was not about a temporary move, in fact it was the exact opposite.

As soon as my testimony ended, Jim was called to rebut me. But Jack Casey nailed him on a salient point—if the move was supposed to be temporary, then why did Jim agree that we discussed putting an addition on my house to accommodate Mom and all her belongings?

Jim had an answer but it was obvious that Jim Patrick's testimony was for his wife, not for the court.

And that was pretty much that. The judge adjourned then saying he was going to retire to his chambers to review the testimony and then make his decision. As we watched the judge retire from the bench, Jack and I conversed about the testimony, how lopsided it was in Mom's favor and what a great job she did on the stand.

I told Jack that as far as I was concerned the testimony that had the most impact came at the end of Mom's cross examination, when Rowlands asked Mom about the thrust and goals of Nancy's lawsuit against her.

Rowlands: *"What do you think she (Nancy) is trying to do?"*

Ella: *"I think she can't stand the idea that she doesn't have the say in my doings anymore."*

Lessons Learned

1. *Make sure your attorney is skilled at courtroom work in addition to knowing the law. Jack Casey did a thorough job on both counts and it showed.*
2. *Expect the opposition to use any means, fair or foul to trip you up. Don't discuss your case or tactics in public, and don't allow strangers to "help" you.*

CHAPTER SIXTEEN

Will It Ever End?

By now you probably are thinking, ***"How predictable. And They Lived Happily Ever After."***

Sorry, life isn't like that.

When Judge Egan retired to his chambers, Mom turned to me and said, "I'm starving."

We briefly discussed either waiting on the judge's decision, which in retrospect we should have done, or trying to find something to eat in the immediate area which didn't appear too likely since it was way past the normal lunch hour.

But Mom hadn't eaten since 6:30 a.m., and now it was about 4 p.m. That's nearly 10 hours, and that is a long time for anyone to go without eating, much less a 92-year-old who has just endured an exhausting trial.

Jack and I agreed that John Tuttle could take Mom, Jennifer and Heather to the Purple Pub, our favorite restaurant in the area that I spoke of in an earlier chapter, which is about 20 minutes north of the Albany Courthouse. Jack and I would wait for the judge's decision, call and let the family know what was happening, and Jack would give me a ride to meet them as soon as the judge adjourned court.

So off they went and down we sat.

The judge emerged about fifteen minutes later and asked where Ella went. I told him what he should have known without asking, that she hadn't eaten in nearly ten hours and went for food.

"Bring her back," the judge ordered.

I protested that I could receive the verdict for Mom and relay it to her. If we won, it was over, or so we thought; if we lost we would file an appeal on the spot. But at the moment it was far more important that she get something to eat. No way. The judge ordered me to get in touch with John and return Mom to the court. I went out into the hallway and called John on his cell phone just as they arrived at the Purple Pub. They couldn't believe Mom was being ordered back to court, but John turned around nonetheless and headed back to Albany.

As I returned, Jack was exiting the courtroom his face contorted in anger. When I asked what was wrong he told me that my brother-in-law and the judge were joking it up big time inside. "It seems Jim Patrick's father and the judge's father were old friends," Jack replied.

An icy cold fear began to grip my insides. Mom was saying ever since we were served in January that Jim Patrick's local connections probably were playing a part in the inexplicable legal decisions that came from the Albany Supreme Court, and now it was being thrown in our faces.

I walked inside, saw the judge and my brother-in-law finishing a conversation and slowly drifting apart. I didn't like the looks of it one bit. The judge asked if Mom was on her way back and Jack answered for me. "They were just about to sit down," Jack said. "They've left and are on the way back."

Judge Egan wanted to know where Mom had gone and why. So Jack told him, adding, "It's a family tradition."

I sat down to wait and then got another shock. While it is normal to have a bailiff in a courtroom when a case is in progress, there were none for the bulk of this case. An Albany police officer drifted in and out during the testimony, but he didn't seem to be assigned to that courtroom in particular.

But now there were two police officers inside the courtroom. A few minutes later the doors opened and I turned around, expecting to see John and Mom coming back. Instead, there were two more police! The icy feeling in the pit of my stomach increased, if that was possible.

In later months as the debate on universal health care and other government intrusions into our daily lives were played out in the news media, I couldn't help but remember the feeling I had inside the Albany County Supreme Court. I realized that if the judge's decision went against Mom, it was going to get ugly very quickly. Mom said many times that she would not go to Hawthorne Ridge or any other facility willingly or quietly, but the last thing on earth I wanted to see that day was my mother being taken into custody and committed to an Alzheimer's home.

Yet there was no way she was going to get out of that courtroom if the judge said she was staying. By now, I was as fearful as I have ever been about what the government could do, and just might do. I would caution anyone who thinks that government control of our lives—pre-cradle to grave as the saying goes—is something benign and beneficent, that they would think differently if they were in that courtroom on March 27. I realized then that Mom's life was not in her hands, my hands, her doctors' hands, or Jack Casey's hands.

The judge held my mother's future in the palm of his hand, was the sole arbiter of her fate, and just ten minutes earlier he and my brother-in-law were chumming it up like old fraternity brothers. You don't ever want to be in that position, with no recourse if the ruling goes against you.

A few minutes later Mom, John, Jennifer and Heather returned and Mom sat down at the defense table. The judge reconvened the court and went straight to the heart of the issue.

Judge Egan: *"I have considered the testimony of Elizabeth Smith-Boivin, Nancy Patrick, Wilson Winter, Courtney Patrick, Ronald Winter, James Patrick and most importantly, M. Ella Winter."*

The standard by which this petition is to be judged is whether or not Ella Winter is incapacitated as that term is defined in the Mental Hygiene Law.

The burden of proof in these proceedings is on the Petitioner to prove by clear and convincing evidence that the alleged incapacitated person is in fact incapacitated."

I was sitting at the defense table, keeping my face as unemotional as possible, but at this point I felt like jumping up and yelling ***"No kidding, judge! It's about time!"***

That is exactly the standard that should have been applied from Day One, and if it was applied Mom would have been spared months of stress and unhappiness. But I didn't say anything or let on how I was feeling.

The judge continued: *"Ella Winter is here in the courtroom. I have had the opportunity to watch and listen and observe her. She walks by herself* **(remember the wheelchair?),** *is well dressed and can see, hear and talk. She has answered all of our questions appropriately and expressed her own opinions. She may be 92, but she is not incapacitated."*

Judge Egan then added: *"That is not to say that she doesn't need some assistance. I'm sure she needs someone to help her go to the doctor and shop and attend to her finances. There are the physical realities of being 92. She does not, however, need a guardian."*

"This petition is dismissed."

I'd like to say that it was over then but it wasn't.

The judge didn't rap his gavel and officially close court, so people were slow to realize that the formal hearing was over. But within a few minutes the impact of the judge's decision sank in and once again, as if the entirety of the previous 7 hours had not occurred, my siblings and assorted minions surrounded Mom, even as I was trying to get her out of the courtroom so we could get her some food.

I'm not sure what was in the judge's mind, but as I tried to get Mom to the door, he asked that I stop and said in effect that the reconciliation process should start there in his courtroom. Frankly I didn't care what happened in his courtroom any longer just as long as it had nothing to do with us. What I did care about was Mom's health and since it was now about 5 p.m., she hadn't eaten in nearly 11 hours!

But Nancy crowded in, grabbed Mom and started rubbing her back as if whatever ordeal Mom went through was caused by anything, and anyone other than herself. Mom stood stiffly as her antagonists tried to make believe it hadn't all happened, and it was nearing 5:30 by the time we finally got Mom downstairs.

Of all the comments that were made in the half hour after Mom's victory, there were two that none of us heard, even in a whisper from Nancy, Skeeter, Courtney, Jim or their lawyers. Not one of the people who just put Ella Winter through the battle of her life said, "I'm sorry, Mom."

And after the way Ella clearly showed her competence by skillfully parrying every single attack by Nancy's lawyer, it apparently never occurred to them to say, "Congratulations Mom. You certainly didn't appear to be demented on the stand. We're really happy the judge found you competent." The things that weren't said that day were as significant as the things that were said.

In time we got Mom out of the courtroom and into the elevator. John went ahead, retrieved his car and pulled it up to the sidewalk right outside the courthouse door. Mom got in, and John and I walked to the back so we could place our suit coats in the trunk for the trip to Connecticut.

Just then the Nancy Patrick legal team and entourage exited the courthouse, and it was one sorry looking group of people. Faces were grim, eyes were downcast and there was no joy in Albany. I thought then that if they really cared about Ella they would be overjoyed that she acquitted herself so well on the witness stand and was declared competent. But that case was never about Mom, or her competence, as future events would soon reaffirm.

The entourage walked within a few feet of us and I could not resist singing a few bars of the Beatles' ***"I'm A Loser,"*** to which John immediately told me to hush. "We don't want to gloat," he said. "Your Mom has been through a difficult day."

Well, maybe ***he*** didn't want to gloat, but after what my family went through for the previous three months I wanted to gloat a whole bunch. When I was on the witness stand Jack Casey asked me how I would handle the future with my family. This question was asked in the context of previous questions that Rowlands asked my mother on what she would do if Nancy withdrew her suit. (This was after more than four hours of testimony against Mom.)

I told Jack that in the previous three months my brother and sister repeatedly and maliciously attacked my home and family, akin to an electronic home invasion. I said that if they had the backbone to try in person what they did over the phone, I could have and would have called the police. I added, however, that I would sit down with Mom and work something out.

But that statement was based on the supposition that my sister would withdraw her complaint and acknowledge the error of her ways. She didn't do either.

Not only did Mom not get an apology, neither did I or the rest of my immediate family, who had been under as much stress as Mom. But out on the sidewalk I acquiesced to John's better manners. We got in the car and headed for the highway.

It was so late by now that we gave up on any idea of going to the Purple Pub. We drove up Rt. 787, and picked up Interstate 90 east toward Boston. We crossed the Hudson River and as we headed up the hill toward Columbia I took a last look in the side view mirror and saw the tall buildings of downtown Albany receding in the distance.

It was one of the most beautiful sights I have ever seen.

I suppose that in the interests of fairness there is an issue that should be related here. I have been critical of Judge Egan because I believed, and I still do, that he should have dismissed Nancy Patrick's lawsuit at the first hearing. It was meritless, there was nothing to support the allegations contained in it, and in the long run, after many thousands of dollars were spent, it *was* dismissed.

I believe its lack of merit was apparent from the outset.

Nonetheless, Mom thinks Judge Egan is the best thing to hit the earth since sliced bread. She is not interested in the legal technicalities as much as she is interested in how she was treated when she took the witness stand. She dismisses Nancy and her lawyer with a wave of her hand, but she will tell you in an instant that Judge Egan put her at ease, and she felt very comfortable testifying before him.

"He told me to turn to him and talk just to him," Mom says. "I didn't have to look out on the courtroom and all those people. I didn't have to look at Nancy or her lawyer. I just talked to the judge and I told him my whole life story. I think it made a difference to him that I could tell him so much about myself."

So, I will continue to believe that the case progressed much further than it should have, and Mom will always believe that Judge Egan rescued her from a fate that to this day makes her shudder.

That subject matter makes for good discussions in our home, but after we left Albany we still didn't feel safe, at least not for a while. We arrived at the toll booth at Exit B-1, picked up the ticket and headed east on the Governor Thomas E. Dewey Thruway. We paid the toll at the Canaan Barrier booths and continued toward the Massachusetts border.

No one in the car took an easy breath until we passed the sign that said ***Welcome to Massachusetts.*** Then we all let out a collective sigh of relief. We stopped at the first rest stop on the Massachusetts Turnpike and Mom got a MacDonald's hamburger and milk for her victory dinner.

It was twelve hours since she last ate, she went through an emotionally brutal day, she was verbally assaulted in the courtroom by two of her children and other family members, and when her burger arrived she literally inhaled her food. We chatted a bit, and toasted Mom's victory with diet colas and shakes, then resumed the trip to Connecticut.

I'd like to say that it was over then but it wasn't.

One of the last things Judge Egan said after he dismissed the case was that the court evaluator, Chad Balzer, should submit an invoice for his expenses. I thought his total bill couldn't be more than two or three thousand dollars at the most.

But the court evaluator's bill was nearly $9,000! In the following weeks we found that true to form, my sister, who wanted Mom to pay all the legal fees for the case, but lost that option when the judge dismissed it, wanted Mom to pay Balzer's bill in its entirety too. Jack Casey suggested that we petition to have Nancy Patrick pick up the bill since she filed the suit, it was proven to be without merit, and we never asked for nor needed the court evaluator's services.

So it was back to the judge, more arguments, more time, and more money. Jack noted that the evaluator was charging $300 per hour for his services, more than Jack charged for his time when he was arguing in court, and that the judge didn't even use the lengthy report the evaluator submitted. In fact, no one asked for a report from the evaluator, other than his impression of Mom's mental abilities. And even though we offered numerous times to drive to New York to meet with the judge and the evaluator, we were instead forced under threat of a court order to allow him to drive to Connecticut, with us paying even while he was just driving!

Nancy, who continued her spiteful phone messaging, left the following on May 1, 2009, after Jack filed notice that Mom would fight being stuck with the evaluator's $9,000 bill.

"If you're talking about the court evaluator who was appointed by the court, not by me, I have no control over him. He's giving you the price for you not bringing Mom here for him to talk to."

When I passed that one on to Mom she was stunned. The court evaluator was appointed because Nancy brought a meritless suit against her own mother, and now Nancy was denying any responsibility for either her own actions, or the cost associated with them. To add insult to injury she was claiming that the bill would have been less if we brought Mom to New York for an interview, which is exactly what we offered for nearly two months prior to the trial!

In a registered letter sent to us in April, Nancy tried to convince Mom that she was being lied to in our home and only Nancy was really looking out for Mom's "best interests."'

"I was trying to protect you from what I think is a bad situation. Chad the court evaluator said ... it was obvious to anyone that you were being fed constant false information about me."

Actually, Balzer's report said nothing of the kind, but there was no reason to let the truth get in the way of an ongoing soap opera script. And Nancy ended her letter with a flippant shot at her mother, *"I forgot to mention that **my** attorney bills were paid in full before Friday.* (The week following the trial.) *I would never have **you** pay for anything that is **my responsibility**. You should already know that."*

Except her legal bills, court evaluator's fees, miscellaneous expenses and the cost of forcing Mom into an Alzheimer's ward. Nancy apparently was willing to pick up the cost of anything else.

Her May 1 phone message ended with Nancy claiming that any issue of payment to Chad Balzer had ***"No bearing on my part. I don't know what you're talking about .... I feel so sorry for my Mom."***

She may have felt a twinge of guilt after the trial, but she was not sorry enough to avoid suing her mother, and not sorry enough to pay the bills that wouldn't exist except for her lawsuit. Nor was she sorry that she continued to press the legal action right through a full-day trial that ultimately showed with unquestionable clarity that Mom is in command of her faculties.

Nancy also was in a bit of a bind to find a way to explain Mom's comment on the witness stand that she hadn't called Skeeter or Nancy while the suit was in progress, because you don't *"talk to the enemy."* Nancy's lawyer tried to pin that on me during the trial but Mom made it clear that it was not me who was driving her thinking.

But within a month Nancy found a way to work the blame for her actions back on me. The next few lines of her May 1, 2009 message were priceless.

"Courtney did not come from Boston to berate Mom. She came to support Mom and try to protect her.

"Skeeter did not come from Florida to be an enemy to Mom, he came to try to protect Mom, and to protect her assets, and to protect her from you."

"Whatever's going on with your family and what you're doing to Mom, it's sad, it's pitiful. ... My Mom has never been mad at me for more than 10 minutes in her whole life until she got into your house, and now suddenly I'm the enemy?"

As I noted previously there is enough material here for a fledgling psychiatrist's entire career.

Somehow, my sister managed to overlook the fact that this entire issue erupted because she refused to give Mom's checkbook back to her. Then, when Mom stood up for herself and exercised her rights as a free and independent citizen, it was Nancy who filed suit against her.

It was Nancy who falsely claimed Mom was suffering from and being treated for Alzheimer's, that she was demented, and that her mental state had deteriorated to such a degree that she shouldn't come to court because she wouldn't be able to comprehend the action against her or take part in her own defense.

This was the same Ella Winter who was adjudged competent by a slew of medical and legal professionals, including the New York Supreme Court judge who heard the lawsuit that Nancy Patrick brought against her own mother.

And in that suit, Nancy sought to amass all of her mother's assets into an account, not in Ella's name, but in Nancy's name, and only Nancy's name. Maybe Mom hasn't been angry with her daughter for more than ten minutes in the past, but she sure is angry with her now! Of course, there was that little matter of being sued by her own daughter, who not only attempted to "marshal" all of Mom's resources, but stated repeatedly in the lawsuit that she wanted to be Ella's guardian with power to place her in a nursing home.

The messages from Nancy Patrick were remarkable in their rancorous, even sadistic commentary, and that they came from a person who appeared to be in total denial.

She continued, ***"What do you think I am? What do you think I am?"***

Actually, I hadn't given that concept any thought at all. But since she brought it up, I'll just note that actions speak louder than words.

Nancy called again later that day again trying to claim that her daughter, who drove from Boston to testify against Ella, did so only because she feared that she would never see Mom again. I have already relayed the essence of that message, along with my questions about why Courtney tried to put Mom into an elder facility when Mom obviously didn't want to go. If she wanted to talk to Mom, she only needed to wait for a break in the proceedings.

But this is where the lunch issue came up too.

"And when she was trying to say goodbye you wanted to rip her away and take her <u>to lunch!</u>

"And guess what the judge said? BACK OFF! You know why? Because you're a jerk! You're such a total jerk I can't even believe it.

"My daughter and your brother came to that courtroom to see their mother, because you haven't let them see their mother or talk to their mother in almost five months. What kind of human being are you?"

OK, aside from the confused identity issues—Mom is also Skeeter's mother, but she is Courtney's grandmother—and that Judge Egan never said, "back off," this is another one of those ever-so-revealing commentaries. Nancy Patrick had, by May 1, completely driven from her mind the fact that she, her brother and her daughter all testified against Mom in a case that she and she alone brought against her mother.

And despite the image she attempted to convey on the day of the trial—the doting daughter who was rescuing her mother from God knows what so she could be placed in an elder facility—her actions don't stand up to scrutiny. At the end of the trial as we were attempting to see to Mom's needs, in this case, feeding her, Nancy could have cared less that Ella didn't eat for nearly 12 hours; she just wanted to make some kind of show for the judge and the judge to his eternal discredit allowed Nancy to do it.

But that doesn't alter the fact that Ella was starving, was exhausted, was forced to endure a day-long trial in which her freedom was at stake, was over-stressed, and just wanted a bite to eat. All that was important to Nancy Patrick on the day of the trial, and more than a month later, was that she could find someone upon whom she could unleash her invective.

Obviously, now that Mom is no longer in her area of control, someone else is going to be the target. Fortunately for Mom, she is now out of Nancy's range. Unfortunately for Nancy, I didn't sign up to be the replacement whipping boy.

In the end, Balzer came down to $6,500 and Mom, wanting this over with once and for all, agreed to split it. In an attempt at some form of reconciliation she asked her son, Wilson Winter III, the horse breeder from Ocala, Florida to kick in one third to ease the burden on her.

He refused.

The really odd thing is that the judge never accepted the evaluator's recommendation. Balzer came to our house on the Sunday before the trial, interrogated Mom for three hours and, like everyone else, found her to be competent.

But that didn't convince the judge to rule that Mom shouldn't have to go through the real ordeal—a day-long trial at which two thirds of her immediate family were trying to force her into an Alzheimer's facility when she was perfectly happy right where she was. The judge said he read the evaluator's report, but that was it.

Mom didn't hire the evaluator, and we only agreed to see him in Connecticut because we were threatened with a court order if we didn't. We offered numerous times to drive to Albany so Judge Egan and/or the evaluator could meet with Mom there—but they refused to guarantee safe passage. How scary is that? Jack went to court for us one last time on June 5, 2009, and the judge accepted the settlement.

I'd like to say that it was over then but it wasn't.

It was only three weeks later that the investigator from the Connecticut Department of Social Services came to our home to look into the false allegation of elder abuse as I related in the opening pages of this book. Mom met with her, she contacted Mom's doctors, and the case was written off for what it was, another instance of harassment from Nancy Patrick.

But Nancy still wasn't through. Even though Mom moved to Connecticut in December 2008, and moved all her financial accounts, including credit cards, to her new address and new banks, we received a message in June that Nancy used Mom's credit card in late May, without Mom's permission, to make an online purchase.

The credit card company contacted us with information on the purchase and a number to call to report abuse. We did, and they sent a complaint form which Mom filled out. The incident also resulted in Mom cancelling the credit card and filing for a new one. It was just more stress, more harassment, and served only to set Mom's resolve to put off contacting Nancy.

But the attack of delirium that resulted from the social worker's visit ultimately gave us the one item that eluded us for so long regarding Mom's health—a diagnosis for what happened to Mom on December 13, 2008 when she was found to be in what Albany Medical Center termed an Altered Mental Status.

Nancy testified that Mom suffered several of those attacks, always with Nancy present. After a lengthy examination and interview, Mom's doctor Katarzyna Pomianowski, who works with Dr. Gildersleeve, said her examination revealed that Nancy was the source of Mom's fear and stress, the cause of her episodes.

"Mrs. Winter told me how scared she was that 'her daughter is going to get her' and within an hour, developed confusion, disorientation. My diagnosis was reactive confusion/delirium-like state brought on by stress. It is my opinion that stress associated with attempts to place Mrs. Winter in a nursing home is seriously affecting her health resulting in delirium-like symptoms."

But there were more surprises in store for us. I wondered throughout the trial why Albany Medical Center, with a full medical staff, was never able to document Mom's alertness and mental acuity, as we had done.

I also was curious as to why, when Jack Casey was arguing to have the case thrown out on jurisdictional grounds in February that Albany Medical Center, through Nancy's lawyer, supposedly rejected the mental acuity exam that Mom passed with such a high score as meaningless because of its preliminary nature.

Doctor Gildersleeve told us she would be happy to supply whatever follow-up information was needed. I also was told that Mom didn't need further testing because she did so well on the preliminary tests. In later discussions with other medical professionals it was explained to me that forcing Mom to go for in-depth neurological testing was akin to making a heart patient who passed an EKG and a stress test go for open heart surgery "just in case." It just seemed to me that with all the medical expertise available to Mom in Albany Medical Center someone should have been able to come up with a better diagnosis than Altered Mental State.

In fact, someone did.

As I noted earlier, Jim Patrick said that Albany Med wanted to discharge Mom on December 17, 2008, but they convinced the neurology department to keep her for two more days for more tests. In the weeks after the trial, while we were sorting the records from Albany Medical Center, my wife came across two documents that we were seeking since January—the reports on Mom's last two days in the hospital, December 18 and December 19, 2008.

They showed that Mom was given the same preliminary mental acuity screening test in Albany Medical Center that she took in Dr. Gildersleeve's office in February. And the results were exactly the same—a score of 28 out of 30! And right below that entry is another, a diagnosis of delirium, just as Dr. Pomianowski found in June!

Someone in Albany Medical Center knew what was bothering Mom. And those reports were kept from us until it was too late to use them in Mom's trial.

After the issue of Chad Balzer's fee was settled, and before the Connecticut Department of Social Services initiated its examination, we thought we could finally relax. But Nancy resumed phone calls to our house and accompanying backbiting messages. At that point, I decided to put my foot down. I contacted and spoke with doctors and lawyers, the Connecticut State Police, the Connecticut Chief State's Attorney's Elder Abuse division, the Connecticut Attorney General's office, as well as our state Senator and Representative all of whom agree that it is incumbent upon me to be the buffer between Mom and Nancy's vitriol.

I also have a responsibility to the rest of my family, and I can tell you without reservation they are sick to death of retrieving phone messages only to be assaulted by Nancy Patrick's latest issue du jour. So, I blocked incoming calls from most of the numbers that Nancy and her associates used in the previous three months. Nancy got around that one time by using a fax machine phone, but after I received that message I blocked that number too.

But that didn't give us exactly the results we were seeking—a respite from the harassment so Mom could have some time of uninterrupted peace. Instead, Nancy's next step was to have her daughter, Courtney Patrick, call the Connecticut Department of Social Services and again lodge another false complaint of elder abuse against us. I talked several more times with the department head, social worker, and ombudsman about protecting Mom.

Ella's doctor gave us her diagnosis of stress induced delirium in writing, including Mom's specific fear of Nancy Patrick. When I received a call from the Social Services department about Courtney's complaint, I needed only to remind them that Mom's granddaughter travelled from Boston to Albany to testify against her grandmother. When I did, that diversion went away.

Mom's case is now in the files in Connecticut, the state police are aware of it, and we are on solid legal ground, in our own ballpark, finally. In the end Mom was her own best defense and despite the cruel claims in Nancy Patrick's lawsuit, Mom handled herself with strength and determination. On her own merit she won the day—and she won her freedom.

But that victory, like any victory in a hard-fought campaign, did not come without cost.

Ella Winter is safe in Connecticut now and is rebuilding her life. She lives in a farm community that she often says reminds her of Center Brunswick and Waverly, the New York towns where she spent her youth.

She is making new friends, and enjoying being in a home. She eats betters, sleeps better, enjoys the dogs, and the company of her family. She gets her hair done every week, plays the piano, sings hymns, reads her Bible, and socializes. She continues to call her brother Vic and other family members, as well as some of her old friends.

I'd like to say that it is over now but it isn't.

In late October, 2009 I received a phone call from Jim Patrick's daughter Lori from his first marriage. She is a wonderfully outgoing person, we always enjoyed her company and I decided to talk with her.

After exchanging voice mail messages for a few days we finally linked up and spoke for more than an hour about Mom's medical issues, the false claims contained in my sister's lawsuit and outside commentaries, the way Mom feels about her granddaughter testifying against her, and especially the attacks of delirium that come after conflicts with Nancy.

Lori was familiar with the issues I spoke of, and at the end of our conversation said she would contact her father and explain my concerns. I told her I agreed with her decision, and specifically asked that she relay the information about Mom's bouts with delirium. I told Lori that the affect of these bouts is cumulative and I was warned by doctors that ultimately, Mom could lapse into a coma and never recover.

I told Mom about my conversation with Lori, and added that she was going to talk with her father James Patrick, in hopes of ending Nancy's ongoing harassment. Mom was upbeat at the prospects of finally being about to relax and stop worrying about Nancy's next attack.

In retrospect I never should have told Mom about my conversation with Lori. Because within two days of talking with Lori I received an email from James which just picked up where the last attack left off.

Ron,

Lori called me on Saturday to relate your conversation with her Friday evening relative to your mother's health, etc.

To date, I have chosen to remain silently in the background in the hopes that time would help calm the environment surrounding this mess, and, more importantly, your limitless anger toward your siblings. I cannot imagine reacting to family with that much hatred ... Lori tells me that Ella is continuing to experience some of the same delusional episodes that she imagined in Dutch Village whereby the people living above her were trying to break into her unit at night.

There is plenty more but that was enough for Mom. My New York 'family' was still placing the onus for what happened to Mom on my shoulders, denying any responsibility, and most importantly substituting the word ***"delusional"*** for ***"delirium."***

Obviously, nothing changed, and nothing is ever going to change. But that night, once again, Mom had another bout of delirium, and as bad as the others had been this one scared us to the core.

I have never seen her this bad, and I called Dr. Gildersleeve's office for help. All we could do was get Mom to sleep, so the fear and stress could wear off, but we couldn't give her a sleeping pill, either prescription or over-the-counter medication because they can make things worse.

Finally, after nearly two days of being disoriented and unable to speak coherently, Mom started sleeping for longer periods. It took two more days, four total, before she began to look better and feel better.

Ironically, Mom is completely aware of these attacks, and what is happening to her during them. She can sit down afterward and talk about what was occurring around her, and her inability to make herself understood.

The upshot of that attack was a final determination that there will be no more attempts at meeting anyone halfway, partway, a third or a quarter of the way. There will be no more of that. Every time Mom got her hopes up, Nancy dashed it. And each time, Mom suffered for it.

And each time, my family in Connecticut must bear the brunt of the manipulation from New York. We stay up all night tending to Mom, we worry about the impact on her health and well being, and we sit with her nursing her back from the brink.

Mom has given up on any reconciliation with New York and instead focuses on her life in Connecticut.

But she also has moments when she just sits down and asks "why?" There still is a sense of disbelief that her daughter, son and granddaughter tried to put her into an elder facility when she made it so clear that she never wanted to go there—and had a more than viable alternative.

She reminisces about her brother Bob and wonders aloud whether he would still be alive if he was allowed to return to his home—especially if he received some form of hospice or respite care—instead of being told that he too was being institutionalized.

She thinks back to the events leading up to her move to Connecticut and often repeats the testimony she gave in the New York Supreme Court in Albany:

"I can't help it if they (Nancy, Jim and Courtney) took me to Ron's house and I liked it and I stayed there when they went away.

"It just doesn't make sense that I should be mad about it. He is a great cook, and she is a great cook and I have the run of the house.

"I'm happy. So I think that is the main thing.

"Isn't it?

"That I'm happy?"

In early December 2009, as I sat in my office working on this manuscript a silver/gray four-door sedan pulled up to our driveway. It was a sunny day and I could clearly see the male occupant inside, looking intently at our home.

The car was parallel to the house and stayed on the street, so I couldn't see the license plate. But it looked like the state car that the Department of Aging investigator was driving six months earlier.

The car stayed parked at the end of our driveway for nearly ten minutes, neither pulling in, nor pulling away. Finally, it started moving, ever so slowly. I stayed at my desk, keeping an eye on him, and kept the dogs at my side, ready to let them loose if the situation demanded it.

Finally the car pulled out of sight. I was never able to get a clear view of the license plate. I have no idea if it was another visit from the state or something else. But once again our home was put on edge, once again we were reminded that we can never rest easy, never be absolutely sure whether there will be another assault on us, or where it will come from.

I'd like to say that it is over now but ....

The End?

Epilogue

The key to successfully planning for care and living arrangements in elder years, either our own or for family members is awareness.

We must be aware of legalities, we must be aware of medical conditions and their signs, we must be aware of finances in general and our own in particular. We should research the various options available to us in our later years including retirement facilities, assisted living facilities and nursing homes, long before we may need them.

It is obvious after reading **Granny Snatching** that we cannot count on things to simply "go our way" when we reach advanced age. If we really want things to go our way we must have a plan, and have a backup plan for when that one fails. Put money aside if possible for legal costs. Tell a trusted friend what you have planned out so if there are unexplained changes later on someone will know and be in a position to ask questions.

We need lawyers, good lawyers, honest lawyers. We should be in a professional relationship with them years before we need them to watch over our estates, so they will be familiar with our assets and our intentions if they are called upon later. We should be honest with members of our immediate family who would be affected by any decisions on our futures, and we should communicate our wishes, through our attorney if necessary. Family members should at least have access to the attorney, separately if there is tension among them, and be informed of what we have planned. No one, however, should have any right to alter the terms of our future care independently and without our consent.

We should research the costs of elder care facilities in our area, including the costs of retirement homes, assisted living and nursing homes—especially with an eye to increased costs of those facilities over time. Many now require a down payment, often more than six figures, just to be considered for admission, in addition to a monthly payment of thousands of dollars. Can we or our loved ones afford that cost indefinitely?

What comes with the charge for placement in an elder facility? Is medical care available around the clock, are meals included, are there adequate recreation and fitness facilities to keep our relatives active and participating?

Of utmost importance, what happens if we or our loved ones run out of money? What if (or when) we outlive our life expectancy and can no longer afford a facility where we may have lived for years? What happens then? Are we placed on Medicaid, moved to a state approved facility, forced to share a room with one or more other people in the same situation?

These are hard questions but they should be answered long before placement is even considered. Those who are assigned to our care, and I'm talking family members here, should have their own networks of friends and associates who can help when called upon. Ella Winter was aided to a great extent in her fight against her New York family by a long-established network of people who remembered her from her early years, and stepped up when asked.

All across America and in many countries overseas, officials and scholars alike are working feverishly to get a handle on the extent of Granny Snatching and coincident increases in reporting of elder abuse. While the high profile cases have increased public awareness, the bulk of the problem lies in myriad cases involving far less money, but creating difficulties and heartache for families that are no less worrisome.

I was surprised to learn from friends that issues with elder care and asset management are far more widespread than I imagined. A former colleague from Connecticut sent me the following:

Ron, Family feuds are the worst. I KNOW! I too had one with my sister and brother-in-law over the splitting of my Aunt's estate. But the bad blood started earlier because my Dad never liked my brother-in-law.

My wife and I tried to bridge that gap, but it didn't work. The estate battle dragged on for four or five years and split my sister, her husband and my wife and I. What a nightmare! It took a while but I try to be as kind as I can to them while they ignore me as if I didn't exist.

I hope your mother gets through all of this with her health! Best ...

Similar messages came from across the country; heartbreaking tales of families that once seemed close, torn apart as elder relatives became increasingly dependent on others.

I found that many of my friends and acquaintances wrestled with the specter of Alzheimer's and was proud to see that they handled it with all the dignity and respect they could muster for themselves and their family members. Some were forced, due to job, family and living circumstances to place an elder relative in an Alzheimer's home. They did all they could to select facilities with excellent reputations that provided the best possible care.

One family spent two years caring for their mother in her home so she would not have to be placed in a facility. But not everyone can accommodate an aging family member for the rest of their lives. I am sure that in the majority of cases they would if they could, but sometimes this is simply not possible.

As I explained to my brother-in-law James Patrick on December 17, 2008, we were positioned perfectly to bring Mom to our home because we made a major shift in our living and working arrangements a few years earlier. We decided to homeschool my youngest daughter, an opportunity for which my wife and I are uniquely qualified.

By doing so, we ensured that I work primarily out of my home office, that my wife works only a few minutes away and has flexible hours that enable her to be home if I have a client call. Thus when we offered to bring Mom to our house, rather than placing her in an elder facility – regardless of which definition my siblings are using today – the only real adjustment involved moving furniture, lots of it to be sure, but nonetheless it wasn't as if our entire lifestyle was revised.

I'll repeat, because it bears repeating, not everyone can do this. Not everyone wants to do this, and not everyone should do this. It worked for us and it can work for others, but it simply will not work for everyone.

Similarly, while there are many good elder care facilities, and nothing in this book is intended as a slap at any facility, it is unfortunately true that not every facility provides quality care, and not all staff members in such facilities are the people you really want tending to the needs of your loved ones. Elder abuse allegations and arrests surface periodically, but the many difficulties involved with documenting elder abuse, including incapacitated individuals and in some cases fear of retaliation, make it difficult to gather hard statistics. There are, however, some national figures that give us an indication of the scope of the problem and the speed with which it is growing.

A 2004 nationwide survey of data from state Adult Protective Services revealed 565,747 reports of suspected elder and vulnerable adult abuse the previous year, a 19.7 percent increase when compared with 482,913 reports four years earlier.

This represents 8.3 reports of abuse for every 1,000 older Americans. In more than 89 percent of the cases the alleged abuse was reported to have occurred in a domestic setting!

Meanwhile, both the raw numbers and percentage of Americans classified as elderly are climbing and within a few years, as the bulk of the Baby Boomer generation passes the sixty-five-year-old mark, the numbers will increase at a near exponential rate. By the year 2030 an estimated 78 million Americans will be classified as elderly.

Since the concept of "Granny Snatching" often involves more than one state, an effort also is well underway to create a uniform national guardianship law. But even with a uniform law, there will continue to be cases where the rights of an elderly person are at risk. It is a safe assumption that money will be the root cause on at least one side of the dispute.

So what can be done? As the Boy Scouts say, Be Prepared! Know what people mean when they use common terms regarding elder care and medical conditions. I have listed a few of the most common legal and medical definitions in the following Appendix.

It also is common for claims made in legal actions to be, shall we say, somewhat excessive. In divorce actions for instance, the breakdown of a marriage often is defined in terms that can range from inflated to outrageous. So if you find yourself in the midst of a legal action, expect that many of the allegations against you will be quite personal, inaccurate, and having little to do with the core issues in the lawsuit, except to provide a diversion.

In that case you must learn to prioritize, stick to only the issues that affect the outcome of the case, and don't allow yourself to get bogged down in superfluous arguments that solve nothing but run up the legal bills.

The case of Nancy Patrick vs. Ella Winter was similar to a divorce action in the sense that the claims made by Nancy and other family members in support of institutionalizing Ella often had only the most tenuous attachment to reality. These were not verbal claims made in the heat of debate, but rather specific written allegations contained in the documents filed to support her case.

Nancy Patrick's lawsuit also claimed in essence that I had plotted to move my mother to Connecticut under false pretenses, that once she arrived there I cocooned her away from all other contacts and fed her a regular diet of misinformation on Nancy's intentions.

Even though her intent was spelled out clearly in the allegations and **"POWERS SOUGHT"** in her lawsuit, Nancy Patrick tried to explain it all away as some sort of legalese. However, the very first paragraph under **Property Powers Sought**, Paragraph 1, states, ***"marshal the income and assets of M. ELLA WINTER, and establish bank, brokerage, and other similar accounts in the name of the guardian."***

The thrust of the rest of the lawsuit was a flood of allegations regarding Mom's health, her mental status and my intentions. Ultimately, we proved these allegations to be false, even though they continued to be repeated after the lawsuit was dismissed.

In the long run, Nancy Patrick's claims, and those of others who testified against Mom, were disregarded and discarded by Judge Egan once he heard the case and interrogated Ella Winter himself. They also were disproved to a large degree by Ella's handling of her interview with Court Evaluator Chad Balzer. In fact, Balzer's report highly commended Ella, but as we will see, it also contained flaws that left Judge Egan with little recourse but to reject its recommendations.

The primary reason why Nancy Patrick's lawsuit was dismissed was because Ella showed herself to be competent in virtually every interview and test. She was the best evidence in her favor and having met her there was little the court could do but rule in her favor. But in addition to Ella's competence, there was another reason why we were able to deflect so much of the venom that was directed at us. We had—and have—records: phone records, emails, medical records, receipts and calendars that showed by day and date where we were and what we were doing, going back more than a decade.

These records were available, but in many cases not used during Ella's trial because the goal in that proceeding was to prove

Ella's competence. Going into the individual allegations, especially those aimed at me, would have had no impact on the outcome of the trial, but would have prolonged it and cost Mom even more money. Nonetheless, they exist, are available should they be needed in the future, and they go a long way toward resolving "he said-she said" disputes. Having documentation is essential to prevail in a legal proceeding.

That is a salient point that was either missed or not considered when my siblings and their families decided to sue Mom and take us all to court. You can make all the commentaries you want outside the courtroom, but when you take the stand you better have proof of your commentaries or you will lose, and possibly worse.

As I noted at the outset, there never was a single medical record included in the lawsuit against her that showed Mom had been diagnosed with or treated for Alzheimer's or dementia as her daughter claimed. Albany Medical Center knew Mom was mentally competent and that she was suffering bouts of delirium that it attributed to her being in the hospital. The records from Albany Medical Center are proof of this. An in-depth analysis of this delirium by Mom's medical provider in Connecticut showed that it had less to do with a hospital, and far more to do with her fear of her daughter.

But that is only one of the many issues that were raised in Mom's trial that we are able to disprove simply because we have the documentation that disproves them. Some of this documentation came from unexpected sources, including court evaluator Chad Balzer's report. He conducted a three-hour interview with Ella, at least half of which was in her company alone.

He wrote: ***"I asked Ronald and Jennifer to allow me to meet privately with Ms. Winter (Ella) which occurred for a large part of the interview, approximately 1.5 hours."***

That statement alone knocks the stuffing out of any claim that we were manipulating and influencing Ella. Balzer noted that Mom had occasional difficulties recalling specific dates or names, however,

"Ms. Winter was fully oriented to our conversation for the entire three-hour interview. She was engaged and appropriately responded to the many questions asked of her. She also asked me appropriate questions understanding my role in this proceeding. Every answer to my questions was specifically responsive, and included pertinent information."

Remember, Mom was ninety-two years old at the time of his interview, and Atty. Balzer moved up his arrival time by two hours without notifying us. Normally, Mom would have been taking a nap during much of the time she was under interrogation. Yet she had little difficulty handling his inquiries and responding with her own.

Balzer's time sheets show that after he interviewed Ella and returned to New York, he had additional conversations with both Nancy and Skeeter, ostensibly to inform them of his findings. Unfortunately, neither appeared to be willing to drop the lawsuit.

Skeeter already filed an affidavit in the case that was notable only for its fabrication. He claimed for instance in Paragraph 5 of his affidavit that, ***"I contacted my brother Ronald and he offered to care for our mother at his home in Connecticut until long-term plans could be established."***

This is patently inaccurate. Phone records show I talked with my brother one time, on the night of December 14, 2008 when he called to tell me that Mom was in the hospital. That was the extent of our conversation other than what I have previously written – that we discussed convening a family meeting between Christmas and New Year's to discuss Mom's future.

The only conversation I had with anyone – other than my wife —prior to Mom's move that involved her living in Connecticut was with James Patrick on December 17. I did not talk with my brother after December 14 until he arrived in Connecticut on December 30. His penchant for inserting himself into places and conversations where he didn't actually appear or take part is troubling, but his comments are not supported by the records.

The records from Albany Medical Center also provided much needed backup for Mom's claims to competence. Although Atty. Balzer had access to them, I was disappointed that when he referred to the discharge forms he neglected to mention that Mom was treated for Hypokalemia—potassium deficiency.

The Transfer Discharge form stated that on Dec. 17, 2008 "the patient was noted to be Hypokalemic" and she was given intravenous potassium. That factor was not noted in Balzer's report.

Rather, he played up the hospital's suppositions that Mom's Altered Mental Status could have been related to senile dementia or even secondary to her stay in the hospital. Those were *suppositions* listed on the discharge statement of Dec. 19, 2008, and as we later learned, someone at that hospital already knew what was wrong with Mom.

Although he interviewed Mom and gave a clear and concise report of her competency, Balzer ended up trying to please both sides by recommending that the judge find Mom competent, but NOT dismiss the suit against her. This, however, would have left Mom at the mercy of her daughter on several fronts, not the least of which was Nancy's attempt to have Ella pay all of the legal bills, including Nancy's.

It also ignored the fact that the judge kept the case going by claiming that he couldn't be sure Ella was competent when she transferred her postal address, bank accounts and other affairs permanently to Connecticut late in December 2008, and early in January 2009. When the judge found Ella competent, there was no longer a jurisdictional issue. He didn't have it, and he knew it. He couldn't "split the baby" in an attempt to appease both sides. If Ella was competent, then Nancy Patrick had no case.

When interviewed by Chad Balzer after his trip to Connecticut to see Ella, Nancy continued to assert that Mom was suffering from Alzheimer's and should be placed in a nursing home as it states in her lawsuit. ***"Nancy confirmed the allegations as set forth in the petition,"*** Balzer noted at least twice in his report.

"Nancy told me that she and her mother had been best friends since Nancy was 20. Nancy indicated that she had talked to her mother or had seen her mother every day since she was 20 years old, until Ella went to Connecticut on Dec. 22, 2008."

Now, Nancy turned twenty in 1970. Considering that Mom and Dad often came to Connecticut to visit us for several days up to a week at a time beginning in 1983, I can say unequivocally that Nancy hardly ever called to talk to Mom while they were with us. And if you consider that Nancy is fifty-nine years old as of this writing, and was fifty-eight going on fifty-nine when Chad Balzer interviewed her, that means she claims to have talked with Mom every day for more than thirty-eight years—which is longer than she has been married!

If that claim was accurate, Nancy must have called her mother every single day of her honeymoon, and every single day when she and her family went away on vacations, and every other day for all those years regardless of where Nancy was or where Ella was. Regular family contact is nice, but if Nancy's claim was even remotely true it would long ago have gone from normal contact to an obsession.

I can't help but be reminded through this statement that there are two major times of separation between a parent and child in each of our lives: when the umbilical cord is cut; and when the apron strings are cut. According to Nancy's claims, only one of these events took place in her life.

Nancy also told Balzer that ***"if she could confirm that her mother was happy and doing well, she would be OK with her mother residing at Ronald's home in Connecticut."*** But Ella wrote a heartfelt letter to Nancy on March 11, 2009 explaining in detail that she was happy where she was and imploring Nancy to drop her lawsuit.

That exact issue was addressed in the trial when Nancy was being cross examined by Mom's lawyer, Jack Casey. Nancy claimed on the witness stand, under oath that she would never put Ella into a nursing home, *"and I will swear to that on any Bible."*

But Nancy already swore to the truthfulness of her lawsuit in which Paragraph 9 under **Personal Powers Sought** specifically stated that Nancy sought the power to **"arrange for her** (Mom's) **admission to a skilled nursing facility ..."**

When Jack pointed out that paragraph to Nancy in court she blew off her entire lawsuit by claiming that she filed it because I was preventing her from seeing her mother, and that it was all just legalese that didn't accurately represent what she wanted or believed. Meaning her entire lawsuit was not just frivolous, but vexatious too, and she knew it when she raised her hand and swore to the truthfulness of its contents.

But as Jack persisted in his cross examination Nancy engaged in semantics over the questions of renewed communication and visitation with her mother.

Casey: *"Has it been communicated to you through your lawyer that if you withdraw this petition all communications will begin again between you and your Mom?"*

Nancy Patrick: *"No."*

When Casey asked again, Nancy admitted that she did receive that communication but not from her attorney. Rather it was directly from her mother in the letter that Mom wrote on March 11.

Casey persisted in his questioning, asking several times in several ways if Nancy would drop the lawsuit if she was allowed to resume visitation and communication.

Casey: *"As you sit here right now, if your mother is willing to engage in communication and visit with you as it was before, would you withdraw your petition?"*

Nancy Patrick: *"No."*

Casey: *"So the answer is no you won't withdraw the petition and you want to go forward. Is that correct?"*

Nancy Patrick: *"Yes."*

And that was the totality of Nancy Patrick's position. She wanted what she wanted, and what she wanted was control over her mother in all facets of her life. She didn't care if Mom lived in Connecticut and if we took care of her twenty-four hours a day, seven days a week, so long as Nancy Patrick retained control. But as we have seen, that was not to be.

Mom's letter was an anguished outpouring, offering complete reconciliation, but also setting down the terms, mother to daughter. Nancy disregarded that letter just as she disregarded the medical testimony, legal affidavits and even Balzer's own report. Nancy continued to disregard anything that did not agree with her agenda, and continued to maintain that she, and only she, should regain control over Ella's finances, despite Mom's fierce opposition to her efforts.

Balzer had access to Mom's letter to Nancy and clear evidence that Nancy was saying whatever seemed to work at the moment, but not living up to her statements.

Balzer's report also said ***"It was Nancy's expectation that Ella would only be staying with her brother in Connecticut for three weeks while Nancy and her husband were in Florida. They brought some of Ella's belongings so that Ella would feel comfortable visiting for three weeks."***

Once again, as shown by Ella's testimony, and a timeline of the comings and goings of my siblings in January 2009, there not only was no discussion with us prior to Ella's move to Connecticut that the visit was temporary, but a meeting after Nancy's Florida vacation was not feasible. The documents proved the realities of the case, not the verbal claims.

No one at any time spoke of a three-week visit and there is no record of any such conversation, even in the myriad messages left on my voice mail. And, from a purely common sense angle, I would never have rearranged my home for three weeks, nor would we have packed Mom's room with her entire allotment of clothing that would take her from the winter, into the spring and summer.

We would not have brought furniture, including her television, her easy chair and ottoman, her wall paintings and photos, to our home. We have more than enough televisions here for Mom to watch whatever she wants and plenty of paintings and pictures for the walls.

Ella also told Nancy, Skeeter and Courtney directly in phone conversations between December 22, 2008 and January 24, 2009, the night the process server brought the lawsuit to our home, that she was happy in Connecticut and wanted to stay where she was. And lest we forget, it was only twenty-four hours from the time that Ella was dropped off in Connecticut, with a large amount of her personal belongings, that Nancy began emptying her apartment in Dutch Village, once again documented by Nancy's own emails to me.

The apartment management required a thirty-day advance notice of a lease termination so the official date when Mom no longer had access to her apartment was January 31, 2009. But everything she owned had long since been shredded, taken, given away or otherwise removed, the utilities were disconnected, and Mom had nowhere to live if she had gone back to New York—other than Hawthorne Ridge. Nancy even kept Mom's set of keys; she couldn't have gone back to her apartment if she wanted to, at least without permission from Nancy who was busy working to send her elsewhere.

Balzer's report also noted that Nancy claimed the doctors at Albany Medical Center said Ella could not go back to living alone in her apartment. But Nancy didn't offer to let Ella live at her house, and Ella maintains to this day that she would never have accepted such an offer, due to the volatile nature of her relationship with her daughter.

So the question remained, exactly where was Ella supposed to go after three weeks in Connecticut?

The logistics of moving Ella to Connecticut for only a three-week stay, and the accompanying claim that a family meeting was to take place immediately thereafter, were impossible. Skeeter already had gone back to his horse farm in Florida. He was scheduled to take a lengthy business trip in mid-January and said he was not coming back north until Memorial Day.

But even faced with overwhelming evidence that her statements did not hold water, Nancy continued to maintain that there was only one version of the truth, and it was hers.

Balzer's report also confirms our position that Nancy spoke with Ella after her move to Connecticut, far more than she claimed in her lawsuit.

He writes that Nancy said, ***"Since Dec. 22, 2008 when Ella went to Connecticut, Nancy has only been able to speak to her three times and leaves daily telephone messages which are unreturned."***

Once again, the Big Lie is repeated and repeated. Nancy spoke with Mom at least three times between Christmas Day and New Years, and spoke with her again several times in January. It was their conversation on New Year's Day when Nancy refused for at least the third time to give Mom back her checkbook that convinced Mom to rescind Nancy's Power of Attorney.

But it was Mom's Jan. 7, 2009 conversation with Nancy when Mom informed Nancy of her actions that Nancy erupted on the path that led to the lawsuit.

Balzer wrote that ***"Nancy indicated that she spoke to her mother while she was in Florida in December 2008 and January 2009."*** (This directly confirms our position and contradicts Nancy's statement from the previous paragraph that she had spoken with Mom only three times).

However, it also should be noted that by Nancy's own statements she was not in Florida until Jan. 2, 2009 and was emptying Mom's apartment from Dec. 23, until she left for Florida. But there still was no disruption in the contact between Ella and Nancy at this time.

Most significantly, Nancy admitted to Balzer, that ***"Ella told her that she thought things had changed and that Ella was staying in Connecticut. This upset Nancy ...."***

So, by Nancy's own admission, Mom made it clear weeks before Nancy filed suit against her, that her move was not considered temporary. This combined with Nancy's own admission that she spoke with Mom even after she filed the lawsuit, meaning she also spoke with Mom while she was preparing the lawsuit, completely negates the claim that the suit was filed only to overcome the lack of communication between Nancy and Ella.

Skeeter's claims of impeded contact with Mom were similarly revealed to be false simply by referring to phone records, and his statements. He spoke with Mom after his horse-selling trip, telling her about the condition of the market, even the weather. Skeeter returned from that trip after the lawsuit was initiated and he spoke with Mom only days before she was served. Again, the claim that the suit was initiated because Mom was not communicating with her family was false and the documents prove it.

The claims in Nancy Patrick's lawsuit, both those referring to Ella's mental condition, and the expanded claims of neglect and danger to her if she stayed in Connecticut were patently inaccurate, and ultimately Ella prevailed in a court of law. But if there had been further testimony required, the overwhelming preponderance of evidence showed that she moved to Connecticut willingly, was staying in Connecticut because she wanted to, and was in no danger in her new home. Ella preferred not to be moved out of her apartment in Menands, New York at all, but if she had to move elsewhere, she was clear that she was happy and well care for in Connecticut.

If you asked me in December, 2008 what I was hoping to achieve after Mom moved in with us, I would have told you that I wanted to give her a warm, safe place to live out her days. I would have told you that even with the problems that existed between me and my siblings I honestly thought "the family" would work together to make her final years the best possible. I did tell everyone in my family that they would be welcome to come visit Mom any time, so long as we were given sufficient advance warning to arrange our schedules accordingly.

That lasted less than two weeks, after which I was accused of a nefarious conspiracy involving stealing Mom's money and holding her against her will. Those accusations were thrown out with the rest of Nancy Patrick's lawsuit, but surfaced again and again as she and other members of her family continued to badger the state of Connecticut Social Services agencies, and send emails maintaining that Mom was delusional, nearly a year after Mom moved.

I had hoped things would be different, but it was not to be. It is unfortunate that as our population ages, many elderly are not allowed to age gracefully with dignity. It seems that some people forget that one day they too will be old, and one day they too will need someone to care for them and look out for them.

As my son Kevin said soon after the troubles began with Nancy Patrick's lawsuit, "They would do well to step back and think over what they're doing. Remember, their children are watching, and will remember."

Appendix I – Definitions

Legal

Power of Attorney: A written document in which one person appoints another person to act as an agent on his or her behalf, thus conferring authority on the agent to perform certain functions.

Powers of attorney can be written to be either general (full) or limited to special circumstances. A power of attorney generally is terminated when the principal dies or becomes incompetent, but the principal can revoke the power of attorney at any time.

Also, a "durable" power of attorney continues beyond the incapacity of the principal. A durable power of attorney can confer either general or limited power. Because no judicial proceedings are necessary, the principal saves time and money and avoids the stigma of being declared incompetent.

Guardian: A person who has been appointed by a judge to take care of a minor child or incompetent adult personally and manage that person's affairs. To become a guardian either the party intending to be the guardian or another family member, a close friend or a local official responsible for the individual's welfare will petition the court to appoint the guardian. The term "guardian" also refers to someone who is appointed to handle the affairs of a person who is incompetent or incapable of administering his/her affairs. This is more often called a "conservator" under a conservatorship

Executor: The person appointed to administer the estate of a person who has died leaving a will which nominates that person.

Unless there is a valid objection, the judge will appoint the person named in the will to be executor. The executor must insure that the person's desires expressed in the will are carried out. Practical responsibilities include gathering up and protecting the assets of the estate, obtaining information in regard to all beneficiaries named in the will and any other potential heirs, collecting and arranging for payment of debts of the estate, approving or disapproving creditor's claims, making sure estate taxes are calculated, forms filed, and tax payments made, and in all ways assist the attorney for the estate (which the executor can select).

Conservator: A guardian and protector appointed by a judge to protect and manage the financial affairs and/or the person's daily life due to physical or mental limitations or old age. The conservator may be only of the "estate" (meaning financial affairs), but may be also of the "person," when he/she takes charge of overseeing the daily activities, such as health care or living arrangements of the conservatee. The conservator is required to make regular accountings which must be approved by the court. The conservator may be removed by order of the court if no longer needed, upon the petition of the conservatee or relatives, or for failure to perform his/her duties.

Living Will: A written document that allows a patient to give explicit instructions about medical treatment to be administered when the patient is terminally ill or permanently unconscious; also called an advance directive.

Domicile: the place where a person has his/her permanent principal home.

Residence: the place where one makes his/her home. However, a person may have his/her state of "domicile" elsewhere for tax or other purposes, especially if the residence is for convenience or not of long standing.

Medical

Alzheimer's: A progressive form of pre-senile dementia that is similar to senile dementia except that it usually starts in the 40's or 50's; first symptoms are impaired memory which is followed by impaired thought and speech and finally complete helplessness.

Charles Bonnet syndrome: A condition that causes patients with visual loss to have complex visual hallucinations, first described by Charles Bonnet in 1760. The syndrome predominantly affects people with visual impairments due to old age or damage to the eyes or optic pathways. This includes vision loss due to macular degeneration and peripheral vision loss from glaucoma.

Hypokalemia: Potassium Deficiency where the body fails to retain the minimum amount of Potassium required for daily functions—it can be fatal if not treated. A person may also develop Potassium deficiency due to extra excretion of Potassium or lower quantity of Potassium in the daily diet.

Symptoms of Hypokalemia include: fatigue; muscular weakness; anxiety, confusion, diminished reflexes, convulsions, stupor or coma; skin blistering, eruptions or dryness; temporary memory loss; heart deterioration; hypertension, sleep loss, depression, constipation; ringing in the ear.

Dementia: Deterioration of intellectual faculties, such as memory, concentration, and judgment, resulting from an organic disease or a disorder of the brain. It is sometimes accompanied by emotional disturbance and personality changes.

Delusion: A false belief or opinion. A false belief strongly held in spite of invalidating evidence, especially as a symptom of mental illness.

Delirium: A ***<u>temporary state</u>*** of mental confusion and fluctuating consciousness resulting from high fever, intoxication, shock, or other causes. It is characterized by anxiety, disorientation, hallucinations, delusions, and incoherent speech.

Sleep Deprivation: Loss of normal amounts of sleep, leading to impaired hearing, sight, brain function, mental alertness, and physical ability, including slow reflexes and clumsiness.

These few definitions will give you a good start, but there is more work ahead to be fully capable of securely planning our futures.

We should educate ourselves on our rights while we are still capable of doing so, and move to protect our assets before they become part of a legal battle. We also should be aware of the signs of elder abuse, and be on the lookout to ensure that our elderly family members are being well cared for, or are taking care of themselves properly.

Physical or mental abuse could be occurring if you observe:

- Recurring or unexplained injuries
- A combination of new and old injuries
- Injuries without underlying diseases, or incompatible with medical history, including cuts, lacerations, puncture wounds, bruises, welts, or discoloration
- Any injury that looks like it may have been caused by cigarettes, caustics, acids, friction from ropes or chains, or contact with other objects
- Poorly treated or untreated injuries
- Injuries in areas usually covered by clothing

- Poor skin condition, poor skin hygiene, or lice
- Absence of hair and/or hemorrhaging below the scalp
- Dehydration or malnutrition that is unrelated to illness
- Loss of weight
- Soiled clothing or bedding
- An environment that is excessively dirty or smells of feces or urine
- Inadequate clothing
- Depression or withdrawal
- Hesitation to talk openly
- Fearfulness of caregivers
- Confusing or contradictory statements by an otherwise competent senior
- Resignation or denial
- Implausible explanations of injuries or conditions
- Unexplained agitation
- Denial of an injured state

Types of Elder Abuse

Physical abuse: Use of force to threaten or physically injure a vulnerable elder

Emotional abuse: Verbal attacks, threats, rejection, isolation, or belittling acts that cause or could cause mental anguish, pain, or distress to a senior

Sexual abuse: Sexual contact that is forced, tricked, threatened, or otherwise coerced upon a vulnerable elder, including anyone who is unable to grant consent

Exploitation: Theft, fraud, misuse or neglect of authority, and use of undue influence as a lever to gain control over an older person's money or property

Neglect: A caregiver's failure or refusal to provide for a vulnerable elder's safety, physical, or emotional needs

Some basic ***Do's and don'ts*** to preserve our assets include:

DO:

- Put money aside for legal fees.
- Develop a relationship with a competent, trustworthy attorney.
- Prepare a plan of action beforehand and make sure your lawyer is familiar with it.
- Familiarize yourself with legal aid options if necessary.
- Develop an understanding of the laws regarding Power of Attorney and guardianship in your state.
- Document everything—and keep records forever.
- Plan for a lengthy legal battle.
- Seek help from your local social services structure.
- Understand the political structure within your community and state.
- Develop political allies (usually through campaign donations).
- Learn the elder laws for your state—and others too.
- Know your rights, especially with regard to legal issues such as power of attorney and guardianship.

DON'T:

- Leave your fate in someone else's hands; instead, spell out your intentions early in writing!
- Be surprised to see efforts made to access your money little though it may be.
- Be discouraged by temporary legal setbacks.

Definitions from: http://dictionary.lp.findlaw.com/; http://www.nlm.nih.gov/medlineplus/mplusdictionary.html; http://www.nursinghomeabuseandneglect.com/;

Appendix II – Lessons Learned

- Document all phone calls, including time and caller. Take notes, including tone of conversation and any highlights, whether threatening, abusive etc.
- Trust no one. Even people who support you can make innocent remarks that can be misconstrued. Keep your comments between yourself and your lawyer. The less you say the less can be used against you.
- Keep phone records, emails, letters and all other correspondence, regardless of how insignificant they may seem at the time.
- If possible, copy voice mails into computer files and onto disks. There is no such thing as too much backup documentation.
- Acquaint yourself with the financial affairs of family members who may wind up in your care. Learn as much as possible before any need arises. Spell out all financial issues, and create a family financial and legal portfolio that outlines your assets while your loved ones are able to assist. Make copies for each family member if practicable. Simultaneously create a planner that outlines the roles each family member will play.
- Expect the unexpected. Expect difficulties and work around them. Acknowledge any friction when it begins and expect that it will play a larger role if a loved one is incapacitated, even temporarily.

- Learn the legal terms and definitions of situations that may face you. For instance, Power of Attorney grants far fewer and less expansive powers than Guardianship. Power of Attorney can be rescinded, but Guardianship has the power of the courts behind it and is much harder to undo.

- Search for a trusted lawyer or firm long before it becomes necessary to use such services. It is important to build a trusting legal relationship such that you are not reliant on relatives' lawyers who do not know you for legal advice.

- Understand the ramifications of turning control over your affairs to another person, even a family member. Write out specifically what you expect from any decisions you make concerning handling your assets and what you expect to occur should you later become incapacitated.

- Medical experts say that 50 percent of Americans will be diagnosed with Alzheimer's as they age, meaning virtually everyone will have to deal with it in one way or another. Take the time and make the effort to spell out in writing, with witnesses also signing, exactly what you expect in the future even if you can no longer participate. Preparation is the key.

- Get a Second Opinion. I cannot stress this enough regarding physical and mental health. Not every opinion is the correct opinion. In Ella's case, the second opinion turned out to be remarkably like the first opinion, but that was not evident when she was facing a trial.

- Do your own research. Do not rely on work that others have done. Double check everything.

- Expect setbacks. The American legal system works but it is not perfect. Expect setbacks, but don't get discouraged when they occur.

- Maintain control over your finances. Keep a separate bank account if necessary just in case of emergencies – such as unanticipated legal issues. And don't shortchange yourself. Legal fees mount quickly and the initial stages of a case may not go your way.

- Don't expect help from places that have a stake in your case. They may have policies that require them to do nothing until your situation is resolved, or they may just have an attitude. Either way, you won't be helped until a final order is entered by the courts. Expect delays where there should be none, and expect no help where help should be given.

- Conserve. Try to find ways to keep the costs down. If you can, drive to the lawyer's office rather than the other way around; if you can do research, do it; if it is not an emergency use mails rather than faxing; use the Internet and email if possible.

- Ensure legal redundancy. That means, if your primary lawyer is out of town, be sure he has a backup in case of emergencies. Make sure your attorney is skilled at courtroom work in addition to knowing the law.

- Expect the opposition to use any means, fair or foul to win their case. Don't discuss your case or tactics in public, and don't allow strangers to "help" you.

Appendix III – Common Signals of Alzheimer's

A common forewarning of Alzheimer's is *permanent memory loss* including important dates or events. Some memory loss is normal, however, and we all have moments when we forget something. The key is that we remember it later. Alzheimer's sufferers won't remember.

Reduced ability to do simple math or follow a plan such as a long-established recipe or the rule of a game we have played many times. Again, we all make occasional mistakes, jump over an ingredient when making a dish we have made before, or make occasional math errors. In Alzheimer's this is a permanent loss.

Another sign of Alzheimer's is *losing track of the passage of time*. An Alzheimer's sufferer may not remember the day, month or even the season. Sometimes they may forget where they are or how they got there. It is, however, common to occasionally forget what day it is or where we are going, but we will remember later on.

For some people, having *vision problems* is a sign of Alzheimer's. They may have difficulty reading, judging distance and determining color or contrast. Normal vision changes can occur due to glaucoma, retina damage, cataracts or eye diseases and may have nothing to do with Alzheimer's. Charles Bonnet syndrome can cause visions that are misdiagnosed as mental disorders.

People with Alzheimer's may have *difficulty following a conversation*. They may stop in the middle of a conversation and have no idea how to continue or have difficulties finding the right word. This also can occasionally happen to people who aren't suffering from Alzheimer's.

A person with Alzheimer's disease may *misplace items*. It is common to forget where we put something, but a person with Alzheimer's will be unable to retrace their steps to find them. They may even accuse others of stealing.

People with Alzheimer's may experience *changes in judgment or decision-making*. For example, they may use poor judgment when dealing with money, giving large amounts to unscrupulous salespeople. They also may disregard their own cleanliness or grooming.

A person with Alzheimer's may *disassociate themselves from favorite activities* as a result of forgetting their previous connection to a sports team or hobby. This can also lead to anti-social behavior.

Alzheimer's sufferers can experience *mood and personality changes*. They can become confused, suspicious, depressed, fearful or anxious if they can no longer recognize once familiar people or places.

Effects of Sleep Deprivation

Millions of Americans suffer from sleep deprivation. If you can lie down in the middle of the day and fall asleep within 10 minutes, then you too are sleep deprived. There are many reasons for this ranging from too much work to simply staying up watching TV.

1. Impaired glucose tolerance.
2. Possible link to obesity.
3. Increased carbohydrate cravings.
4. Weakened immune system.

5. Increased risk of getting breast cancer.

6. Decreased alertness and ability to focus.

7. Hardening of the arteries.

8. Depression and irritability.

Signs of Dementia

A simple task for determining whether someone has dementia can be administered easily.

Observe six areas of activity and check yes or no as to whether the subject can perform these tasks on their own:

1.) bathing

2.) dressing

3.) using the toilet

4.) moving from one room or even one seat to another

5.) control of bowel and bladder

6.) eating with no assistance.

Five or six of these activities performed independently is normal; four out six may be a sign of mild dementia and two out of six could be a sign of severe impairment.

Appendix IV
Resources

Veterans Administration

www.vba.va.gov/bln/21/pension/spousepen.htm#4

Connecticut Department of Social Service

www.ct.gov/agingservices/

National Center on Elder Abuse

www.ncea.aoa.gov/

Nutrition

www.bodyandfitness.com/Information/Health/Research/minerals.htm

Medical information

www.emedicine.medscape.com

Nutrition

www.mayoclinic.com www.mayoclinic.org

Alzheimer's information

www.helpguide.org/elder/alzheimers_prevention_slowing_down_treatment.htm

Bathroom accessories

http://www.premier-bathrooms.com/

ABOUT THE AUTHOR

Ronald Winter is an author, public relations executive, college professor and award winning journalist. He regularly writes and speaks on the military and politics.

Ron is author of the book ***Masters of the Art, A Fighting Marine's Memoir of Vietnam*** published by Random House, and writes Winter's Soldier Story, his website blog column.

His newest work of non-fiction is ***Granny Snatching, How a 92-Year-Old Widow Fought the Courts and Her Family to Win Her Freedom***.

Ron gave up an academic scholarship at the State University of New York at Albany in 1966 to join the Marines and fight in Vietnam as a helicopter crewman and machine gunner. He flew 300 combat missions and was awarded fifteen Air Medals, Combat Aircrew Wings, and the Vietnamese Cross of Gallantry.

After Vietnam he earned undergraduate degrees in Electrical Engineering and English Literature. In a two-decade journalism career Ron was the recipient of several prestigious awards and a Pulitzer nomination.

He was featured in 2004 in the Library of Congress' Veterans History Project; is an adjunct professor of communication at the University of Hartford; is a judge for the annual Connecticut Young Writers competition; and is a director for Michael J. London & Associates Public Relations firm in Trumbull, CT.

OTHER TITLES BY RON WINTER

Masters of the Art, A Fighting Marine's Memoir of Vietnam

ON THE WEB:

Be sure to visit Ron's blog at:
www.ronaldwinterbooks.com

Please visit Ronald Winter's interviews at the Library of Congress online site, "Experiencing War: Stories from the Veterans History Project."

Here's the exact web address:
http://lcweb2.loc.gov/diglib/vhp-stories/loc.natlib.afc2001001.03769/

LaVergne, TN USA
23 June 2010
187170LV00004B/1/P